IMAGES
of America

ROLLING MEADOWS

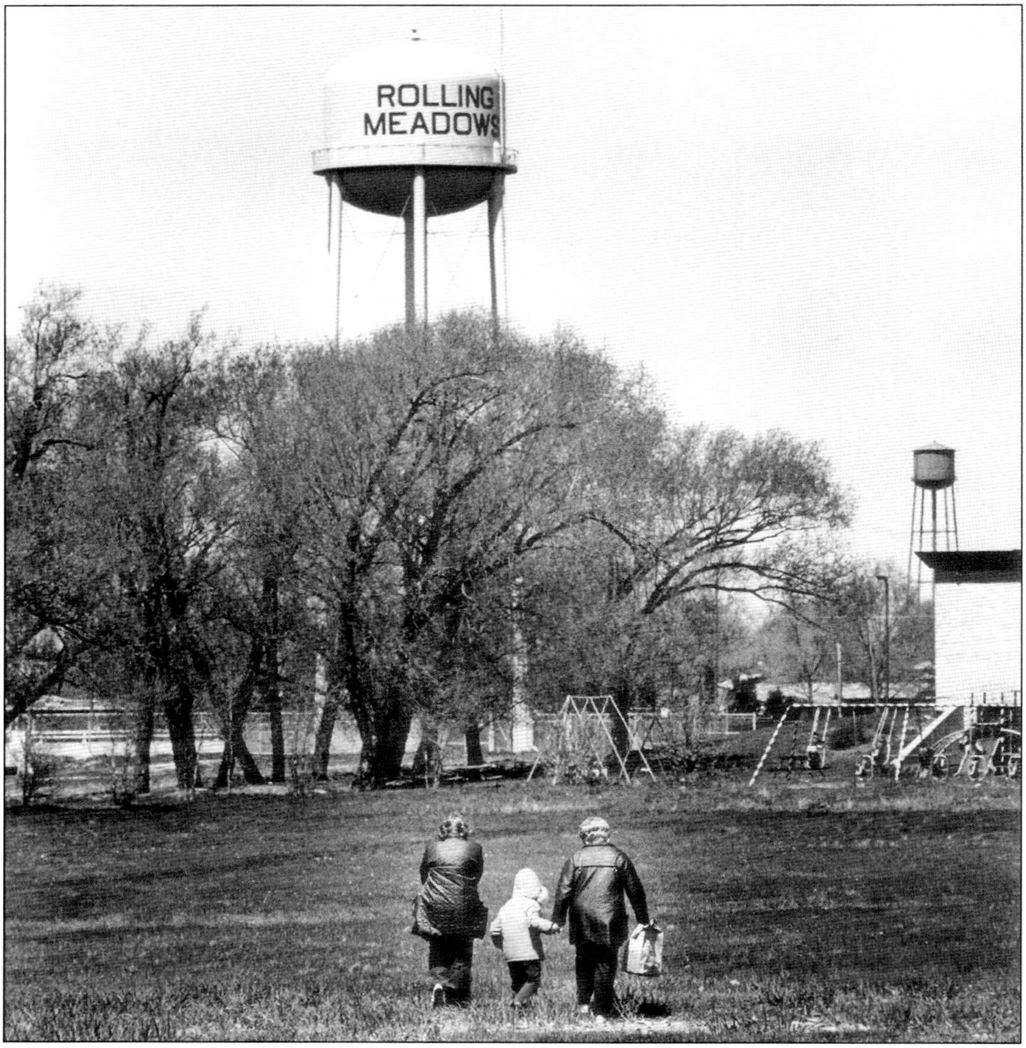

The north water tower in Rolling Meadows has long been a landmark of the city. The developer of Rolling Meadows, Kimball Hill, had set aside land for this water tower years before any of the land around it was operated by the park district. During the early years in Rolling Meadows, this water tower was visible from virtually anywhere in the city. Over the years, however, trees have grown taller and the original one-story houses have added second stories, all of which helps to obscure residents' views of it. But when one walks along Salt Creek and sees the water tower reaching up into the clear blue Midwest sky, one cannot help but see it as a lasting legacy from Rolling Meadows' humble past. (Courtesy of Dom Najolia.)

On the Cover: The cafeteria in Carl Sandburg School doubled as the school's multipurpose room, as evidenced by the stage and curtain. Sandburg was built in 1961 to meet School District 15's growing need for another elementary school, with Joseph Kiszka appointed as the principal. The continued increase in student enrollment resulted in the construction of a junior high wing. Many years later, the school was entirely converted to a junior high school. The multipurpose room, stage, and curtain remain to this day. (Courtesy of Community Consolidated School District 15.)

IMAGES
of America

ROLLING MEADOWS

Ashley Schroeder

ARCADIA
PUBLISHING

ISBN 978-0-7385-9357-9

Published by Arcadia Publishing
Charleston, South Carolina

Printed in the United States of America

Library of Congress Control Number: 2011939445

For all general information, please contact Arcadia Publishing:
Telephone 843-853-2070
Fax 843-853-0044
E-mail sales@arcadiapublishing.com
For customer service and orders:
Toll-Free 1-888-313-2665

Visit us on the Internet at www.arcadiapublishing.com

This book is dedicated to every person, past and present, who has been fortunate enough to call Rolling Meadows home.

Contents

Acknowledgments

Rolling Meadows is a relatively young city compared to its neighbors, several of which have been cities since the middle to late 1800s. Many of the people who live in Rolling Meadows today have either lived here since its inception or were born and raised here. I am proud to say that I am the latter. My personal history is inextricably connected to the history of this city. Much of what I know about Rolling Meadows is from growing up here and being a part of the community, but I would like to thank the people who helped flesh out the rest of the information for this book.

Much gratitude goes to Esther Perica, the wonderful woman who compiled decades' worth of facts, figures, and photographs for her book about Rolling Meadows, *They Took the Challenge*. I must thank her for writing such a helpful resource as well as for advising me in all aspects of this project.

I would like to thank David Ruff, director of the Rolling Meadows Library, who granted me permission to use any information I needed from Esther's book, to which the library holds the rights. His guidance and support of this whole project have been invaluable.

I must thank my parents for being my very best proofreaders. They have always known what I meant to say, even if I wrote something else instead.

Thanks to Jason Smith, the talented writer who allowed me to bounce ideas off of him for the direction and layout of this book. I greatly appreciate his ability to find order in my chaos.

Many thanks go to the people who generously gave their historic photographs to the Rolling Meadows Library's archives. Most of the images in this volume appear courtesy of the Rolling Meadows Library (RML).

Lastly, I would like to thank the residents, city employees, and volunteers of Rolling Meadows who have contributed to the charming hometown feel that this community has maintained since the very beginning. Rolling Meadows is the city it is today because of them.

Introduction

The history of the Rolling Meadows area seems quite removed from how it is today. Originally, the land was used by Native American tribes both as a permanent settlement and as an annual stopping point between summer and winter camp locations. By the 1830s, the US government bought the land from the Native Americans and relocated them west of the Mississippi River. Pioneers from the eastern part of the United States moved west into this "new" land and found the gently rolling prairie to have rich soil that was ideal for farming. Throughout the second half of the 19th century, pioneers swarmed the area, bought up as much land as they could, and farmed it.

The 1900s in northern Illinois saw the development of thriving rural areas. Churches and one-room schoolhouses sprang up to meet the spiritual and educational needs of the farming communities. Barn dances helped to create a real sense of kinship between neighboring farm families, and little pockets of communities outside the city of Chicago grew. Small businesses and public services, like blacksmiths and post offices, formed in these areas, allowing these communities to become somewhat self-sufficient.

In the following decades, farmers began "commuting" to Chicago to sell surplus crops or to make special purchases, such as for weddings or other major occasions. Unknowingly, the farming communities in these rural areas were creating the spatial and economic relationship that would later define Chicago and its future suburbs.

Over the years, those outlying farmlands were passed down through the generations and were broken up among family members as inheritance. Farming families came to realize that developers would soon come calling, interested in purchasing these smaller tracts of land on which to build housing developments. With World War II over and many young married couples looking to purchase their own homes, it was only a matter of time before "empty" land was turned into residential neighborhoods. Truly suburban communities were encroaching on the farmland. Sensing what was to come, farmers from this area moved further west to other farmland, leaving hundreds of acres in the southeast corner of Palatine Township available for purchase, and it was perfect land for development.

Enter Kimball Hill, a law school graduate who, unable to find work in that field, had gone into the housing industry. He had spent years developing housing for World War II veterans and their families. But what Hill truly wanted to do was to build a development of affordable housing for young couples who wanted to remain close to Chicago while having the perks of home ownership and enjoying a patch of land. Hill had his mind set on creating a self-sufficient thriving development with a strong sense of community. He just needed land on which to build.

Just as the farmers were moving out, Kimball Hill made a move on the land. He purchased 537 acres of vacant farmland for his new housing development. Looking at the gently rolling terrain around him, the idea for "Project Rolling Meadows" was born. He imagined a community complete with parks and paved streets, but he needed to start by getting people to move to this new development. And to do that, he had to start by building homes.

Those homes still exist more than 50 years later, and many of the original young couples who purchased those homes still live in them. These residents, along with Kimball Hill, fought tirelessly and gave generously to support and grow the community that was built out of empty farmland. The network of parks, streets, and homes grew into a city that boasts a functioning governing body, a strong sense of community, and a resilient can-do spirit shared by all Rolling Meadows residents.

A city is not created overnight, and incorporation does not just happen. The people of Rolling Meadows had to work hard to establish a homeowners association, let alone a civic government. People had to file paperwork and vote for change. To establish a city hall, residents needed to run for office. To form police and fire departments, people had to volunteer their time and services, as well as dedicate themselves to training. A park district and a public library meant funding, something difficult for a young city to collect. Kimball Hill donated land for facilities to be built on, and residents donated whatever money and time they could to help such city centers get started. The early years of the city were marked by the giving spirit of both Rolling Meadows' founder and its residents.

After the housing was built and the civic departments were established, Rolling Meadows set its sights on bringing industry into town. People from neighboring communities saw Rolling Meadows as just one large subdivision, incapable of any real industry or commerce. But the construction of a large shopping center in the heart of the city and a sizeable industrial park on the city's outskirts brought Rolling Meadows to the public eye and out of scrutiny.

This town has always put a special emphasis on its youth, and through the years that has never changed. One of the most important goals of the early city was to establish enough schools to accommodate each Rolling Meadows child. At the height of enrollment, the city had needed to build and run seven schools for elementary and junior high students. But the city's committed attention to children did not start and end with education. City officials and residents alike worked to build parks and recreational areas for children to play in as well as to provide library and park district programs to stretch their young minds. Rolling Meadows was a city built on family values, something it continues to uphold.

Decades have passed, and Rolling Meadows continues to rise to meet the changing needs of its residents. Local churches, community groups, businesses, and city departments all have the same goal in mind—to serve the educational, spiritual, social, and other needs of Rolling Meadows and its residents.

Community pride and neighborly spirit are as important now as they have ever been. New residents quickly learn what long-time residents have believed all along—Rolling Meadows is the perfect place to raise a family and a great place to call home. Kimball Hill's vision and legacy continue with each new family that moves to town as well as with each family that firmly plants its roots here. Rolling Meadows has come a long way from where it started. Unlike some of the Native American tribes who kept passing through, the residents of this city find it difficult to ever leave.

Rolling Meadows' development from prairie farmland to a suburban city happened in what would seem like a blink of an eye. Although the city was built out of nothing more than softly rolling terrain, in just a few short years, it was catching up with its long-established neighboring cities. Though it happened quickly, it did not happen overnight. And it took more than just a few people to get things moving. It took an entire community of passionate visionary residents. But really, it all started with one man and his vision for 537 acres of rolling meadows.

One

Kimball Hill and Rolling Meadows

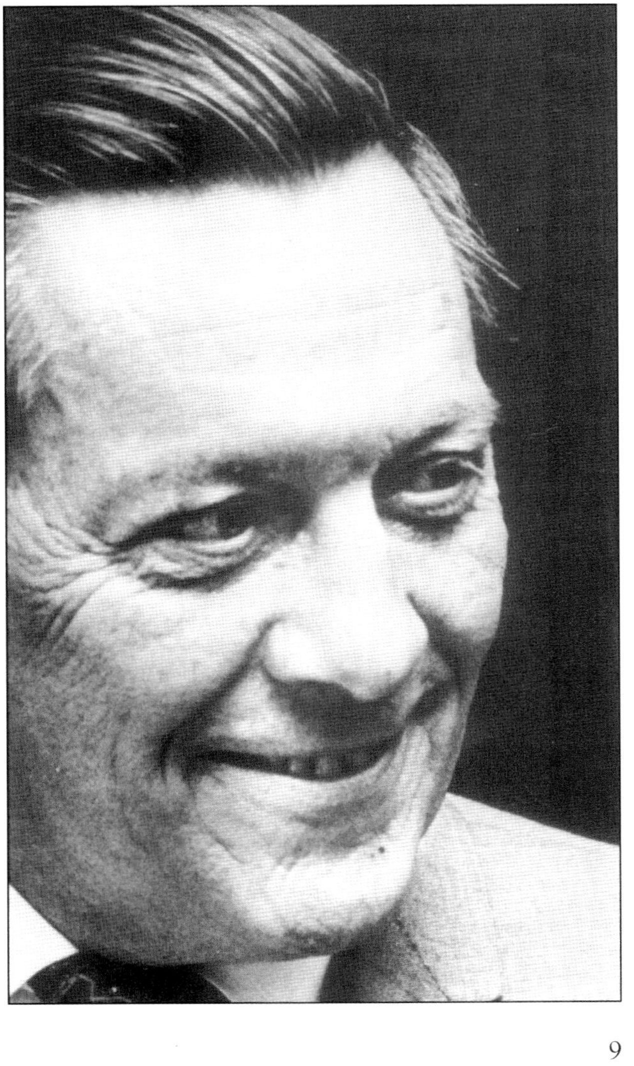

Kimball Hill was a young developer who gained experience developing and redesigning homes in the Chicagoland area for returning World War II veterans and their families. Then his vision shifted to developing low-cost homes for young couples in a brand new development with streets, parks and recreational areas, and a strong sense of community. He purchased 537 acres of rolling farmland in the southeast corner of Palatine Township for this new development. He named his new development after the land—Rolling Meadows. (Printed with permission of the *Daily Herald*.)

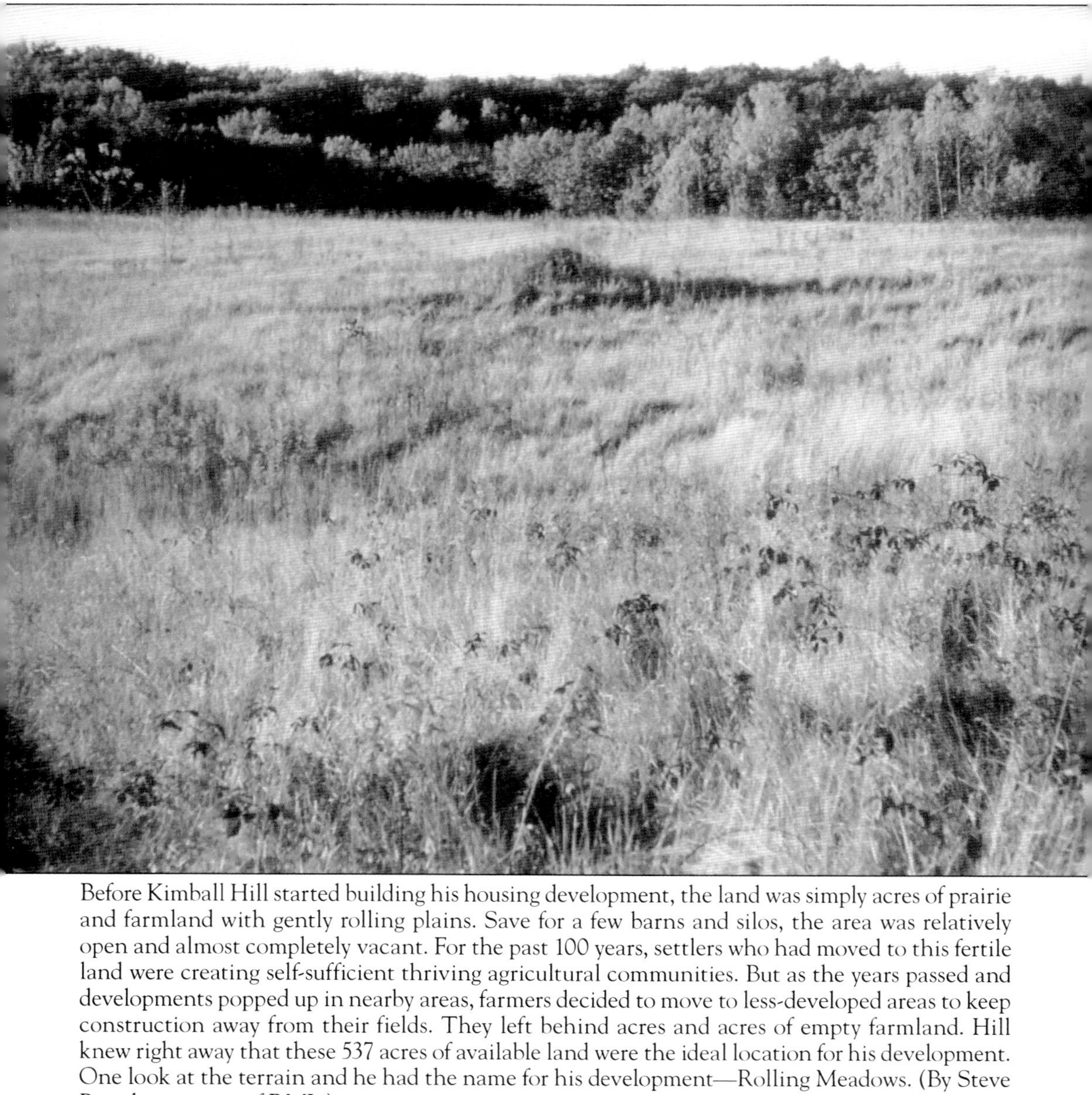

Before Kimball Hill started building his housing development, the land was simply acres of prairie and farmland with gently rolling plains. Save for a few barns and silos, the area was relatively open and almost completely vacant. For the past 100 years, settlers who had moved to this fertile land were creating self-sufficient thriving agricultural communities. But as the years passed and developments popped up in nearby areas, farmers decided to move to less-developed areas to keep construction away from their fields. They left behind acres and acres of empty farmland. Hill knew right away that these 537 acres of available land were the ideal location for his development. One look at the terrain and he had the name for his development—Rolling Meadows. (By Steve Prorak; courtesy of RML.)

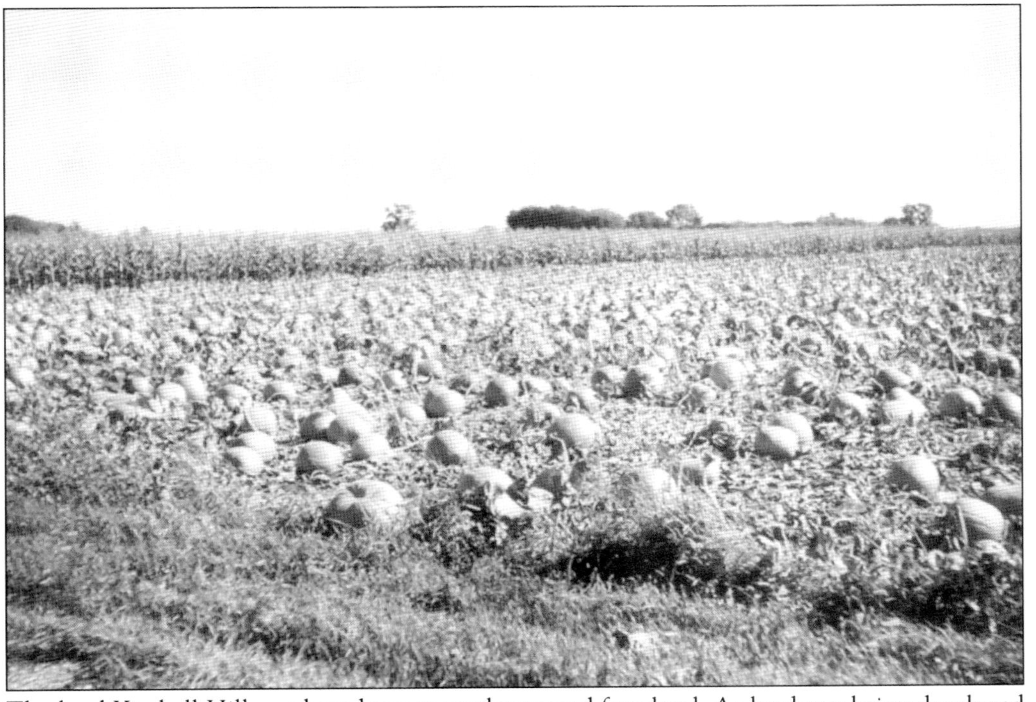

The land Kimball Hill purchased was recently vacated farmland. As land was being developed with housing, other areas remained intact as prairie and farmland. In 1955, the farmland pictured above, what was to become the corner of Owl Drive and Central Road (near where the future Central Road School was to be built), was simply a large pumpkin patch. Below is a stretch of vacant prairie land. (Above by Ronald Brightwell, below by Steve Prorak; both courtesy of RML.)

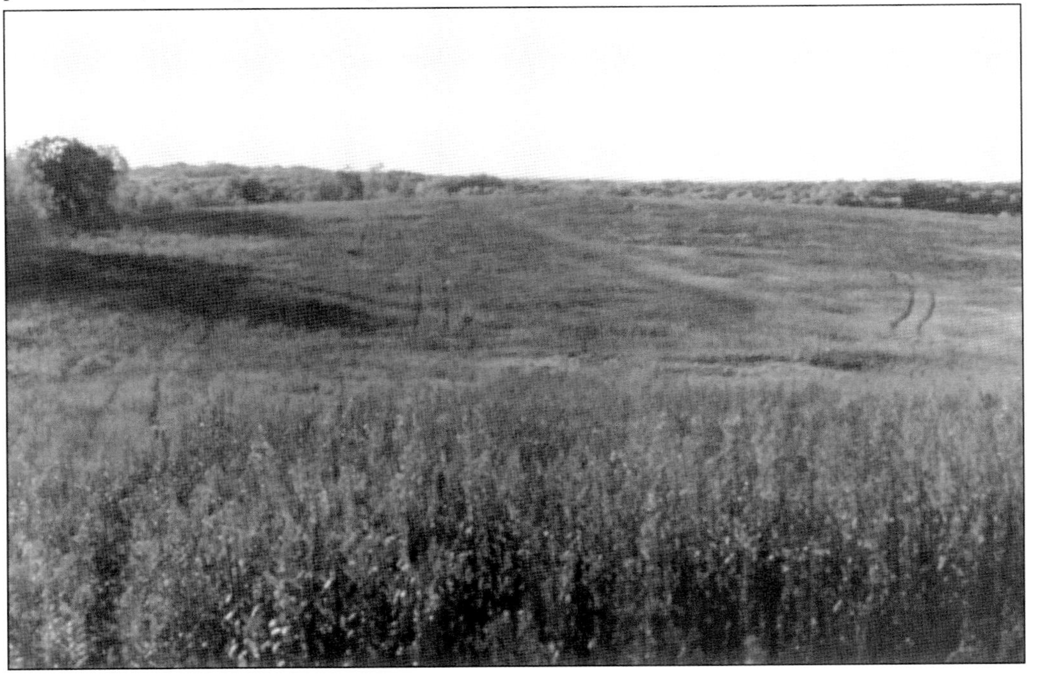

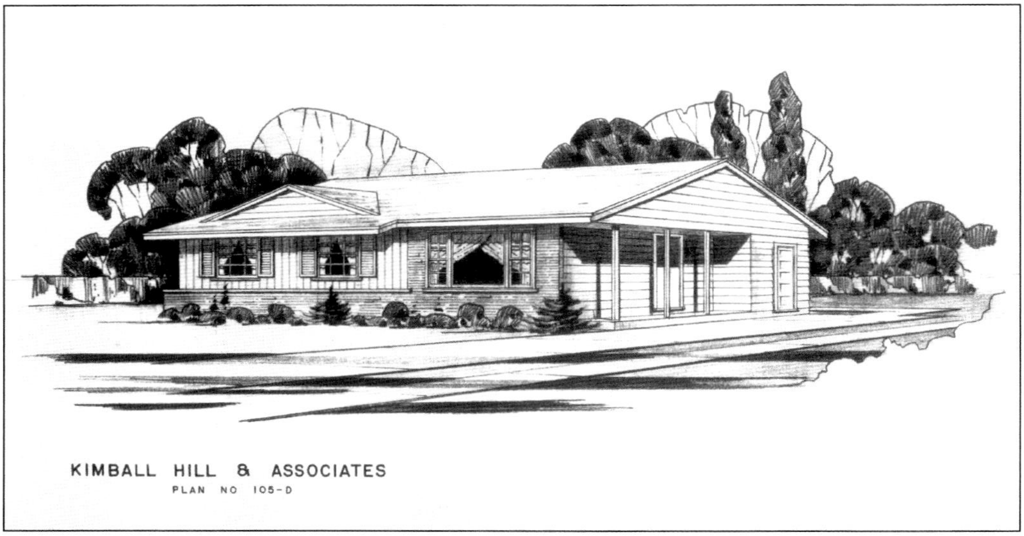

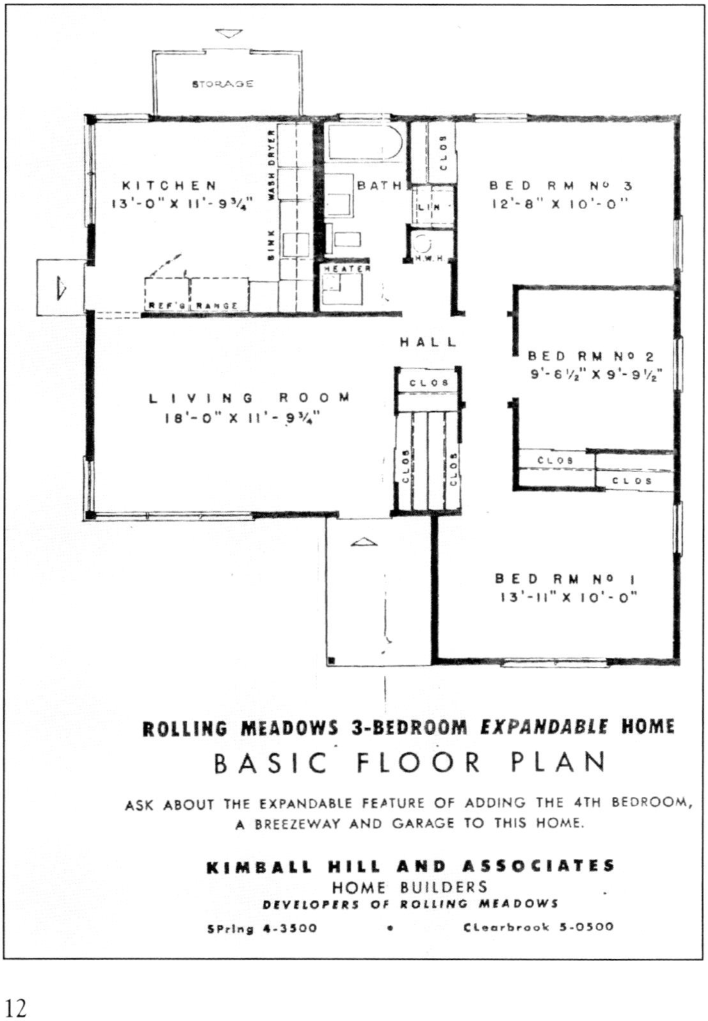

Kimball Hill wanted his housing development to be affordable. His company, Kimball Hill and Associates, designed two- and three-bedroom homes that all had similar floor plans. Since his target buyers were young couples, most of whom had started or were looking to start a family, the homes were practically sized and affordably priced. He did, however, give buyers the option to expand a three-bedroom house design into a four-bedroom home with a breezeway and garage. Above is a sketch for a two-bedroom Rolling Meadows home. It likely shared the layout of the floor plan, left, with the exception of bedroom no. 1. (Both courtesy of RML.)

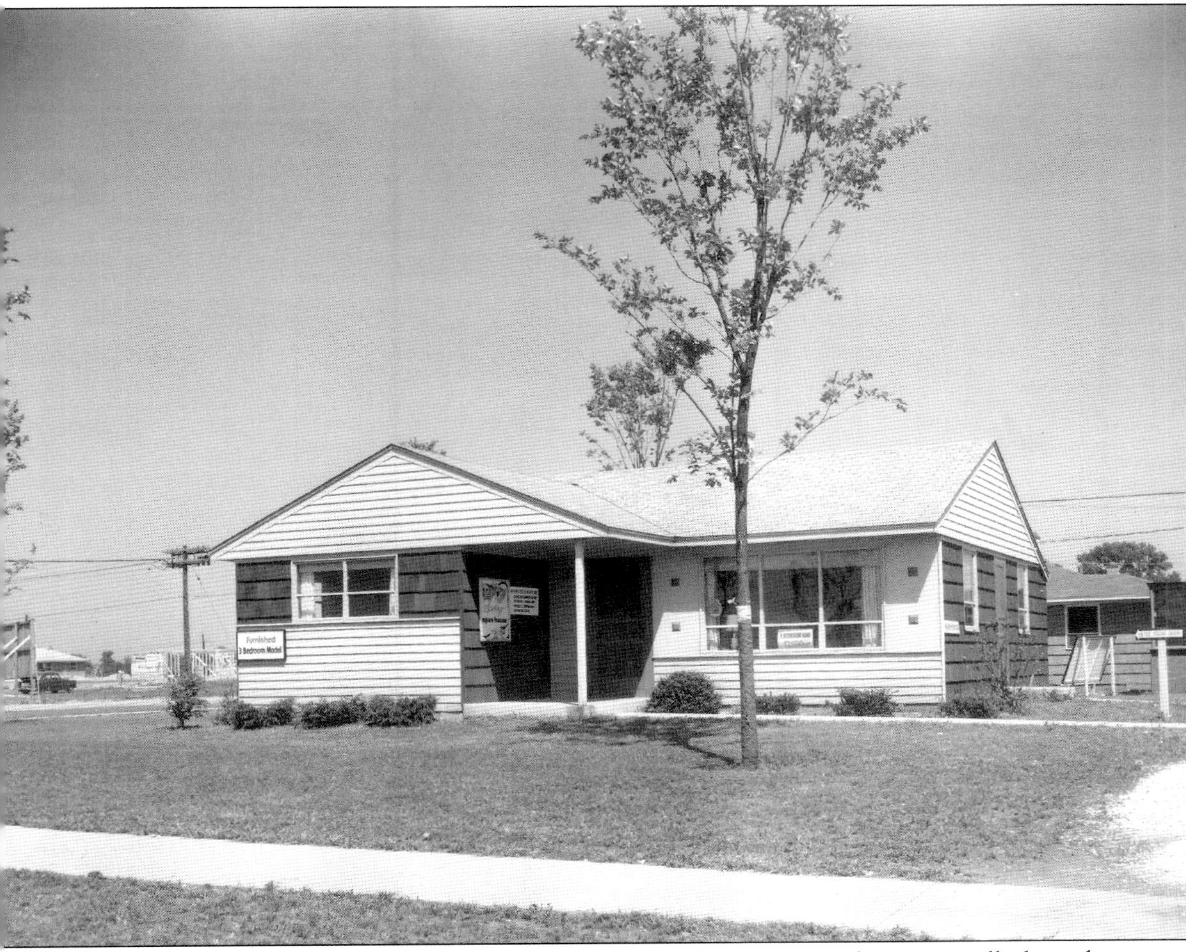

Kimball Hill built a model home in Des Plaines, Illinois, for prospective buyers to walk through. The model home was a spacious, multiple-bedroom, and fully furnished house. The house served as the sales office for Project Rolling Meadows. During open hours, it was staffed by someone from Kimball Hill and Associates who could answer visitors' questions and to initiate intent-to-buy paperwork if necessary. (Courtesy of RML.)

KIMBALL HILL and ASSOCIATES

Creators of Homes Designed for Modern American Living

575 Lee Street, Des Plaines, Illinois — Telephone VAnderbilt 4-2020

Des Plaines, Sales Office - 2347 Rand Road and Ashland, Des Plaines, Illinois VA 4-4156
Model Home Hours: Daily 10 a.m. to 9 p.m. Saturday and Sunday 10 a.m. to 9 p.m.

FINANCING INFORMATION

PURCHASE PLAN -- 25 YEAR LOAN — F. H. A. INTEREST RATE $4\frac{1}{2}$ %

	MODEL	MODEL
Type	A-32	A-33
House and 60 by 167 foot lot	$11,390.00	$12,890.00
Mortgage	$ 9,300.00	$ 9,800.00
DOWN PAYMENT (To be paid at time of signing of formal contracts.)	$ 2,090.00	$ 3,090.00

NOTE: Loan expenses are included in price above

MONTHLY PAYMENTS

Principal and Interest	$ 51.71	$ 54.49
Mortgage insurance premium	4.20	4.20
Fire insurance	2.30	2.30
Taxes (Estimated)	9.00	9.75
TOTAL (Estimated)	$ 66.21	$ 69.74

Additional down payments will reduce monthly payments per $200.00 paid down by $1.11, per month.

Brick Veneer variations are extra; Range in price from $65.00 to $300.00.

Thank you for your visit to our Model Home.

KIMBALL HILL and ASSOCIATES
R. C. Winkle
R. C. Winkle

ASK ABOUT OUR LARGER HOMES WITH MORE SPACIOUS LIVING

Here is a financing information sheet that prospective buyers received when they visited the model home in Des Plaines, Illinois. The sheet broke down the down payment, monthly mortgage payment, and estimated taxes on each style of home (two- or three-bedroom). It also let people know that they would receive a 10,020-square-foot lot, as well as the fact that they had the option to upgrade to a larger home or substitute traditional siding with brick veneer. Many families were surprised by how affordable purchasing their very own brand new home could be. (Courtesy of RML.)

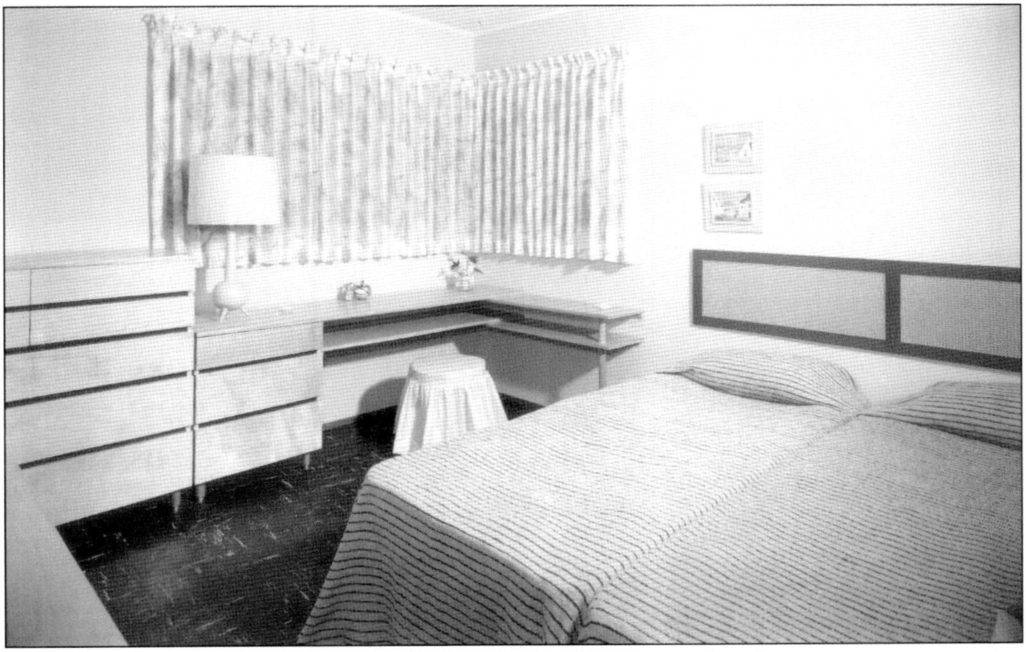

The model home in Des Plaines was fully furnished and accessorized so that as soon as prospective buyers stepped inside, they could envision themselves living in a home, just like this building. One bedroom, the most spacious of them, was furnished with sophisticated, mature fabrics and furniture to distinguish it as the master bedroom. The other bedrooms varied in style. The back bedroom was complete with a school desk and bunk beds, allowing prospective buyers to picture their present or future family filling the rooms in the house. (Both courtesy of RML.)

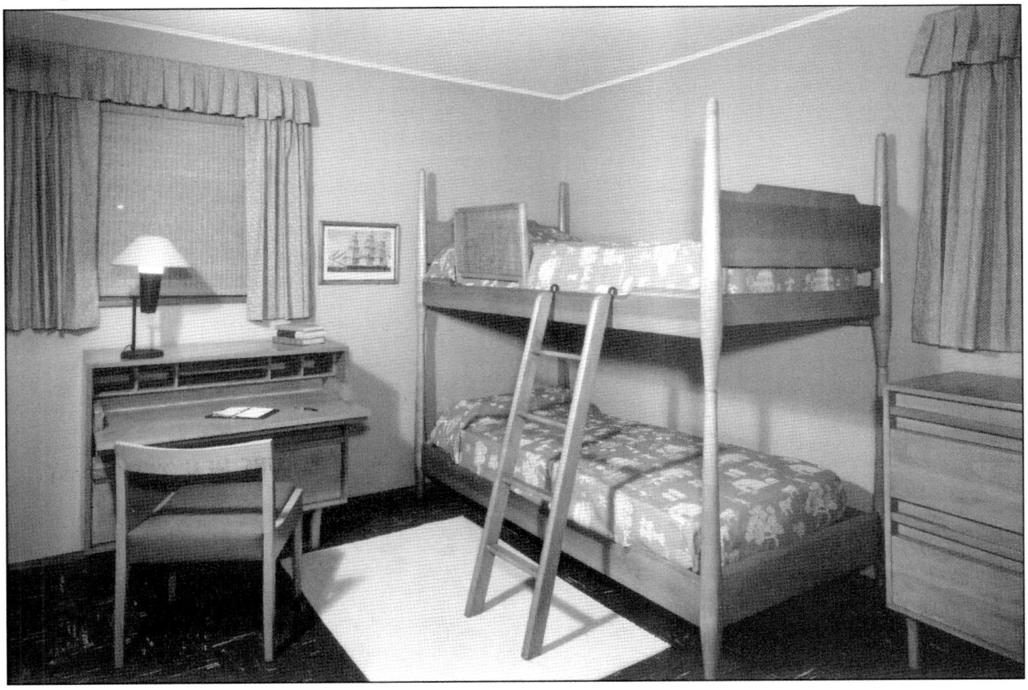

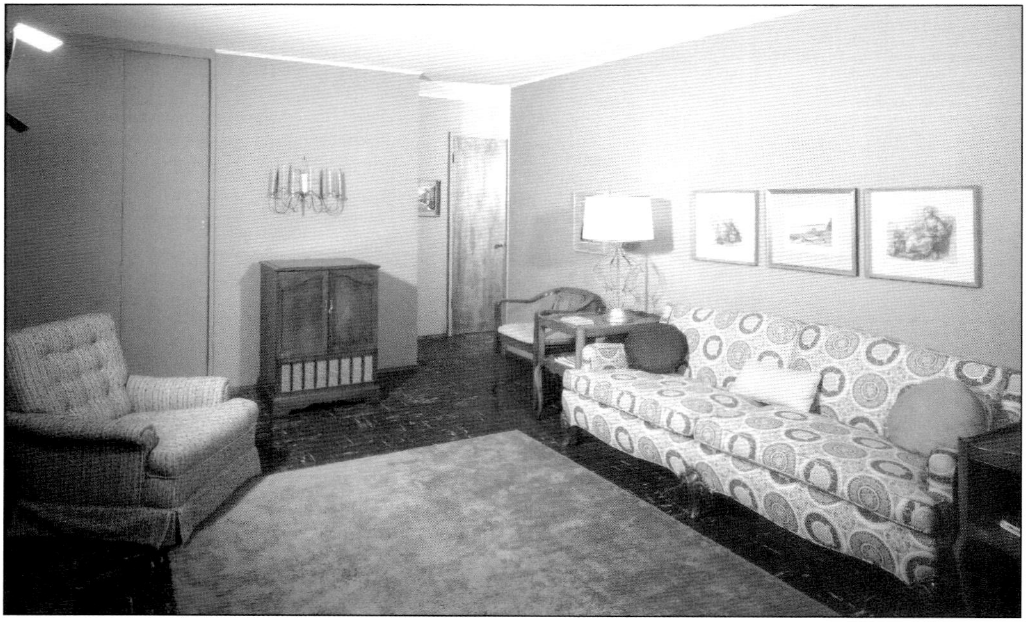

The model home's living room was by far the most spacious of all the rooms. This was the first room prospective buyers would see as they entered the model home, just as they would expect to in their own home. (Courtesy of RML.)

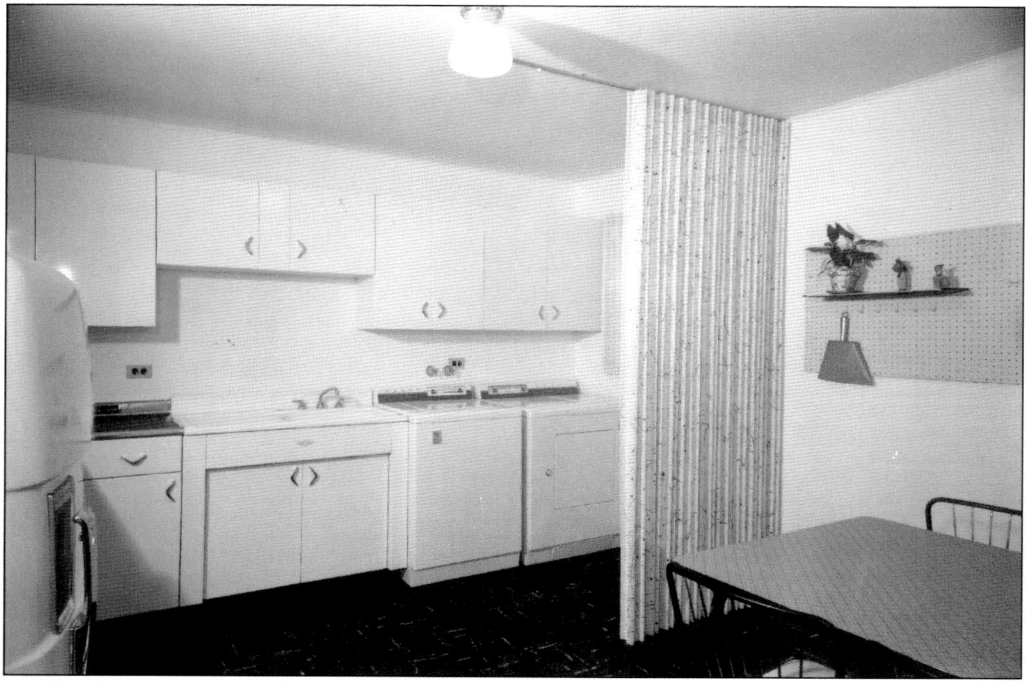

The kitchen was rather deluxe, considering the price of the home, with a refrigerator, range and oven, washing machine, and clothes dryer all in one convenient location. These Kimball Hill kitchens were large enough for a whole family to eat in together, further selling visitors on the idea of purchasing a Kimball Hill home for their family. (Courtesy of RML.)

Much to Kimball Hill's surprise, many people were opposed to rezoning the future Rolling Meadows from farmland to a residential area. Residents from neighboring cities, namely Arlington Heights, were not pleased at the thought of having low-cost housing so close, even though the new homeowners would surely frequent shops and businesses in Arlington Heights. After many petitions and appeals, finally the zoning board responsible for making the final decision voted 12-3 in favor of rezoning. Had the vote remained at 11-4, Rolling Meadows would have never been developed. In these two letters, Kimball Hill writes to families who had deposited money for a new home in Rolling Meadows and were kept waiting for news about rezoning. (Both by Bette Kocian; courtesy of RML.)

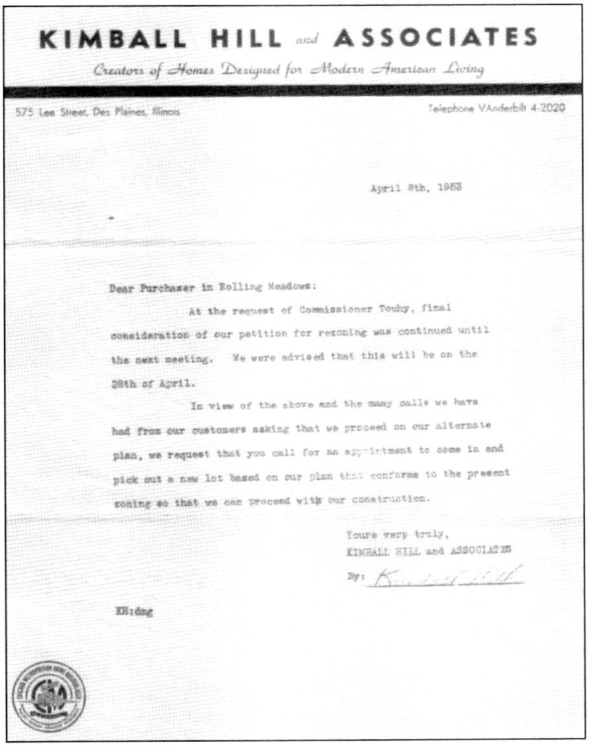

KIMBALL HILL and ASSOCIATES

Creators of Homes Designed for Modern American Living

575 Lee Street, Des Plaines, Illinois — Telephone VAnderbilt 4-2020

April 8th, 1953

Dear Purchaser in Rolling Meadows:

At the request of Commissioner Touhy, final consideration of our petition for rezoning was continued until the next meeting. We were advised that this will be on the 28th of April.

In view of the above and the many calls we have had from our customers asking that we proceed on our alternate plan, we request that you call for an appointment to come in and pick out a new lot based on our plan that conforms to the present zoning so that we can proceed with our construction.

Yours very truly,
KIMBALL HILL and ASSOCIATES
By:

KH:dmg

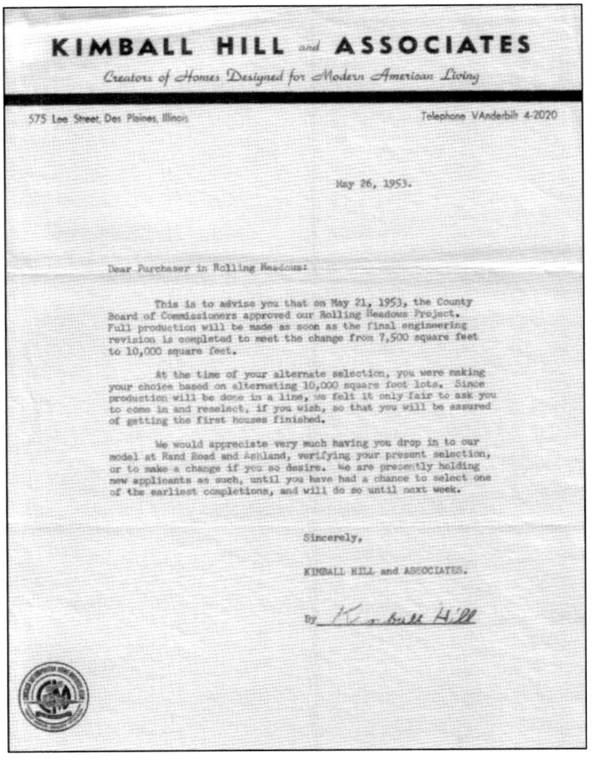

KIMBALL HILL and ASSOCIATES

Creators of Homes Designed for Modern American Living

575 Lee Street, Des Plaines, Illinois — Telephone VAnderbilt 4-2020

May 26, 1953.

Dear Purchaser in Rolling Meadows:

This is to advise you that on May 21, 1953, the County Board of Commissioners approved our Rolling Meadows Project. Full production will be made as soon as the final engineering revision is completed to meet the change from 7,500 square feet to 10,000 square feet.

At the time of your alternate selection, you were making your choice based on alternating 10,000 square foot lots. Since production will be done in a line, we felt it only fair to ask you to come in and reselect, if you wish, so that you will be assured of getting the first houses finished.

We would appreciate very much having you drop in to our model at Rand Road and Ashland, verifying your present selection, or to make a change if you so desire. We are presently holding new applicants as such, until you have had a chance to select one of the earliest completions, and will do so until next week.

Sincerely,

KIMBALL HILL and ASSOCIATES.

By Kimball Hill

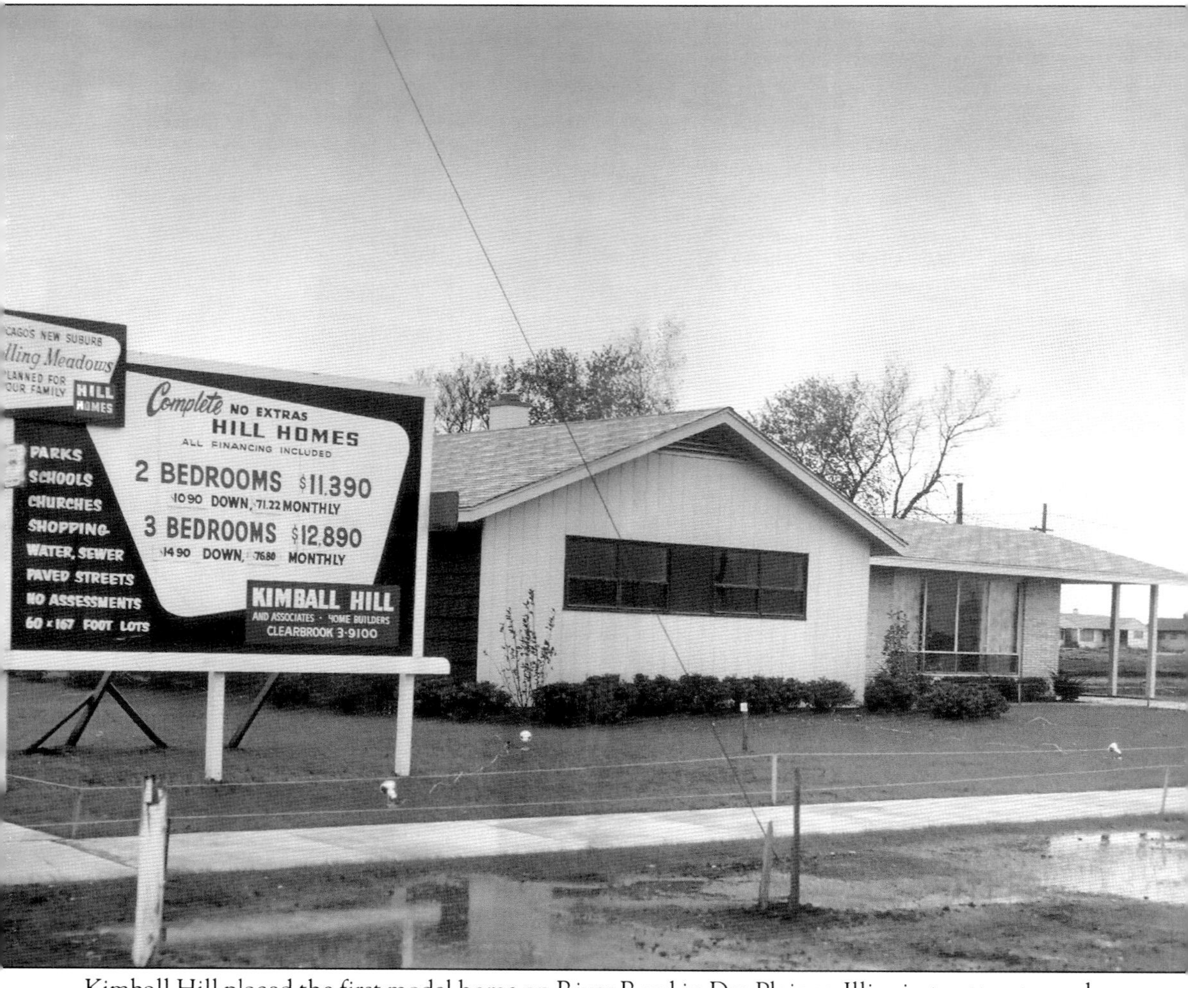

Kimball Hill placed the first model home on River Road in Des Plaines, Illinois, to attract people as they were out for leisurely drives. People were so intrigued by the low deposit prices, between $10 and $25, that some who had no intention to buy soon found themselves filling out intent-to-buy paperwork. This particular model home and advertisement were located on the northwest corner of Campbell Street and Wilke Road, on what would be the eastern border of the future city of Rolling Meadows. (Courtesy of RML.)

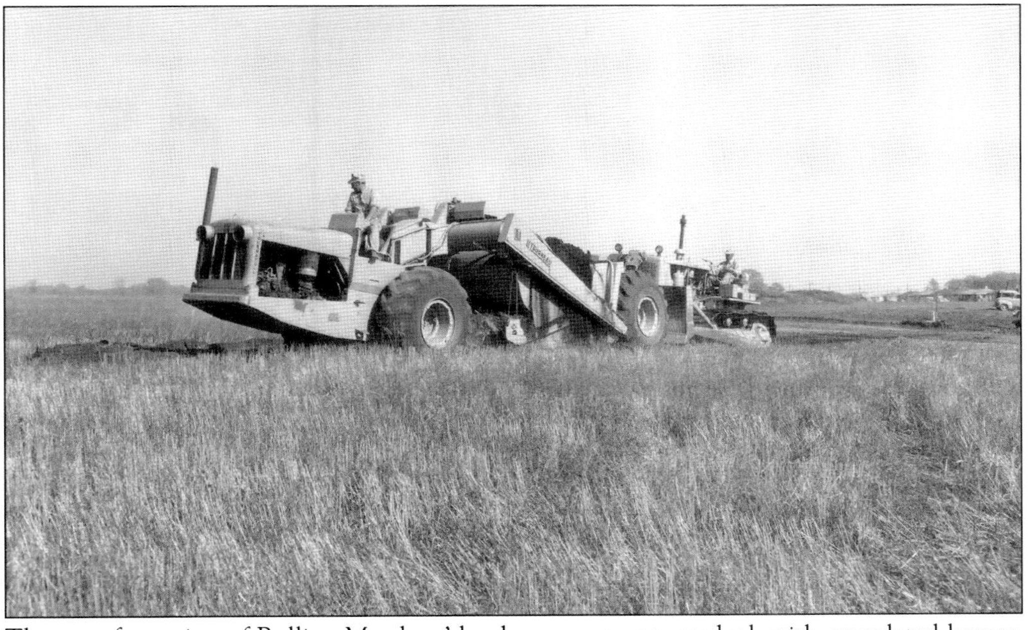

The transformation of Rolling Meadows' landscape was very gradual, with completed homes, construction equipment, farm houses, and prairie existing at the same time. Above, two workers smooth the mounds of dirt behind them with their grading equipment, flanked by prairie on one side and homes (also under construction) on the other. Below, the same equipment drives back and forth over land now devoid of prairie grass to completely level the land for housing and streets. Completed homes appear in the distance. (Both courtesy of RML.)

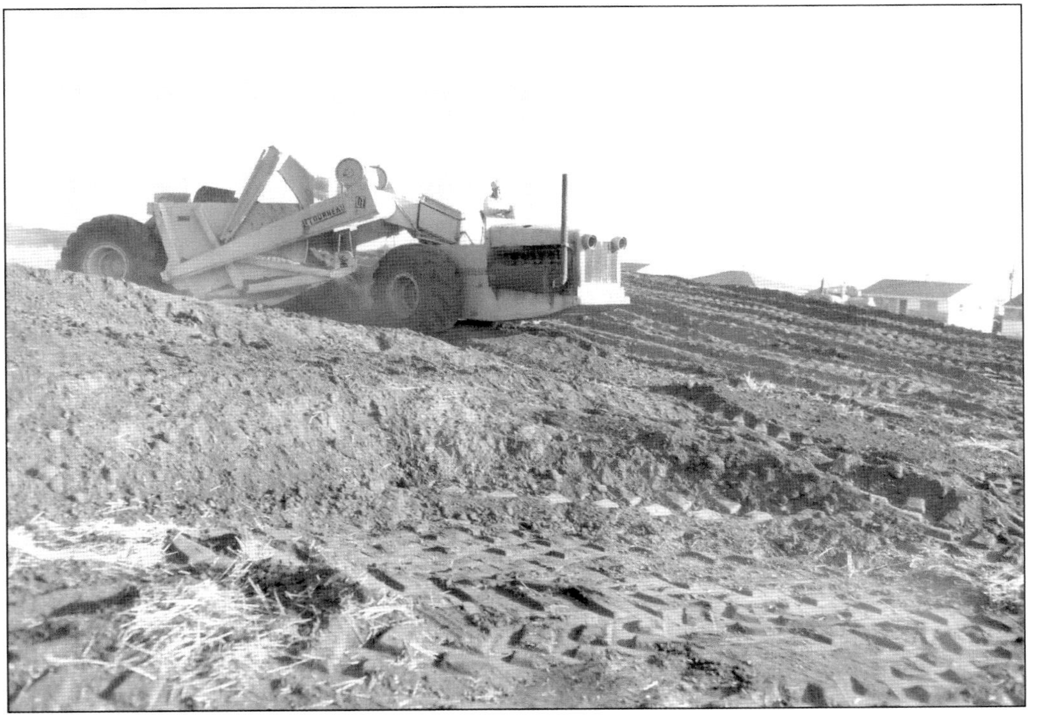

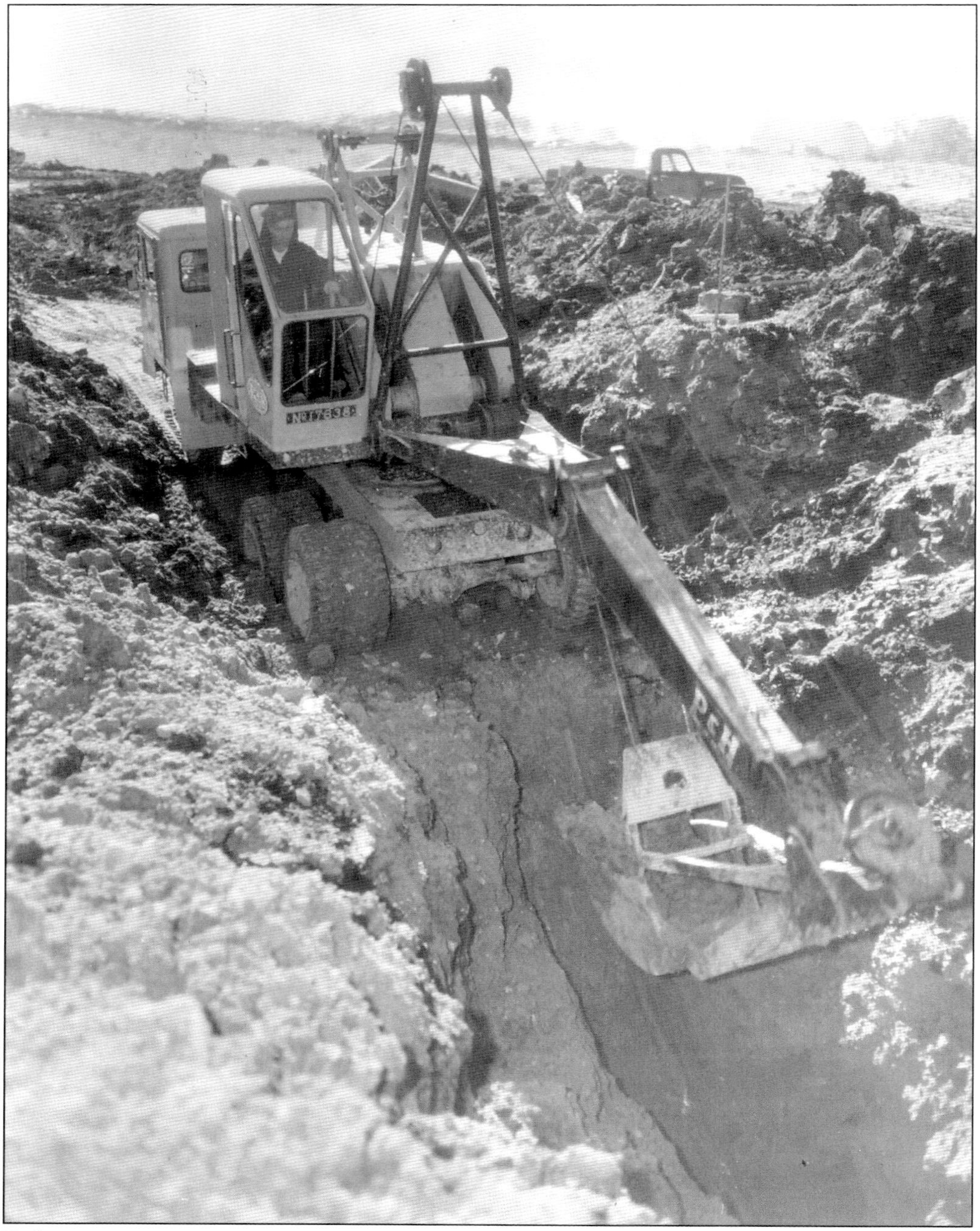

To keep construction moving quickly, workers dug and laid sewer pipes and connected homes to the pipes at the same time that other houses were still being built. Here, excavating equipment digs deep into the prairie land to prepare for the sewer pipes that will likely service the rows of homes in the distance. An old farm building also remains in the distance, again revealing the gradual transformation of the landscape from prairie farmland to a residential development. (Courtesy of RML.)

In the decades before Rolling Meadows was built, it was common practice for each farming family to dig its own well. However, a spattering of individual, separate wells could not provide enough water for an entire development. Several interconnected wells and sewer pipes needed to be installed to service the entire community. Workers labored to complete wells to accommodate the number of completed homes. This construction worker, nicknamed "Curley," was a well-known well digger in the area who worked with Lane-Western. (Courtesy of RML.)

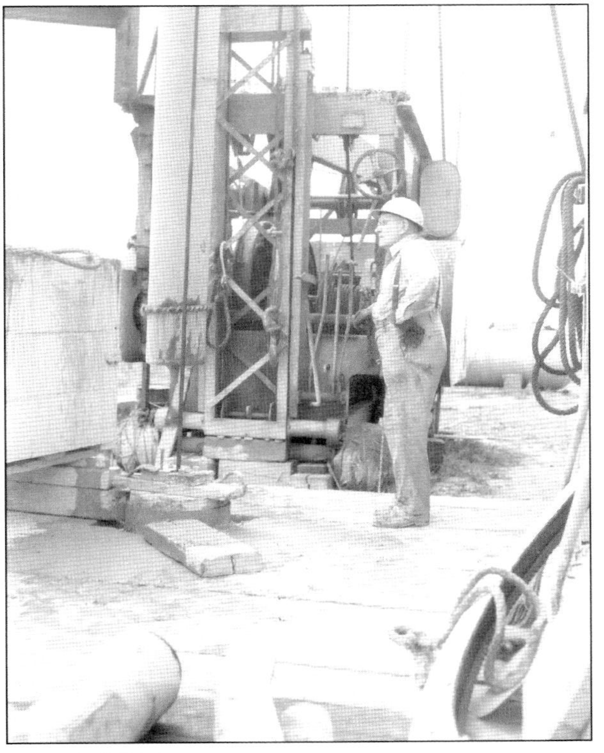

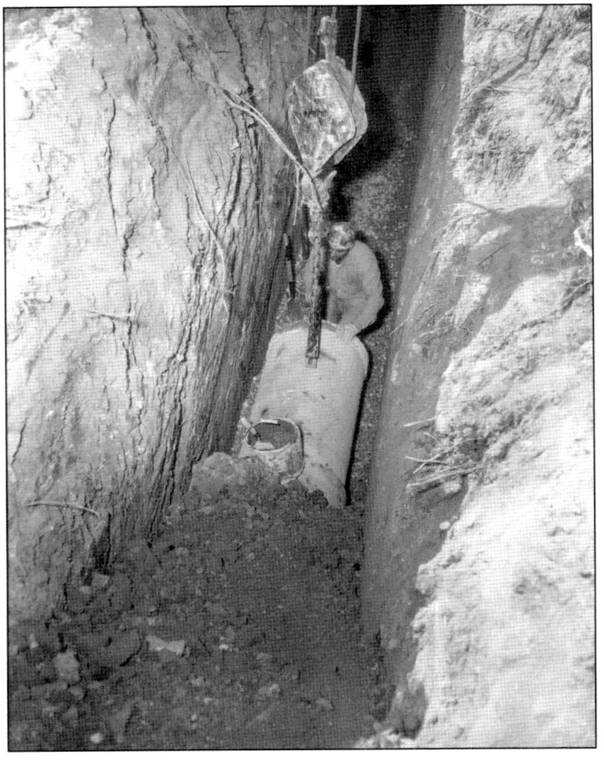

Every housing development requires a water delivery system and electricity. In addition to completing the structure, interior, and exterior of the homes, construction workers needed to focus on digging wells and installing storm sewer pipes. Here, a worker lowers a large sewer pipe and pushes it into its proper place. (Courtesy of RML.)

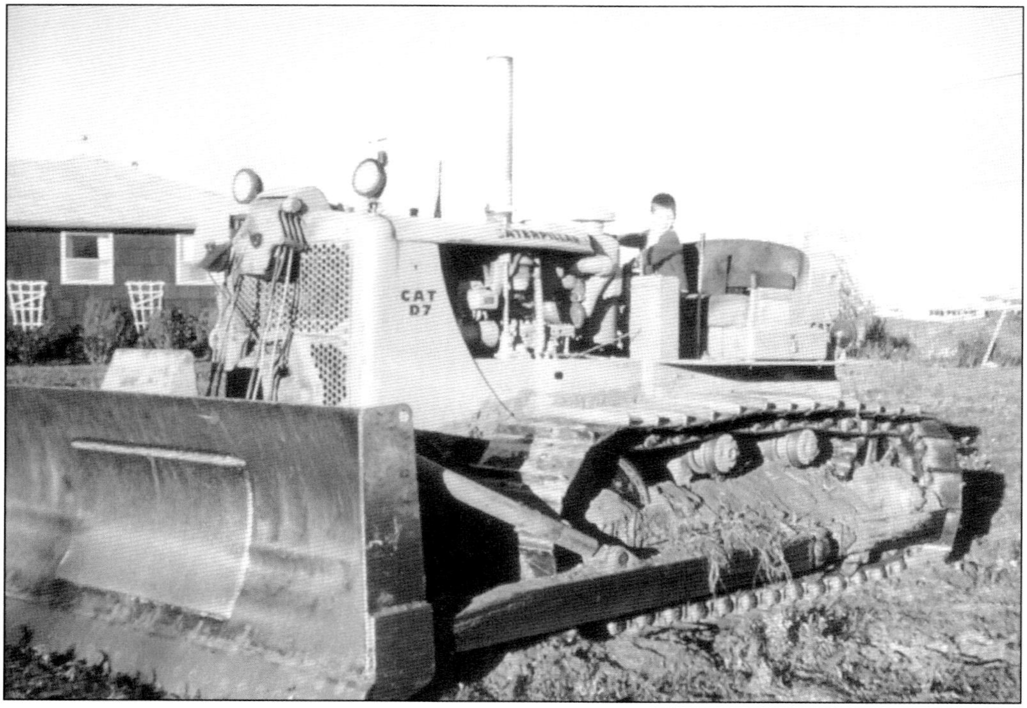

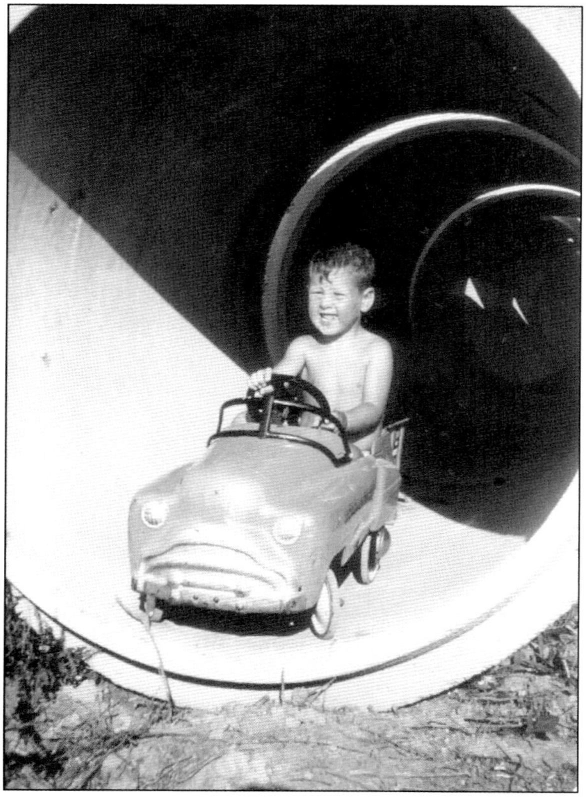

In the first years in Rolling Meadows, before there were paved streets, sidewalks, or driveways, children had a difficult time playing outdoors without getting dirty. They improvised, using construction vehicles and other equipment as playgrounds. Some children, pictured above, would simply climb onto bulldozers and diggers and pretend to drive them. Others would ride through sewer pipes with bicycles, tricycles, and miniature cars. Left, Joe Brightwell drives his "car" through a sewer pipe before it was laid in the ground near Central Road in 1958. (Both by Ronald Brightwell; courtesy of RML.)

Mr. Fletcher of Fletcher Engineering was in charge of all the engineering work for the Kimball Hill housing development. He was responsible for deciding the proper grading for the development, as well as for laying the streets. His company remained the official engineering company of the City of Rolling Meadows for decades after the first house was built in 1953. Here Mr. Fletcher stands, surveying the land in the middle of the construction area. (Courtesy of RML.)

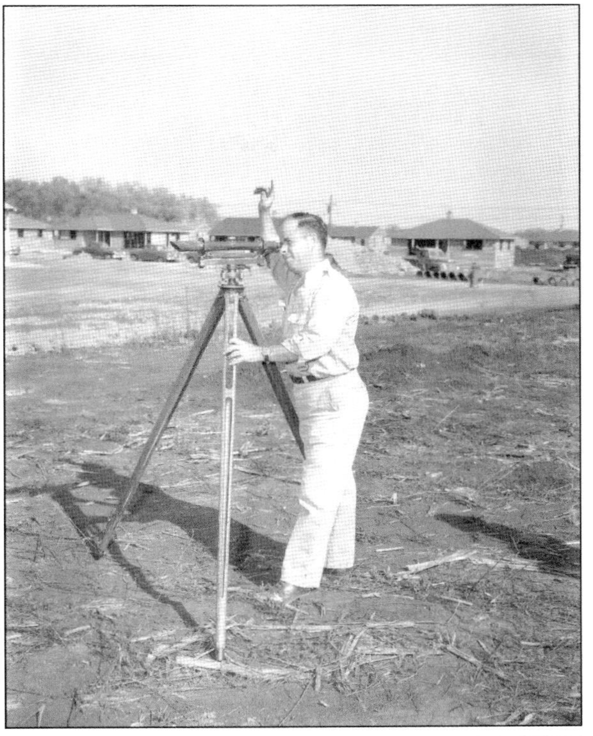

Gottlieb Rauser (left) and Dick Scott, the field superintendent for Kimball Hill, hold a stack of blueprints as they examine and discuss the plans and specifications for each home. Around them, work continues on the rows and rows of homes. (Courtesy of RML.)

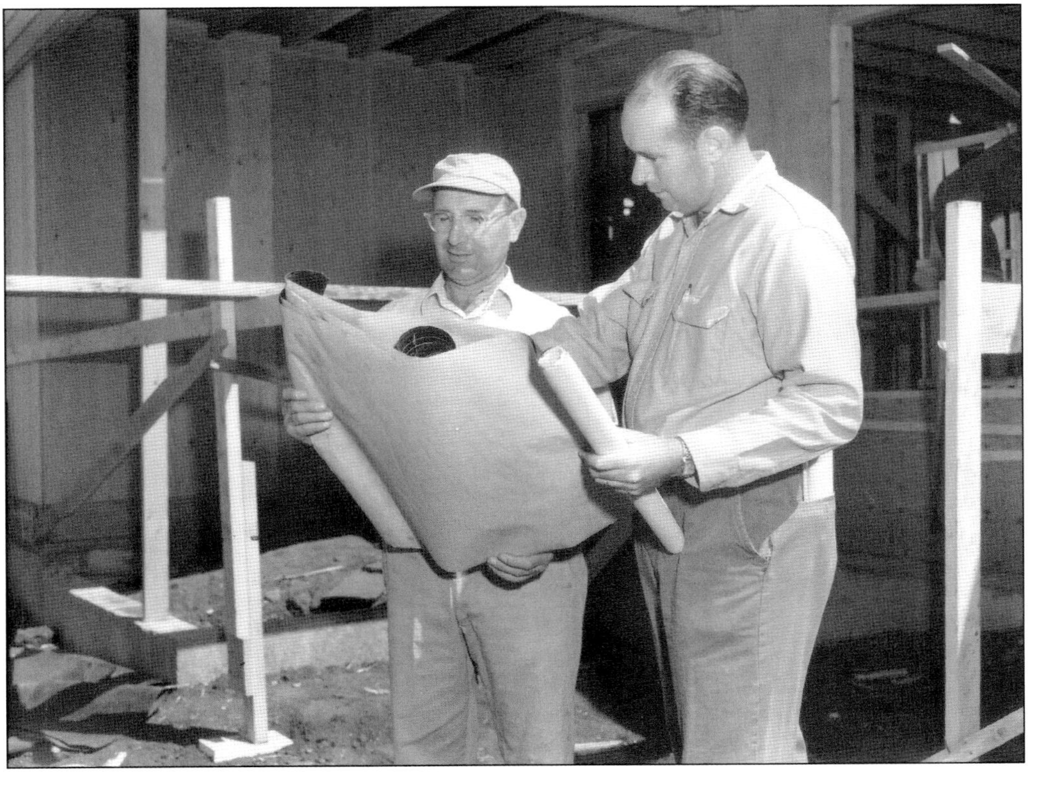

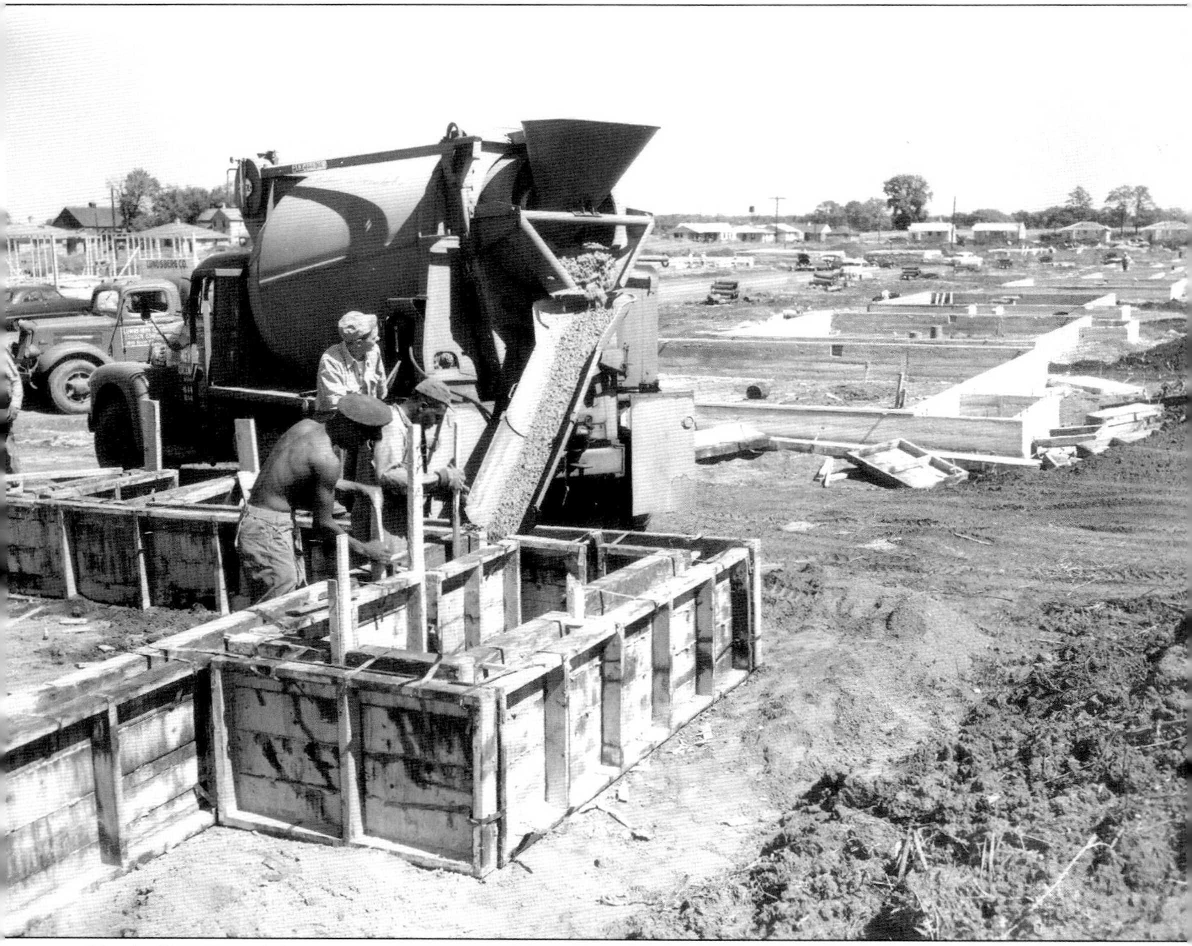

Kimball Hill and Associates wanted the housing development built as quickly as possible so that residents could move in soon after making their down payments. Disputes over rezoning the land from farmland to residential space had delayed construction enough that as soon as rezoning permission was granted, everyone was more than anxious to start work on the development. Builders needed to complete 20 homes per week, so no time was wasted once construction began. The first homes were built in an assembly-like fashion, with multiple homes built simultaneously. Here, a whole block of houses have their foundations poured one right after the other to save time. (Courtesy of RML.)

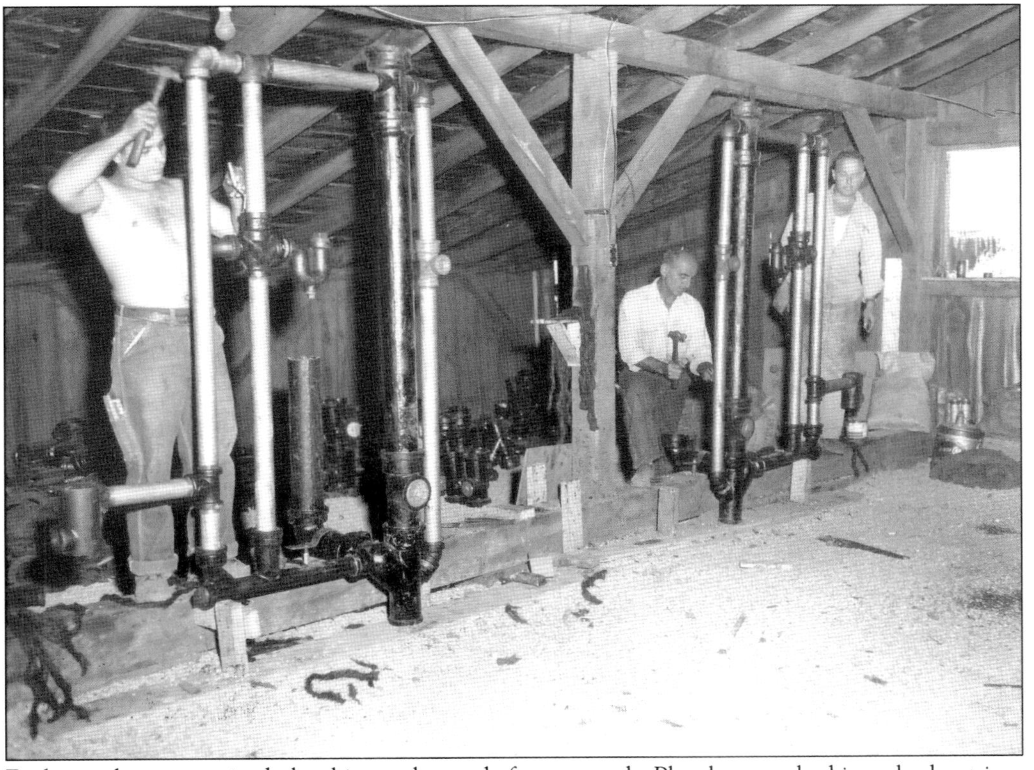

Each new house required plumbing to be made from scratch. Plumbers worked in a shed out in a field near the homes, assembling the pipe structures there. After the plumbing was complete, it was taken out to the houses to be installed as an entire unit. (Courtesy of RML.)

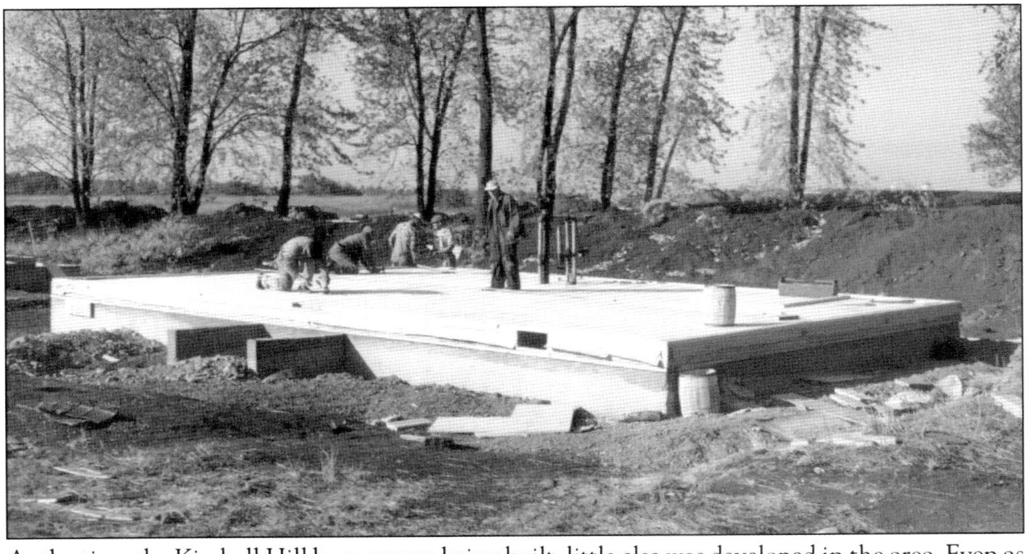

At the time the Kimball Hill homes were being built, little else was developed in the area. Even as workers finalize the flooring for this home, the land surrounding the house looks untouched from its prairie days. Construction workers did not start altering the landscape until after the houses were built and even until after some of the first families had moved in. (Courtesy of RML.)

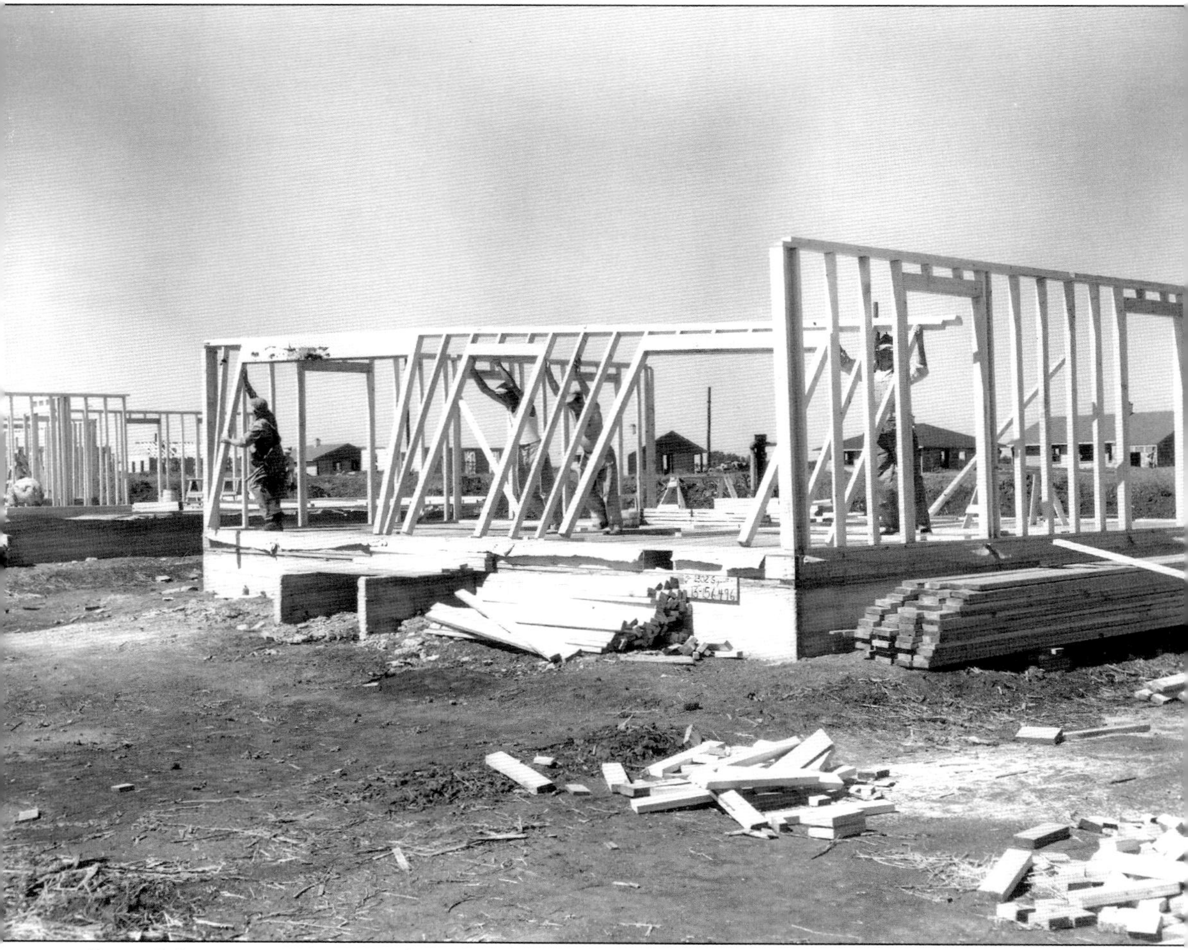

One of the most important phases in construction of these Rolling Meadows homes was the framing. The framing was what gave each home its own character, based upon the developers' designs and how much floor space each homeowner purchased. This particular house appears to be shaping up into a two-bedroom home. The street address is now attached to the side of the foundation, letting workers know that this house will be on Sigwalt Street. (Courtesy of RML.)

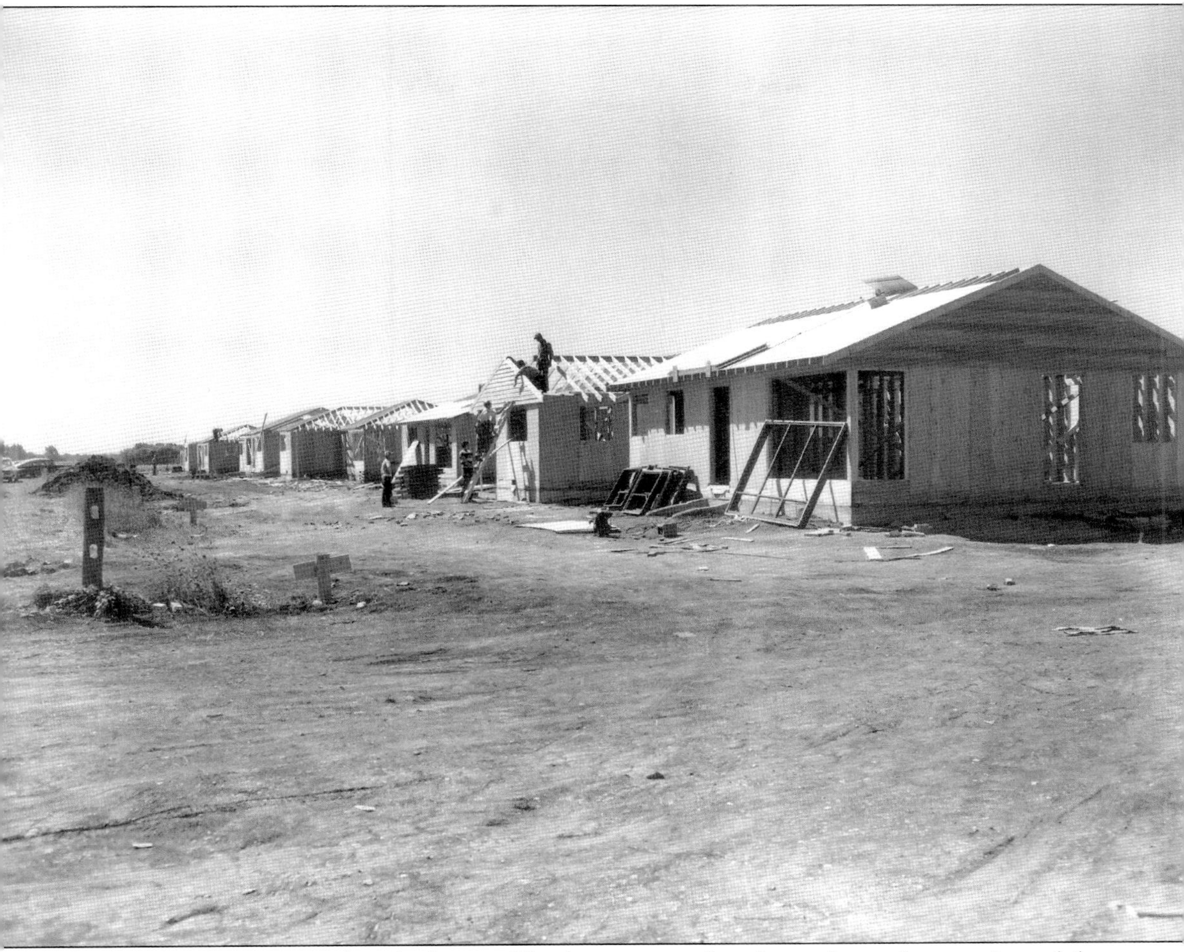

The next step was to seal up the homes. The framing was closed in with wooden panels, and the preassembled eaves were installed. This photograph shows how multiple houses went through the same "assembly" construction simultaneously. Countless workers were needed to complete the homes at the same time as quickly as possible. With the walls closed in, the string of houses is starting to resemble a residential street, a glimpse of what is to come. (Courtesy of RML.)

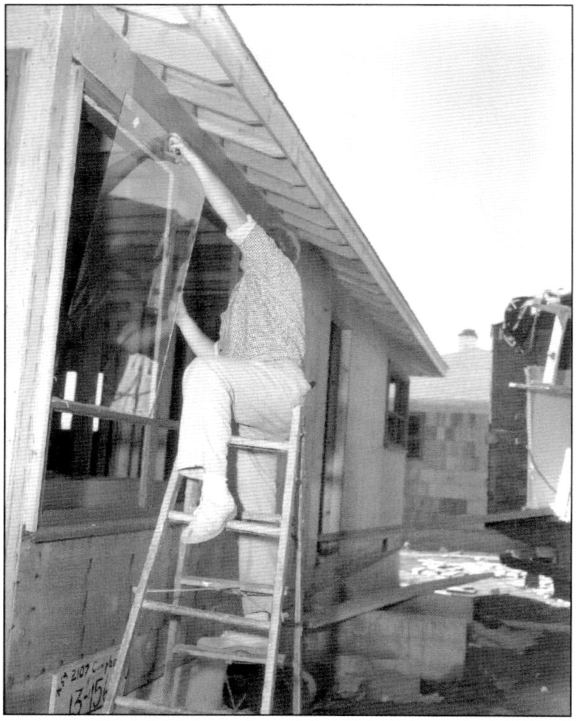

Workers installed windows during the 1950s differently than they do today. Nowadays, precut and preassembled windows are installed, the panes of glass already secure in the framework. Here, in this future Campbell Street home, the interior window framework has already been installed. At left, a worker carefully places each individual pane of glass into the window frame and secures it with glue before attaching the exterior framing. One of the final steps for the exterior of each home was to attach the wood siding and either paint or stain it, below. This home has cedar siding, whereas other homes were upgraded to brick veneer. Here, workers check the siding before staining and sealing it. (Both courtesy of RML.)

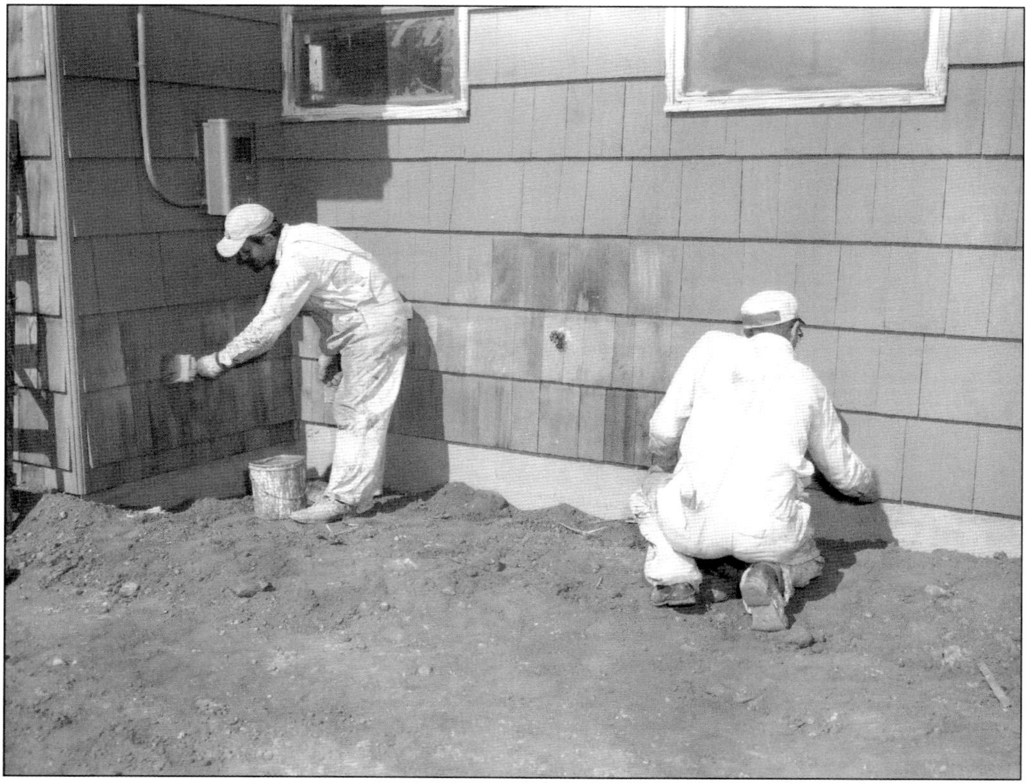

While work was being done to the outside of each home, work continued inside them as well. Electricians, such as this worker, would have to cut and bend pipes at each site to ensure a proper fit for the design of each home. Before any more interior progress was made, both the electrical and plumbing needed to be installed and inspected. (Courtesy of RML.)

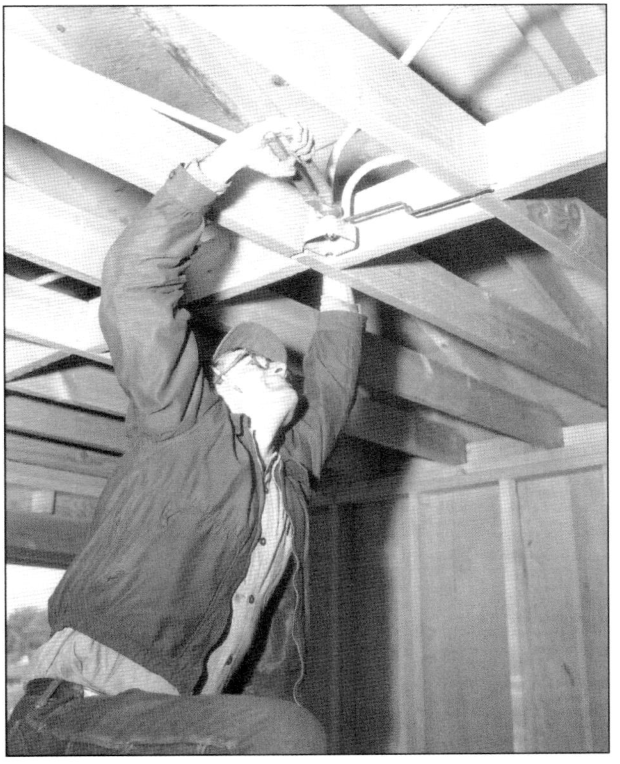

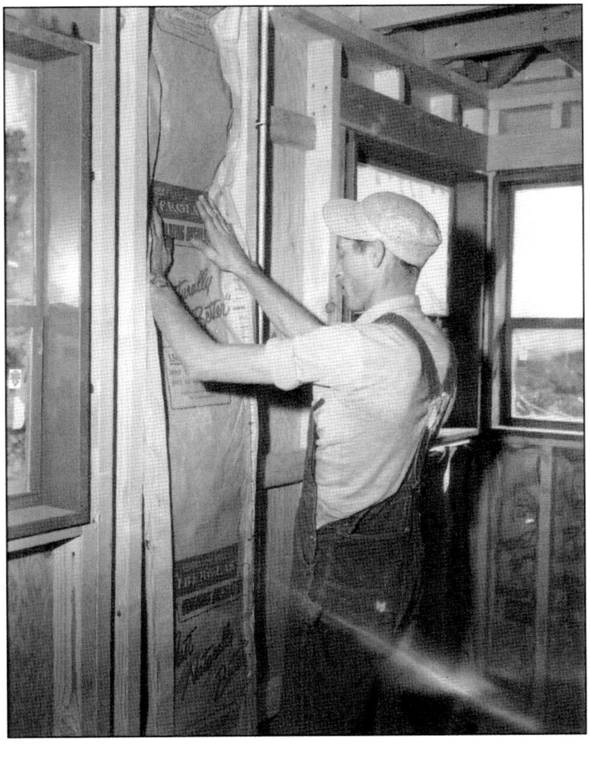

To protect homeowners from the harsh Midwest temperatures all winter long, workers installed insulated panels around the entire perimeter of each home. This was the final step before the drywall was installed and the walls were painted. (Courtesy of RML.)

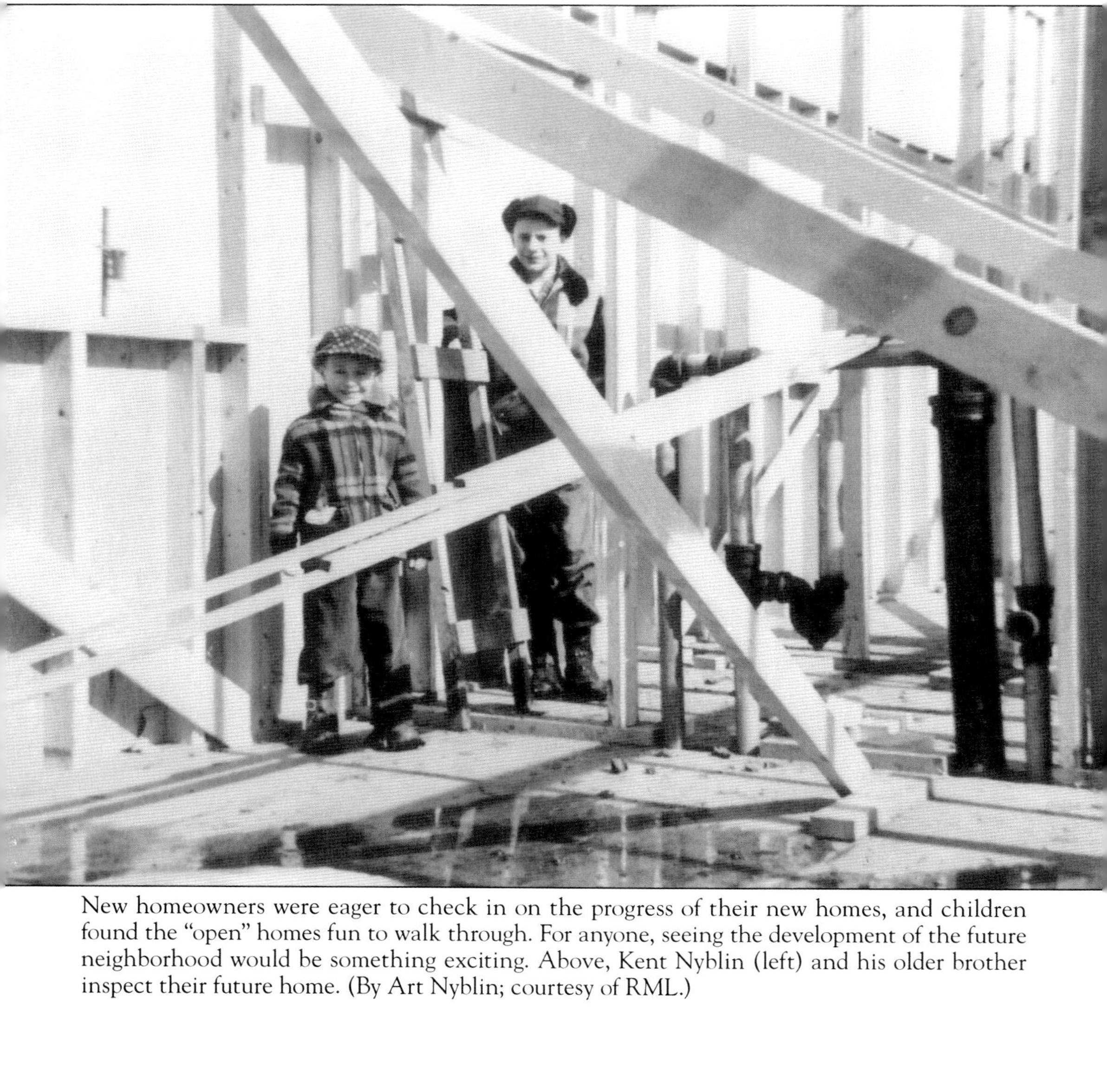

New homeowners were eager to check in on the progress of their new homes, and children found the "open" homes fun to walk through. For anyone, seeing the development of the future neighborhood would be something exciting. Above, Kent Nyblin (left) and his older brother inspect their future home. (By Art Nyblin; courtesy of RML.)

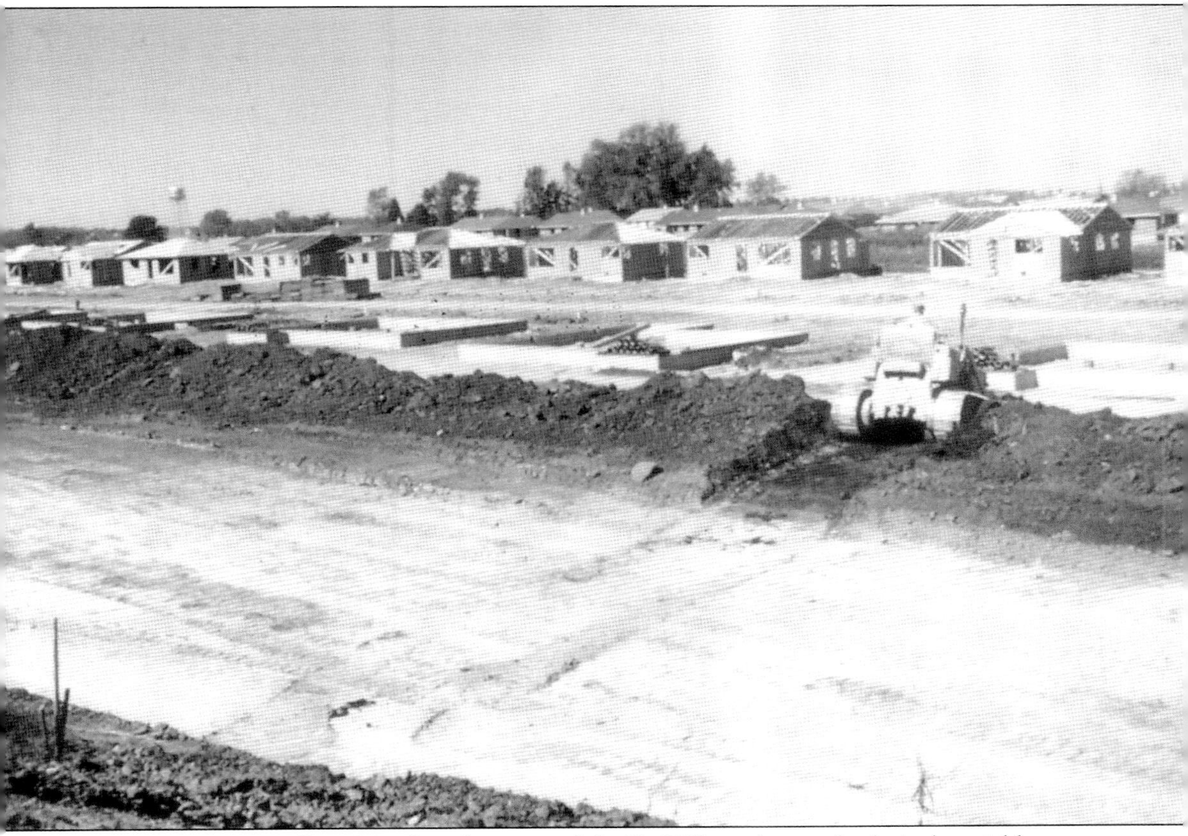

Construction in Rolling Meadows began on July 21, 1953, and moved relatively quickly, at an average of 20 homes per week. The first residents, including the very first family, Victor and Helene Kaseska and their two children, were able to move in by November of the same year. Rain or shine, the dedicated construction workers managed to complete their weekly goal of 20 houses. Here a worker levels and smooths one of the residential streets. (By Emily Berglund; courtesy of RML.)

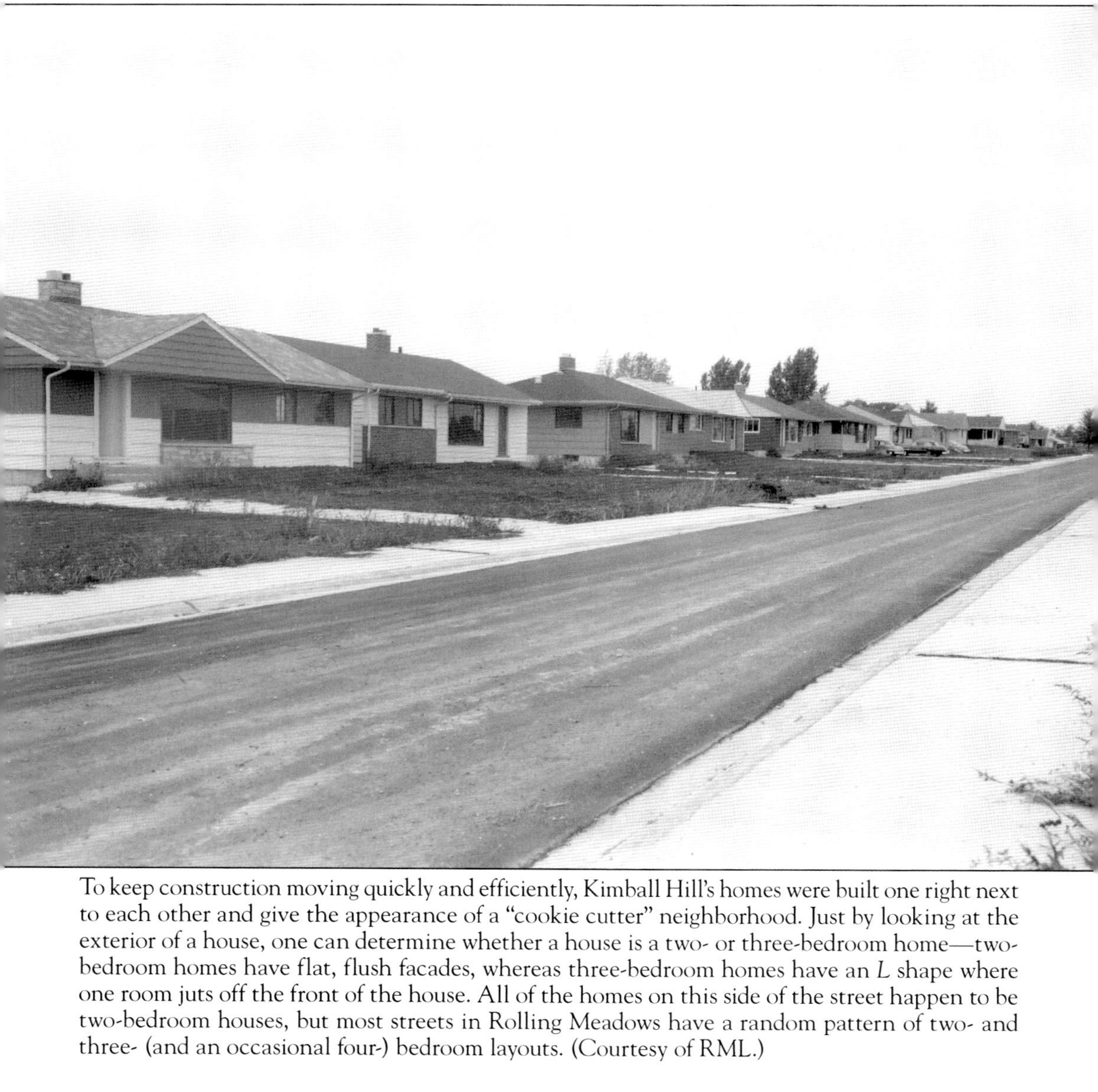

To keep construction moving quickly and efficiently, Kimball Hill's homes were built one right next to each other and give the appearance of a "cookie cutter" neighborhood. Just by looking at the exterior of a house, one can determine whether a house is a two- or three-bedroom home—two-bedroom homes have flat, flush facades, whereas three-bedroom homes have an *L* shape where one room juts off the front of the house. All of the homes on this side of the street happen to be two-bedroom houses, but most streets in Rolling Meadows have a random pattern of two- and three- (and an occasional four-) bedroom layouts. (Courtesy of RML.)

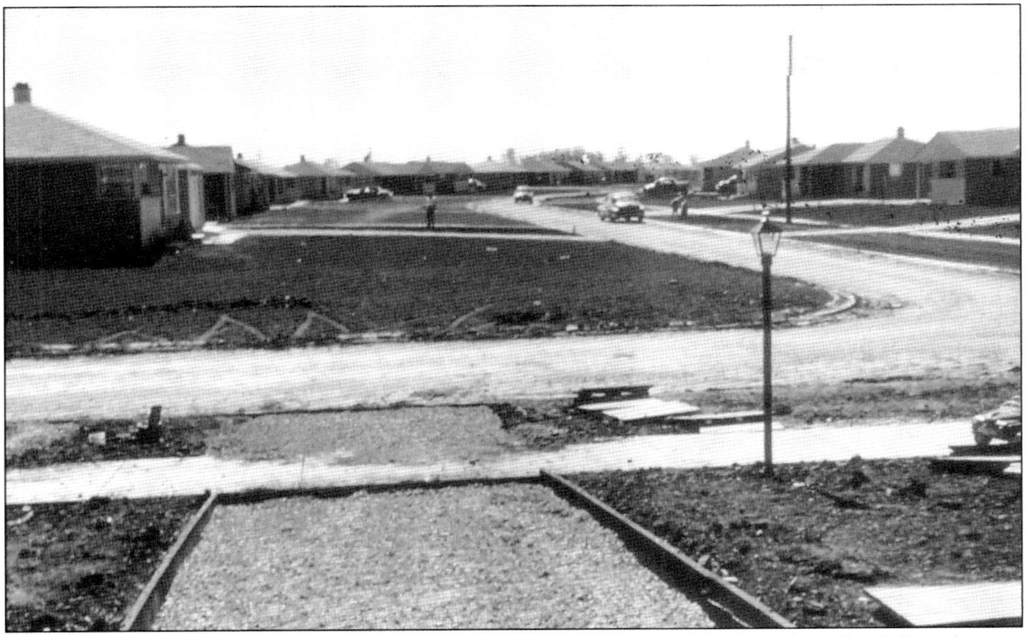

In the early days of Rolling Meadows, there were no paved streets or sidewalks. Many homes did not even have driveways until after residents had moved in. Any amount of rain would produce impossible amounts of mud. Although there were wooden planks laid out in the road for construction and residential vehicles to drive on, cars would often slip off them, and neighbors would work together to pull them out of the mud. Many children lost shoes when walking through it and were forced to play inside. (Above by Emily Berglund, below by Ronald Brightwell; both courtesy of RML.)

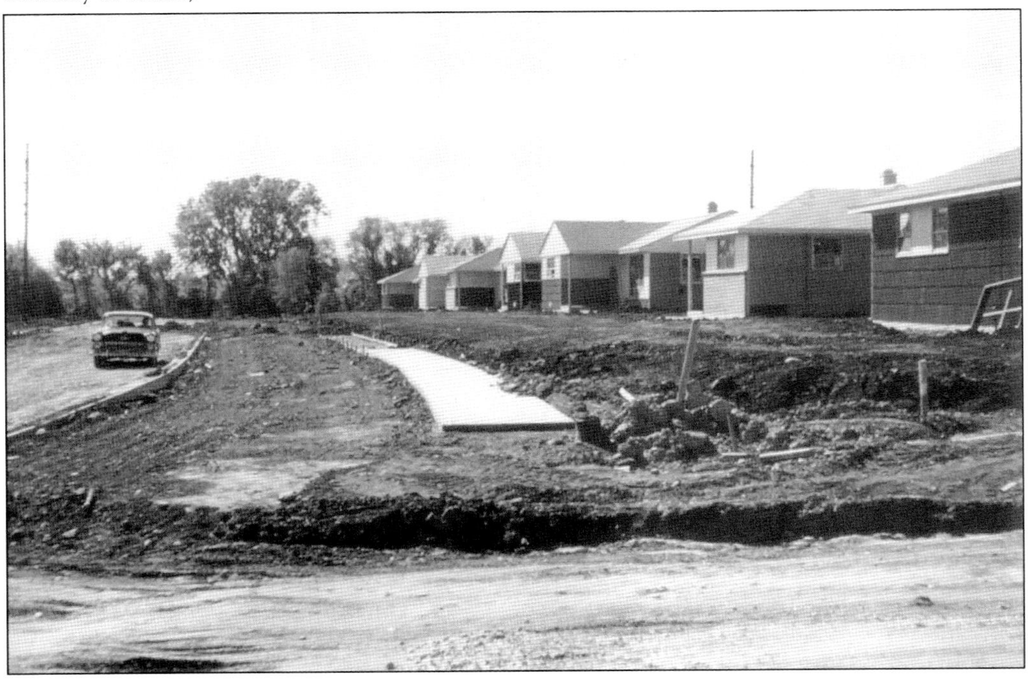

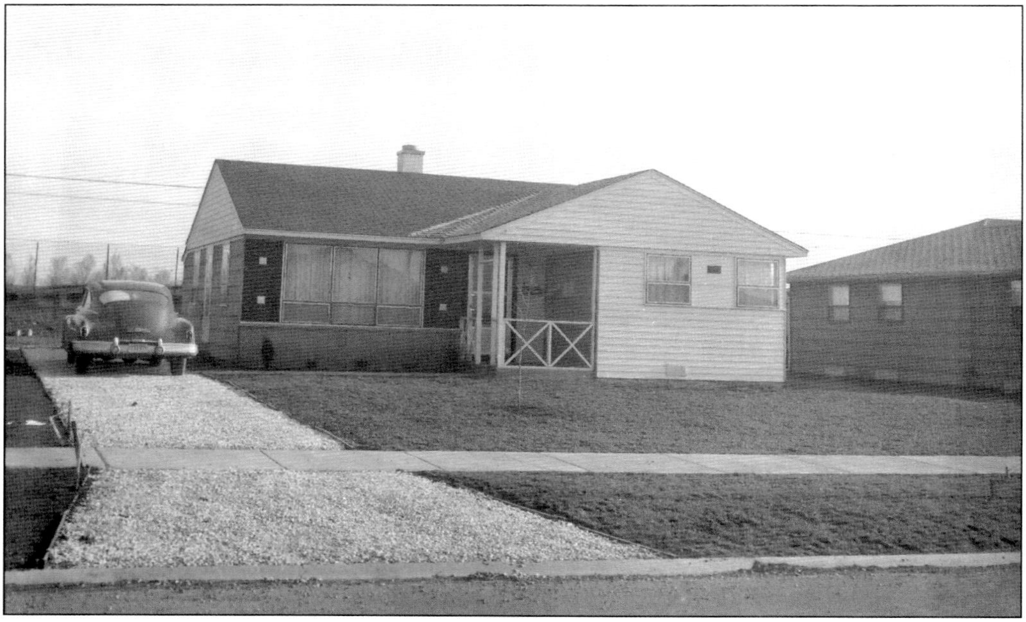

When the first batch of houses was completed, the very first Rolling Meadows residents moved into their brand-new homes. Construction on the house may have been done, but the lots themselves were rather unfinished. Yards, instead of being lush and green, were muddy and dirty, having been worked over with grading equipment from the early stages of construction. However, residents with school-aged children were grateful when sidewalks were installed so that the young students could walk to school without ruining their shoes. Early residents did not let muddy yards (above) or unpaved driveways (below) upset them, as they were still so happy to be living in their very own brand-new homes. (Above by Jim Vandy; both courtesy of RML.)

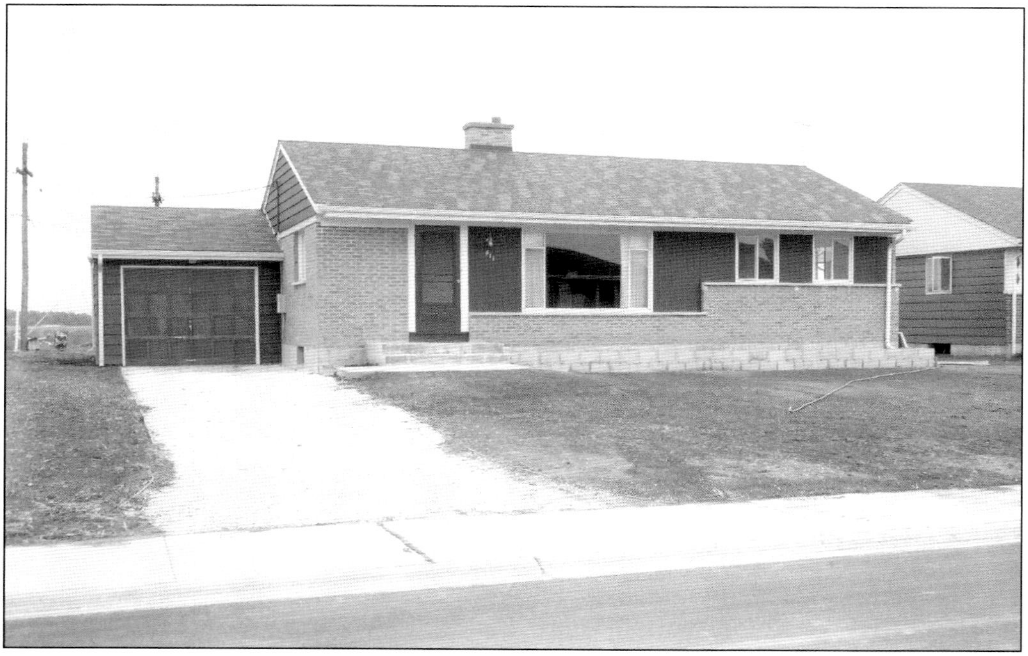

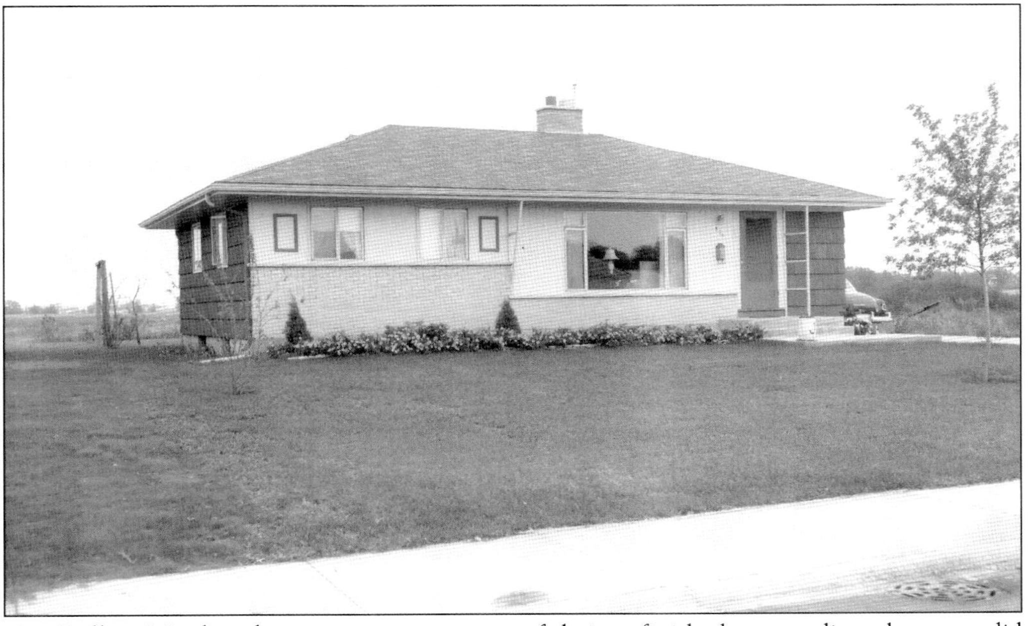

New Rolling Meadows homeowners were aware of their unfinished surroundings, but most did not mind very much. Residents found companionship with their new neighbors as they navigated the "muddy years" together. And, soon enough, construction was complete and each lot had its desired level of curb appeal and personality, making it even better in the eyes of homeowners than the model home they had seen just months or years before. (Courtesy of RML.)

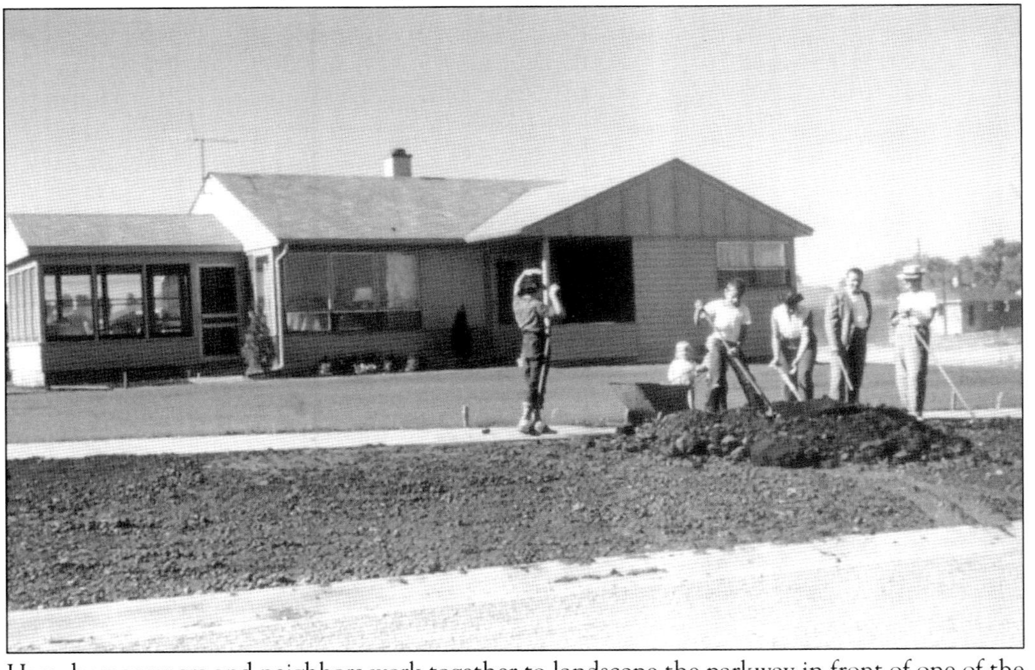

Here, homeowners and neighbors work together to landscape the parkway in front of one of the new Rolling Meadows homes. A strong sense of community grew among neighbors from helping each other with tasks such as these. (By Emily Berglund; courtesy of RML.)

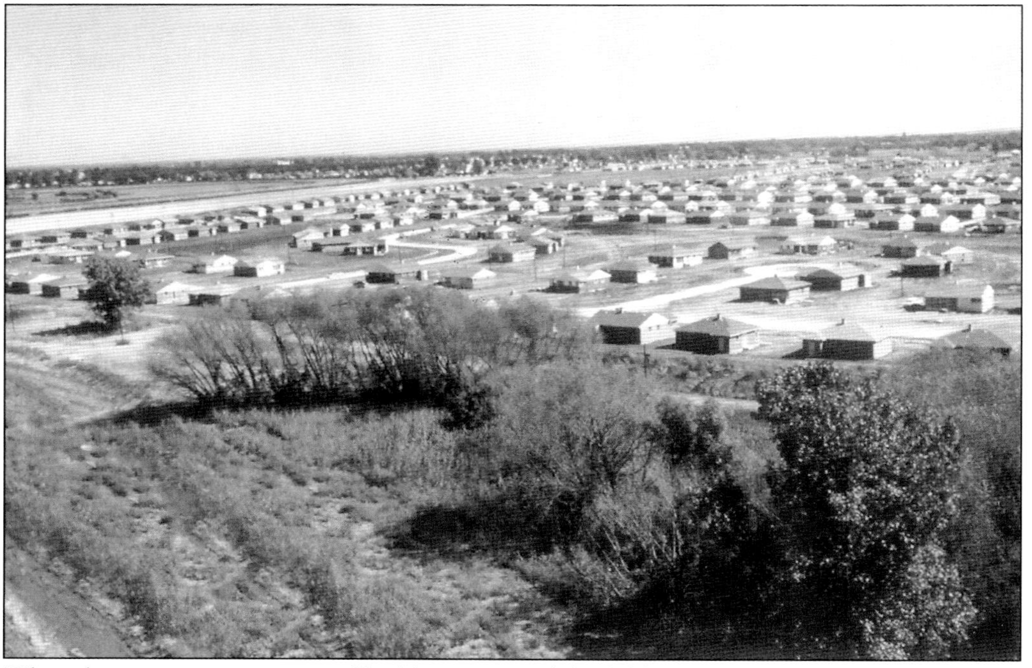

When the construction crews and builders converted the fields of prairie landscape into a housing development, almost all of the trees in the area were removed. Houses and street layouts dictated where trees could be planted. At first, the new Rolling Meadows neighborhood looked empty and barren, a large sea of house after house and street after street, above. But soon developers were able to go in and plant trees throughout the community, thus creating a more lush and scenic environment. (Both by Emily Berglund; courtesy of RML.)

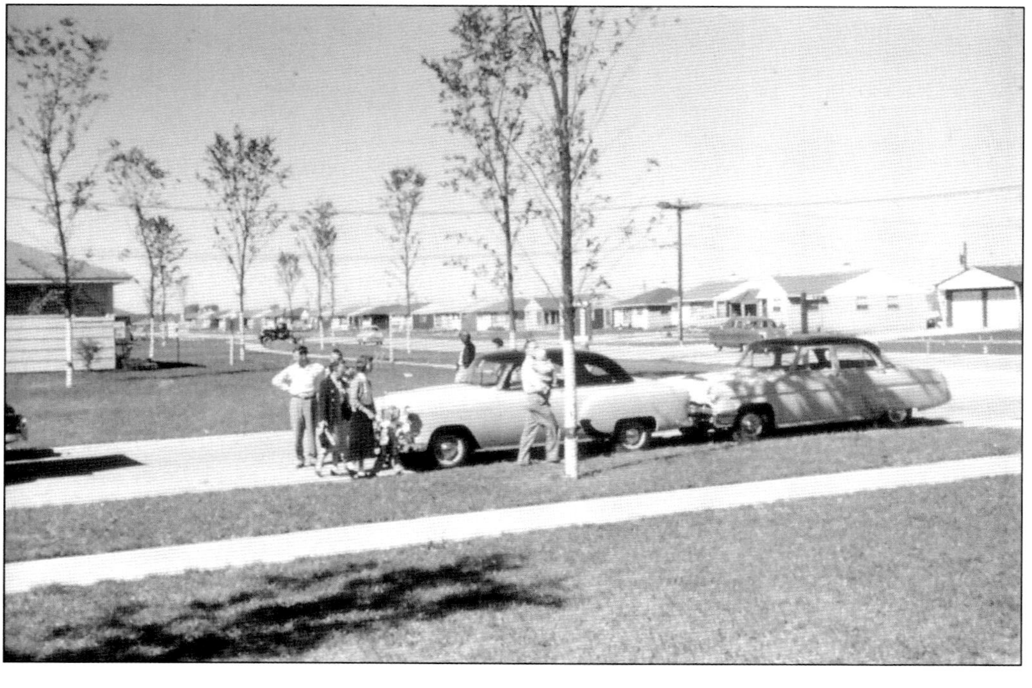

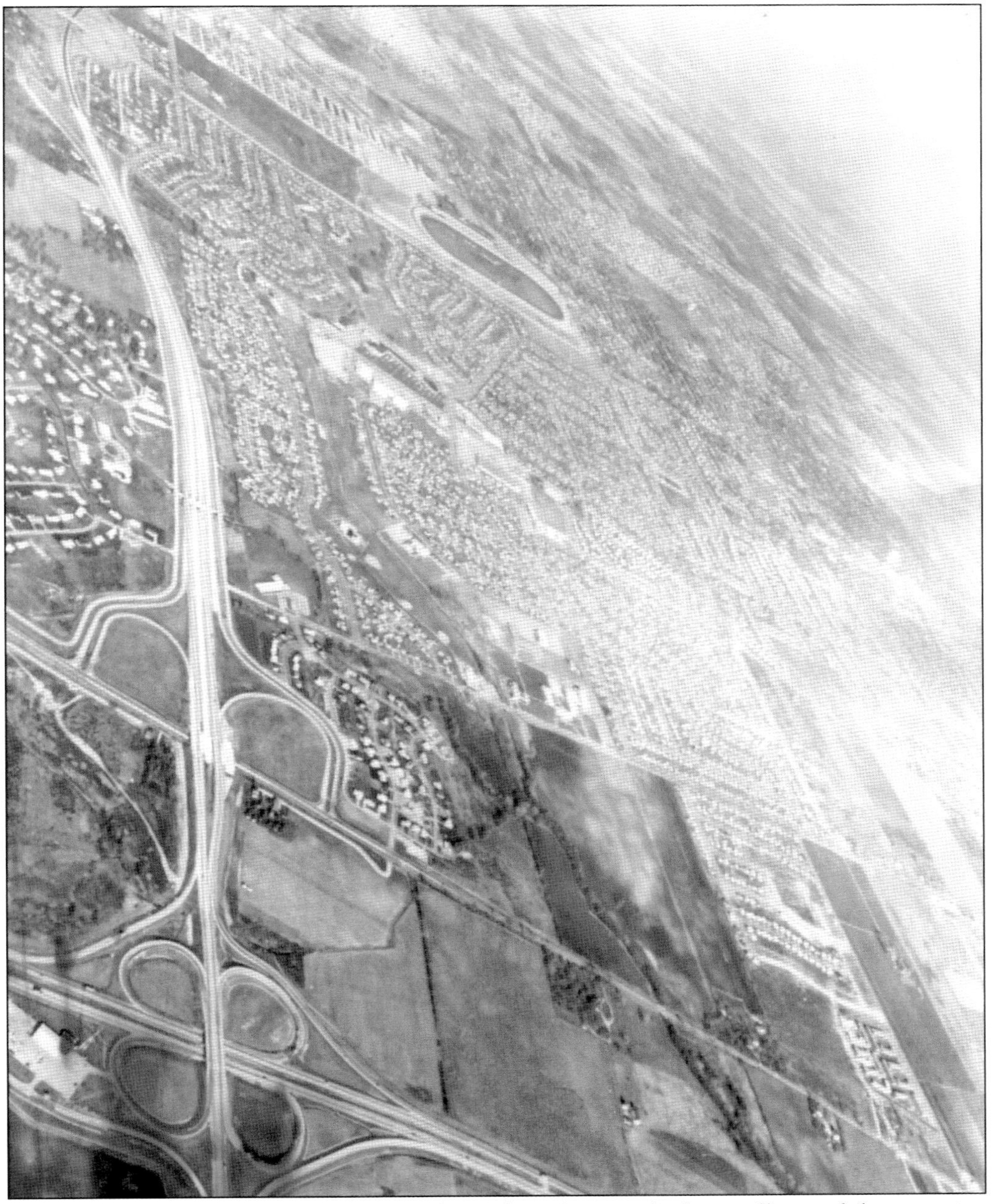

This aerial view of Rolling Meadows in the early 1960s reveals the small size of the new city. At top center are Arlington Park Racetrack and Euclid Avenue, the latter of which denotes the northern boundary of Rolling Meadows. The city extends just west past the wide highway at far left (Illinois Route 53) and south of the expressway at bottom center (Interstate 90). (By Jim McFeggan; courtesy of RML.)

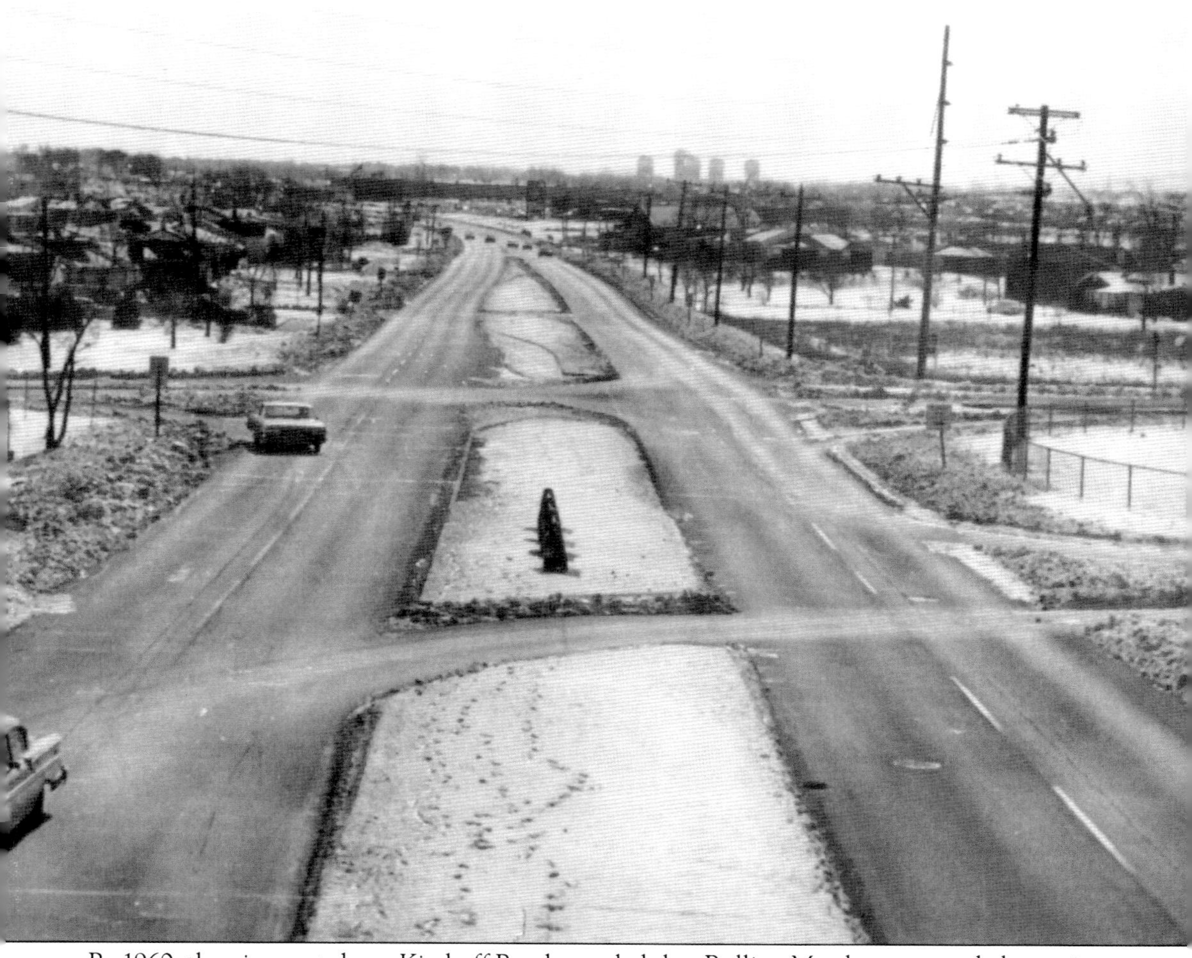

By 1960, the view east down Kirchoff Road revealed that Rolling Meadows was truly becoming a developed, bustling town. Ramps leading vehicles both onto and off of Illinois Route 53 (far right) connected this new town to the rest of the northwestern suburbs as well as to the heart of Chicago. Behind the rows and rows of starter homes is the commercial center of the city, where the stores of the Rolling Meadows Shopping Center and others are located. Although Rolling Meadows is subject to cold and harsh winters, the city's public works department is showing its abilities by the plowed, dry streets. (By Charles Poellien; courtesy of RML.)

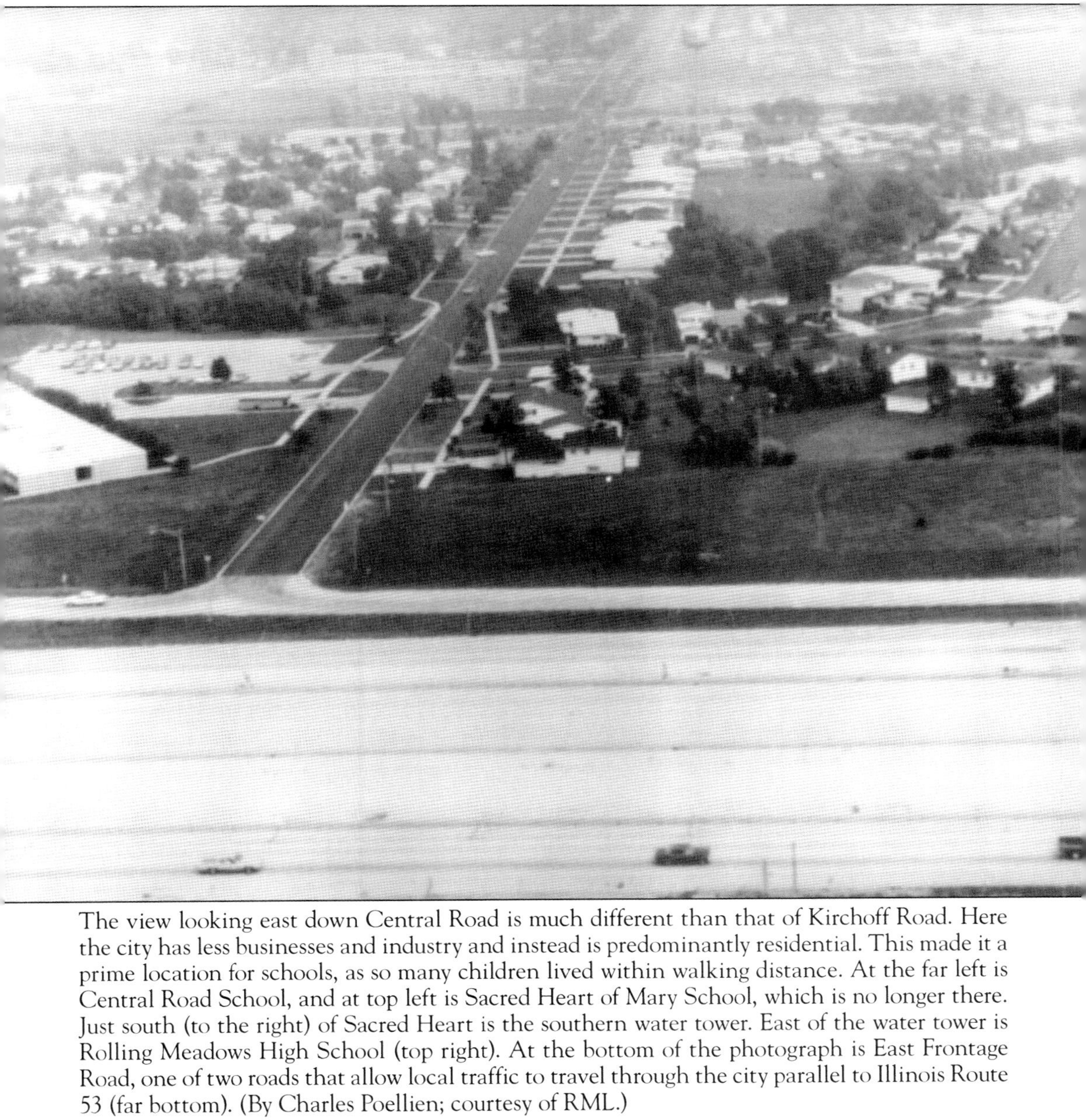

The view looking east down Central Road is much different than that of Kirchoff Road. Here the city has less businesses and industry and instead is predominantly residential. This made it a prime location for schools, as so many children lived within walking distance. At the far left is Central Road School, and at top left is Sacred Heart of Mary School, which is no longer there. Just south (to the right) of Sacred Heart is the southern water tower. East of the water tower is Rolling Meadows High School (top right). At the bottom of the photograph is East Frontage Road, one of two roads that allow local traffic to travel through the city parallel to Illinois Route 53 (far bottom). (By Charles Poellien; courtesy of RML.)

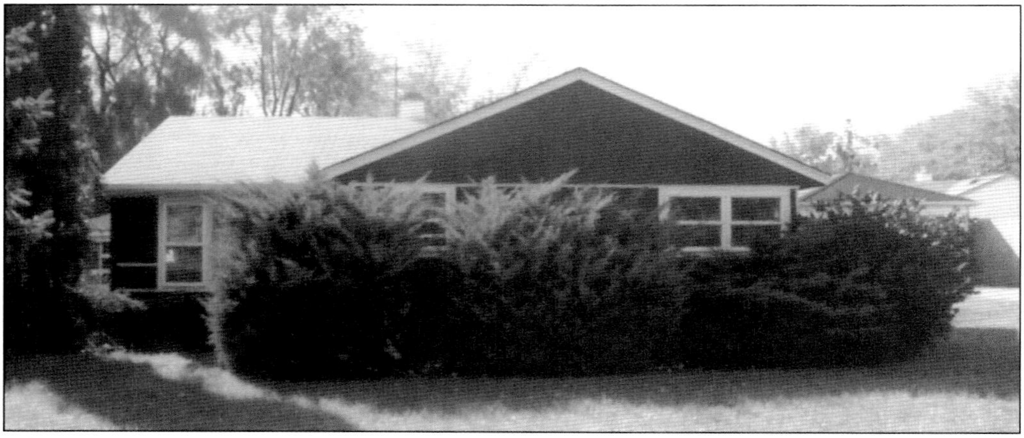

After the initial construction was over in Rolling Meadows, happy homeowners moved into their homes and worked to personalize their new properties. After grass was planted, residents added flowers, shrubbery, and gardens, displaying their pride in their new home and community. The owners of this home used shrubbery for curb appeal as well as for privacy from the busy residential street. (Courtesy of Robin Schroeder.)

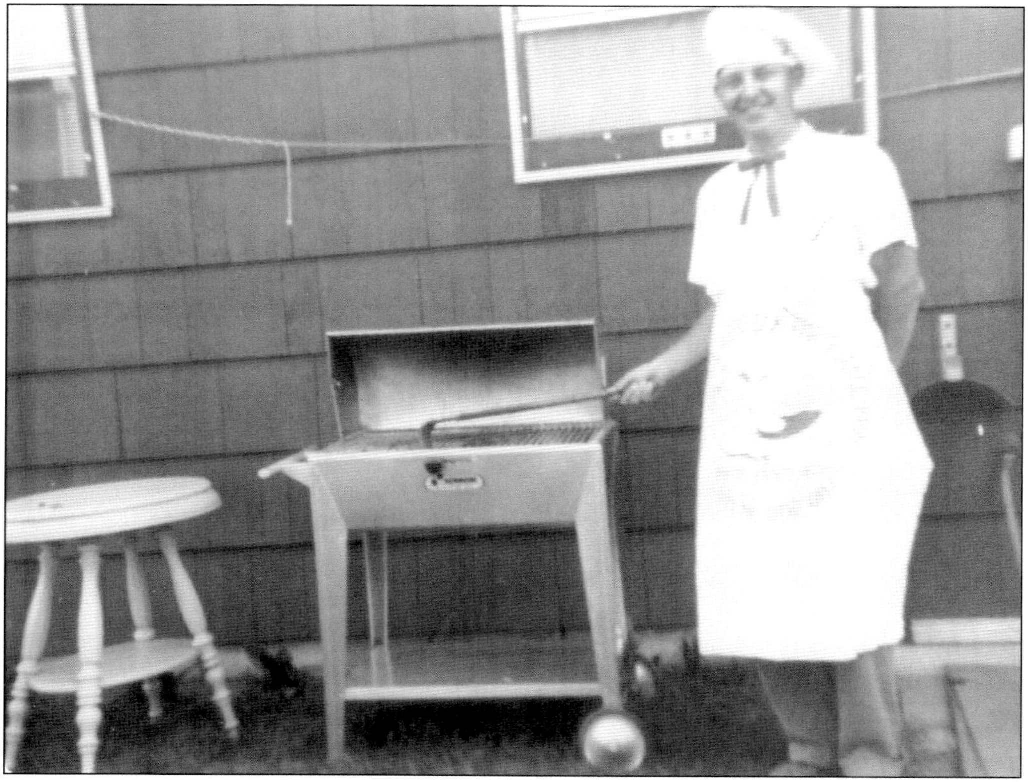

New Rolling Meadows residents had the same idea; they were looking for a sense of community, a place they could call home and of which they could be proud. A homeowner not only got a new house in the purchase price but also a sizeable yard perfect for outdoor activities. Art Nyblin, a happy new homeowner, enjoys his new home and yard while grilling in August 1955. (By Art Nyblin; courtesy of RML.)

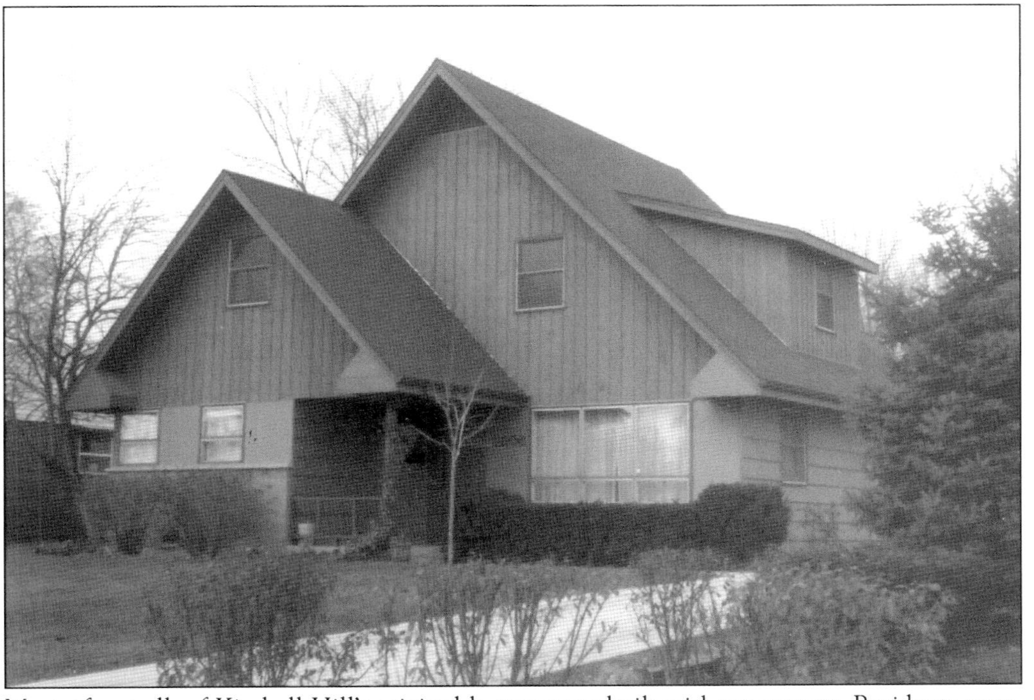

Most, if not all, of Kimball Hill's original homes were built without garages. Residents were, however, provided with driveways on which they could park their cars. By 1955, Rolling Meadows residents were already planning additions to make to their homes. Most homeowners simply wished to attach a closed garage at the end of their driveways to protect their cars from the harsh Midwestern winters. By the 1960s, larger additions were underway. Families that wanted more space but loved their home and community in Rolling Meadows built second-story additions or added a split level off the back instead of moving to a larger home. These are two examples of the common additions found in Rolling Meadows. It is still possible to determine whether these houses started out as Kimball Hill's two- or three-bedroom models from the shape of the first floor of the house. (Both, courtesy of Esther Perica.)

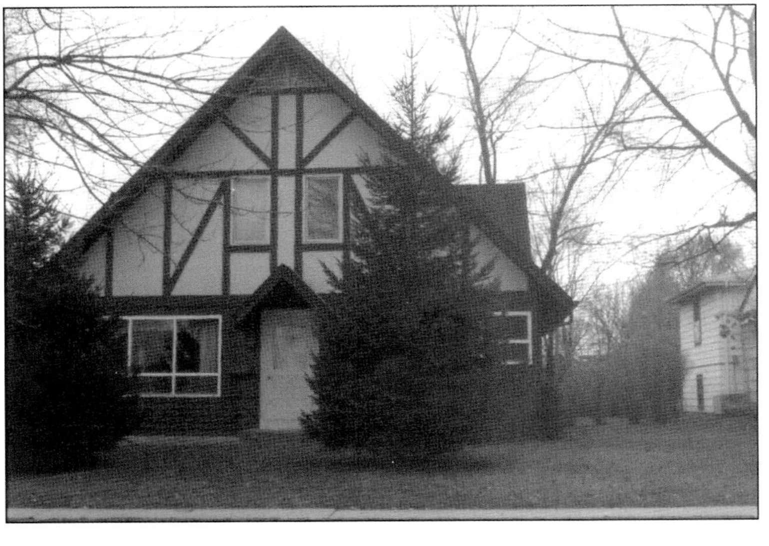

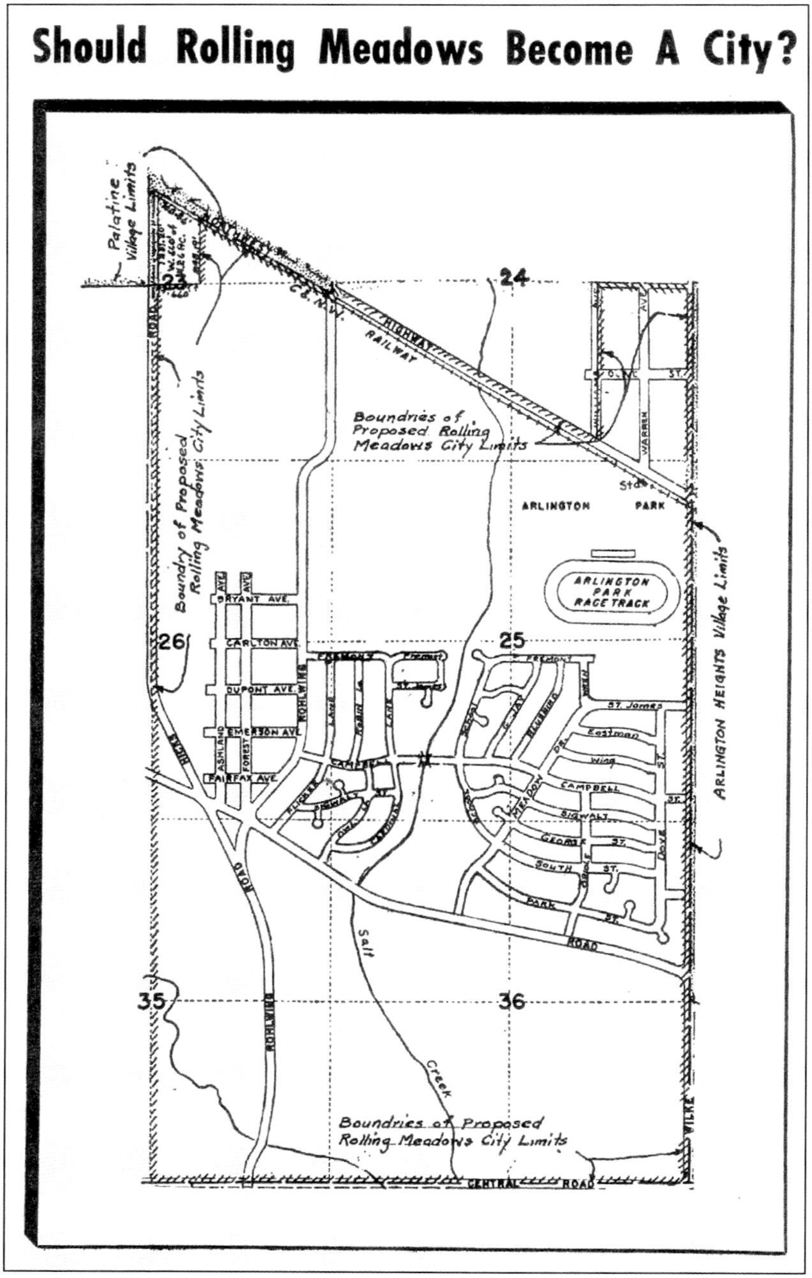

By the end of 1954, the Rolling Meadows Homeowners Association was so considerable that Kimball Hill and residents started to think about incorporation. Originally meant to serve as a liaison between the development builders and homeowners, the homeowners association was hesitant to move forward with incorporation. Louis Ancel and Jack Siegel, the corporation counsel of Maywood (Illinois) and attorney for the Metropolitan Housing and Planning Council of Chicago respectively, wrote a pamphlet describing the advantages of incorporation and distributed it to Rolling Meadows residents. Pictured above is the cover. Ancel went on to help the development legally move forward to become a city. (Courtesy of RML.)

Two

An Official City

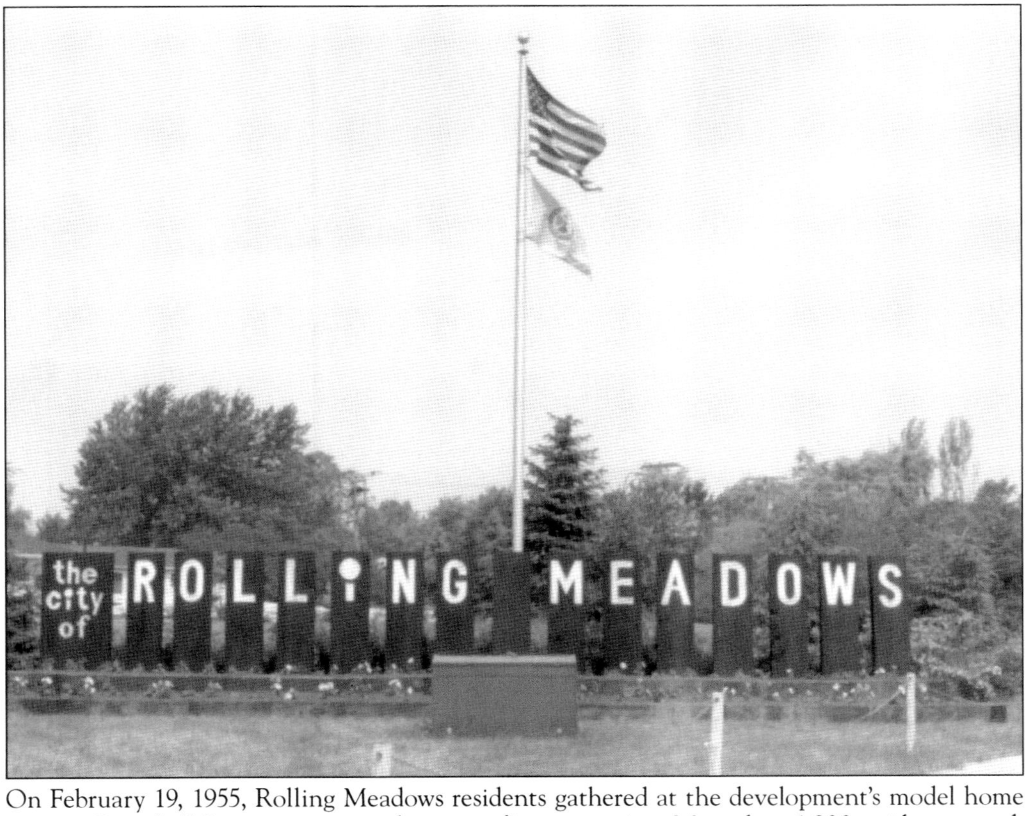

On February 19, 1955, Rolling Meadows residents gathered at the development's model home unit on Campbell Street to vote on the issue of incorporation. More than 1,200 residents voted; 759 were in favor of incorporation, and 447 were against it. On February 26, 1955, county judge Otto Kerner signed incorporation papers for the newly proclaimed City of Rolling Meadows. (By Rick Sutton; courtesy of RML.)

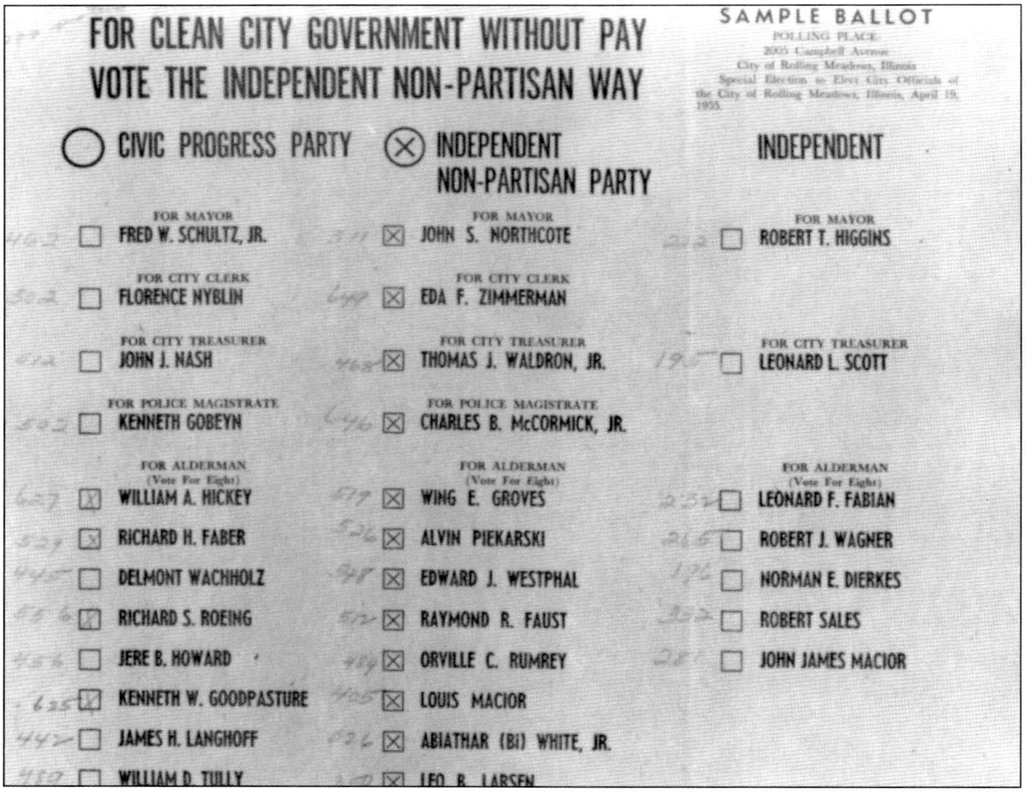

FOR CLEAN CITY GOVERNMENT WITHOUT PAY
VOTE THE INDEPENDENT NON-PARTISAN WAY

SAMPLE BALLOT

POLLING PLACE:
2005 Campbell Avenue
City of Rolling Meadows, Illinois
Special Election to Elect City Officials of the City of Rolling Meadows, Illinois, April 19, 1955.

◯ CIVIC PROGRESS PARTY	⊗ INDEPENDENT NON-PARTISAN PARTY	INDEPENDENT
FOR MAYOR	FOR MAYOR	FOR MAYOR
☐ FRED W. SCHULTZ, JR.	☒ JOHN S. NORTHCOTE	☐ ROBERT T. HIGGINS
FOR CITY CLERK	FOR CITY CLERK	
☐ FLORENCE NYBLIN	☒ EDA F. ZIMMERMAN	
FOR CITY TREASURER	FOR CITY TREASURER	FOR CITY TREASURER
☐ JOHN J. NASH	☒ THOMAS J. WALDRON, JR.	☐ LEONARD L. SCOTT
FOR POLICE MAGISTRATE	FOR POLICE MAGISTRATE	
☐ KENNETH GOBEYN	☒ CHARLES B. McCORMICK, JR.	
FOR ALDERMAN (Vote For Eight)	FOR ALDERMAN (Vote For Eight)	FOR ALDERMAN (Vote For Eight)
☒ WILLIAM A. HICKEY	☒ WING E. GROVES	☐ LEONARD F. FABIAN
☒ RICHARD H. FABER	☒ ALVIN PIEKARSKI	☐ ROBERT J. WAGNER
☐ DELMONT WACHHOLZ	☒ EDWARD J. WESTPHAL	☐ NORMAN E. DIERKES
☒ RICHARD S. ROEING	☒ RAYMOND R. FAUST	☐ ROBERT SALES
☐ JERE B. HOWARD	☒ ORVILLE C. RUMREY	☐ JOHN JAMES MACIOR
☒ KENNETH W. GOODPASTURE	☒ LOUIS MACIOR	
☐ JAMES H. LANGHOFF	☒ ABIATHAR (BI) WHITE, JR.	
☐ WILLIAM D. TULLY	☒ LEO B. LARSEN	

After Rolling Meadows became an official city, it was necessary to elect city officials. Three candidates ran for mayor of Rolling Meadows in the 1955 election—Fred W. Schultz Jr. (pictured below with his Civic Progress Party campaign car), John S. Northcote, and Robert T. Higgins. Northcote was elected as the first mayor of Rolling Meadows. Also elected from the Independent Non-Partisan Party were Eda F. Zimmerman for city clerk and Charles B. McCormick Jr. for police magistrate. This sample ballot has the unofficial poll totals penciled in. (Both by Art Nyblin; courtesy of RML.)

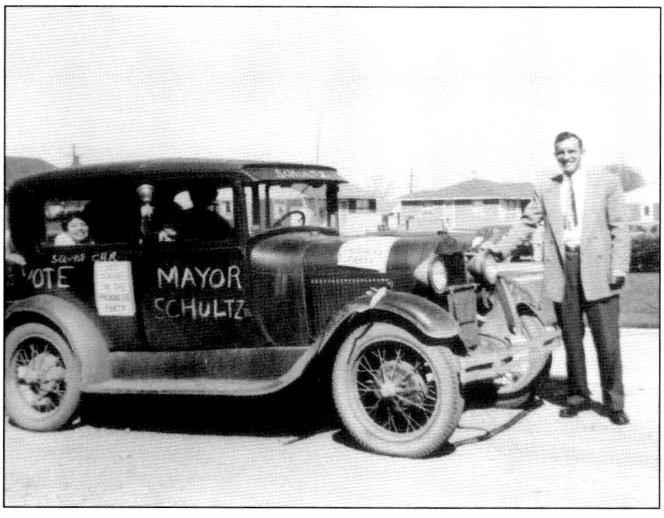

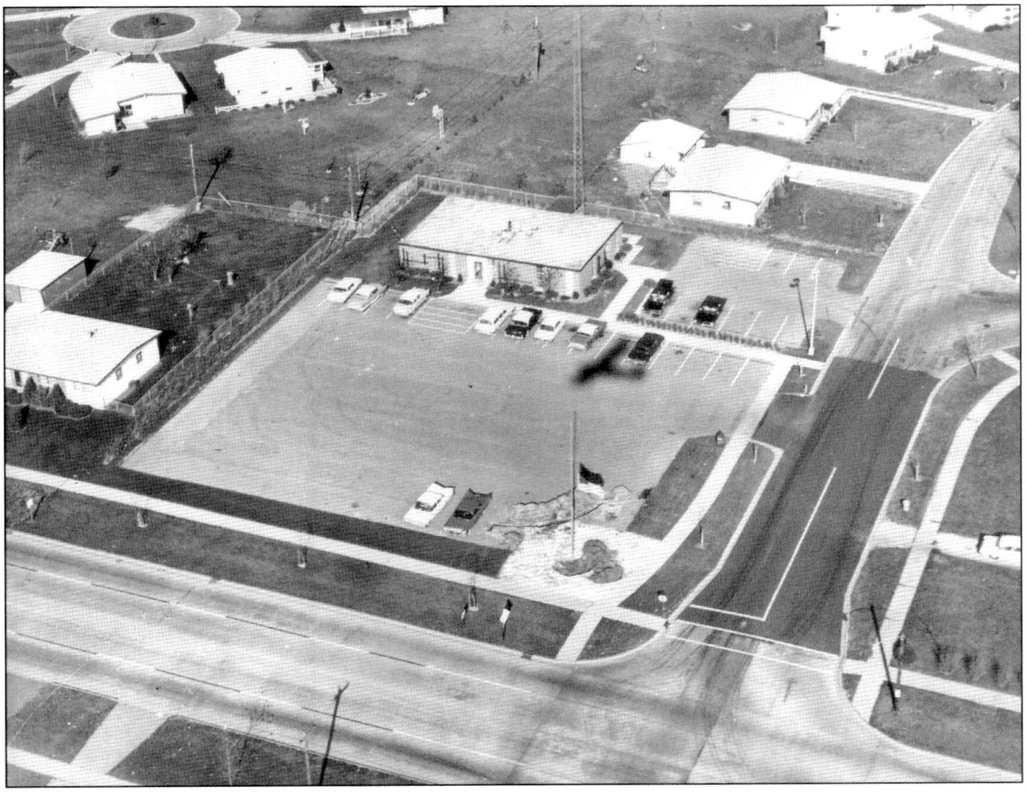

The first city hall building was literally "housed" in one of Kimball Hill's starter homes, which he generously provided for the city's use. The city officials quickly outgrew their headquarters, and a decision was made to purchase land on the corner of Kirchoff Road (above, left to right) and Owl Drive (above, top to bottom), where it still resides today. The building was dedicated on April 15, 1961. The community celebrated with a parade and a full open house of the new building, and all the residents were very pleased with the larger official building. However, by 1969, officials had already outgrown their current quarters and prepared for the first addition to city hall. (Above by Jim McFeggan, below by Capt. Ralph Evans; both courtesy of RML.)

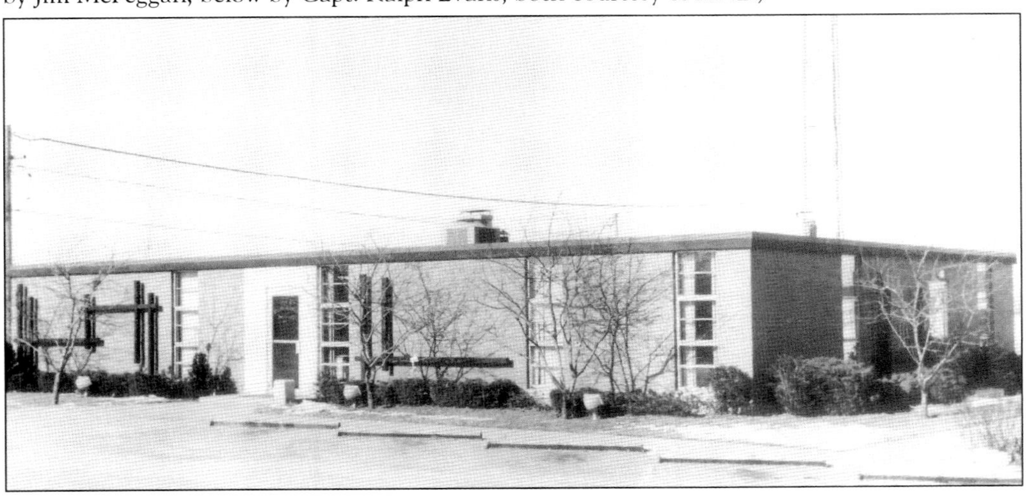

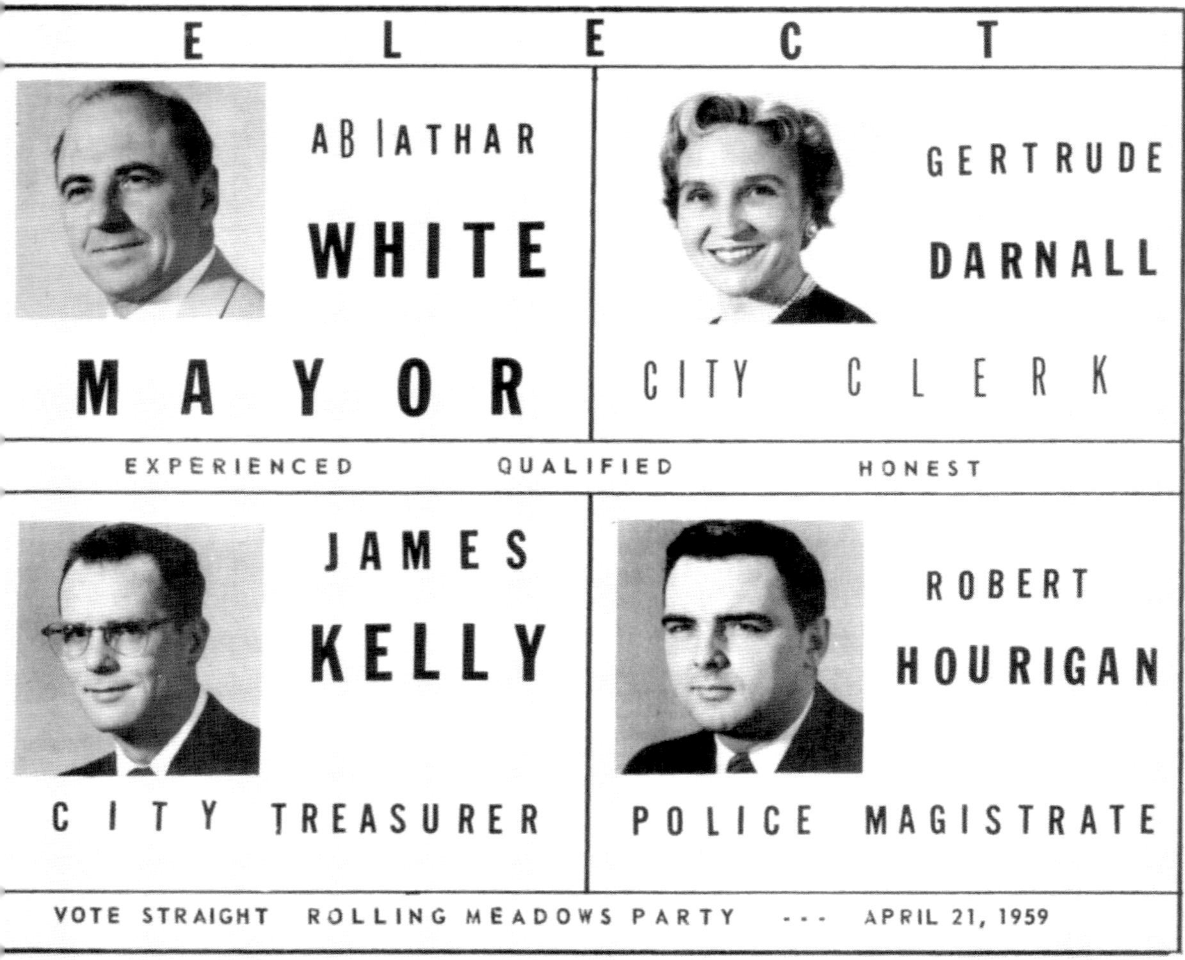

"Vote Straight . . . Party" was a common tagline for city election materials in Rolling Meadows. This particular political advertisement was for the election of 1959 in support of the Rolling Meadows Party. Of the four candidates pictured, only Gertrude Darnall was elected, for her position as city clerk. Abiathar White lost the mayoral spot to John Woods. James Kelly lost as city treasurer to Frank Zupan, and Robert Hourigan lost as police magistrate to Robert Casey. Darnall was reelected in 1963 and again in 1967 as city clerk. She served until 1969, when she resigned and Elizabeth Houldsworth filled the position. (Courtesy of RML.)

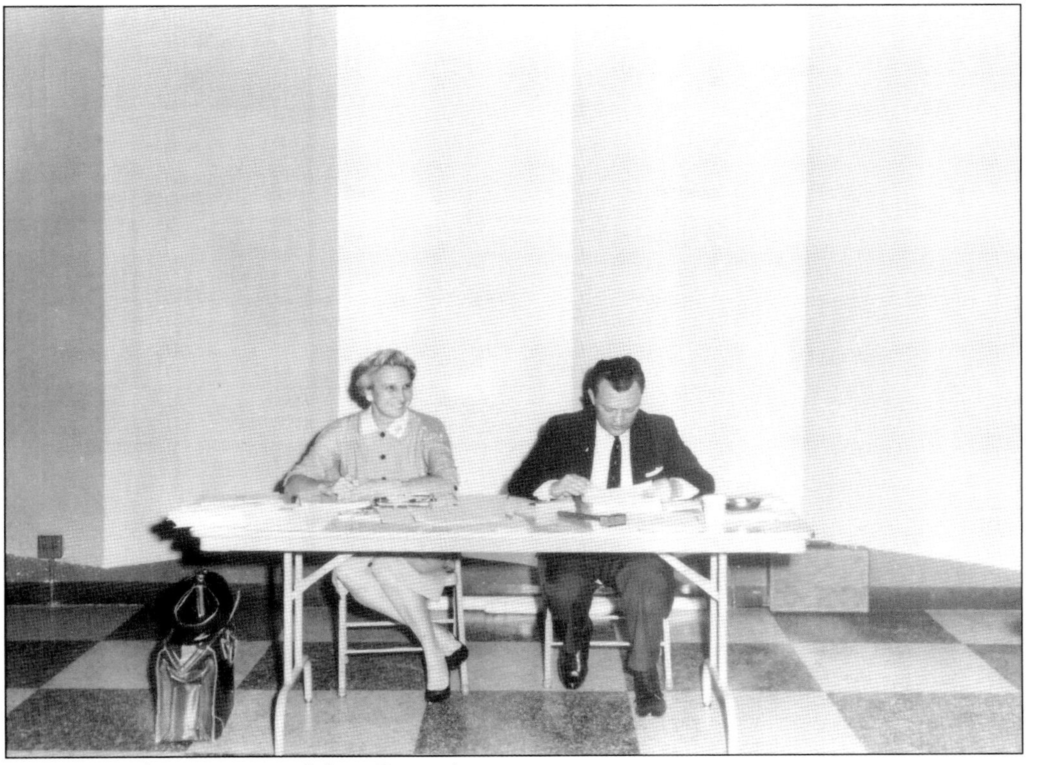

Rolling Meadows Party candidate Gertrude Darnall and Peoples Economy Party candidate John Woods ran for the offices of city clerk and mayor, respectively, and won in the election of 1959. Above, they sit in the basement of the Bank of Rolling Meadows, ready to begin a city council meeting. The bank's large multipurpose room housed civic, political, and social events during the early years of the city. Right, a placard names the city officials as they were in 1965. Much to the disappointment and sadness of his community, Mayor Woods stepped down from his position on December 28, 1965. (Above by Capt. Ralph Evans, courtesy of RML; right courtesy of Esther Perica.)

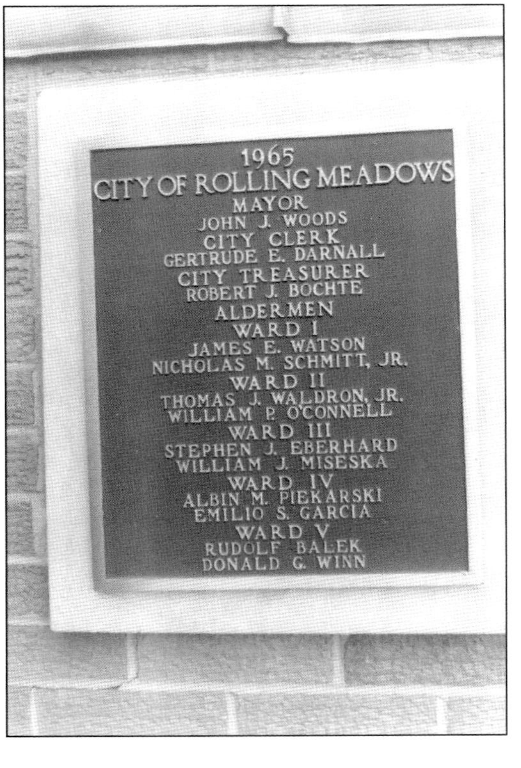

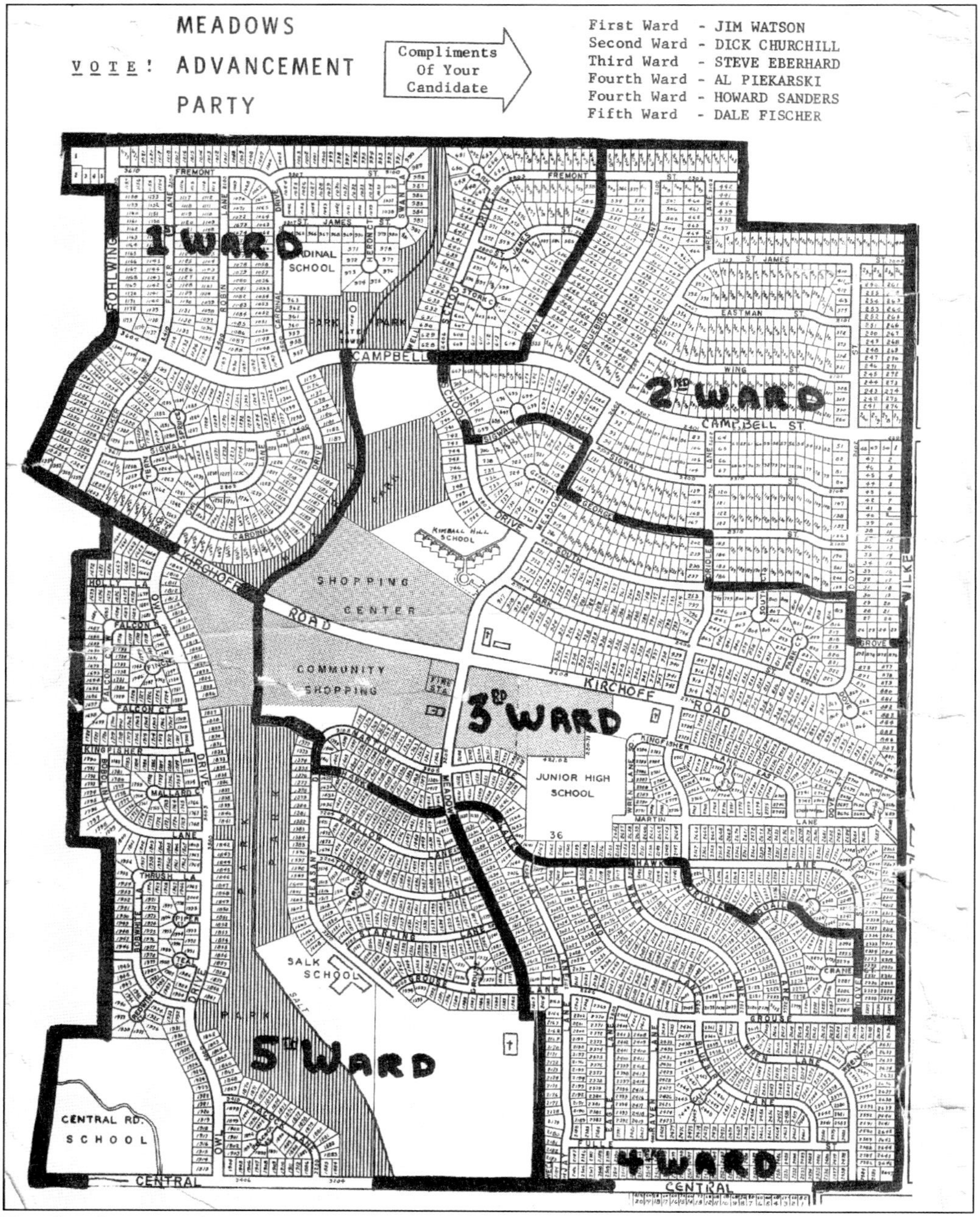

For the election of 1961, a new political party had formed. It was a blend of three previous parties—the Republican Party, the Rolling Meadows Party, and the Voters Interest Party. This new, blended party, called the Meadows Advancement Party, gave out these city ward maps as a political advertising tool. Of the six candidates listed, five were elected. They were James Watson (Ward 1), Stephen Eberhard (Ward 3), Albin Piekarski (Ward 4, two-year term), Howard Sanders (Ward 4, four-year term), and Dale Fischer (Ward 5). The map also gives an indication of the boundaries of Rolling Meadows as they were in 1961 as well as the variations in residential density throughout the city. (Courtesy of RML.)

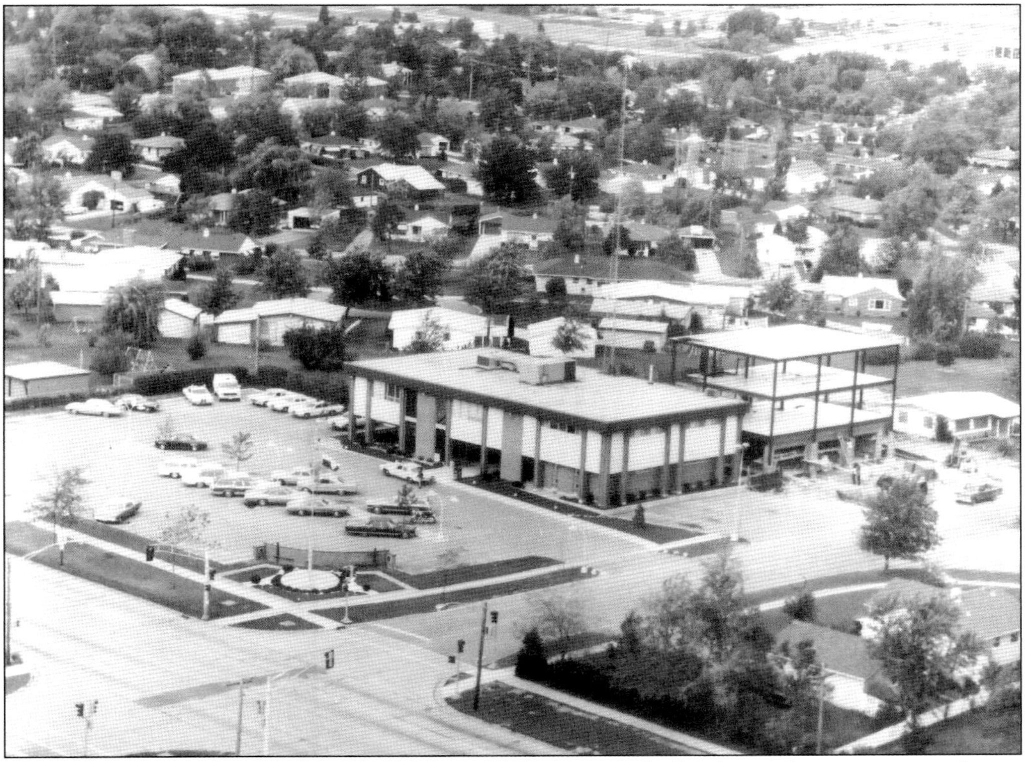

Both of these photographs depict the 1971 addition to city hall. The city's growing population and expanding civic duties required this second addition, which almost doubled the size of the building after the first addition in 1969. Among the new features were enhanced facilities for the police department, additional meeting rooms for civic meetings, and an elevator to accommodate more of the city's residents. The top photograph shows the framework for the new addition on the north-facing facade, while the bottom photograph depicts the building after renovations were completed. (Above by Capt. Ralph Evans, courtesy of RML; below courtesy of Dom Najolia.)

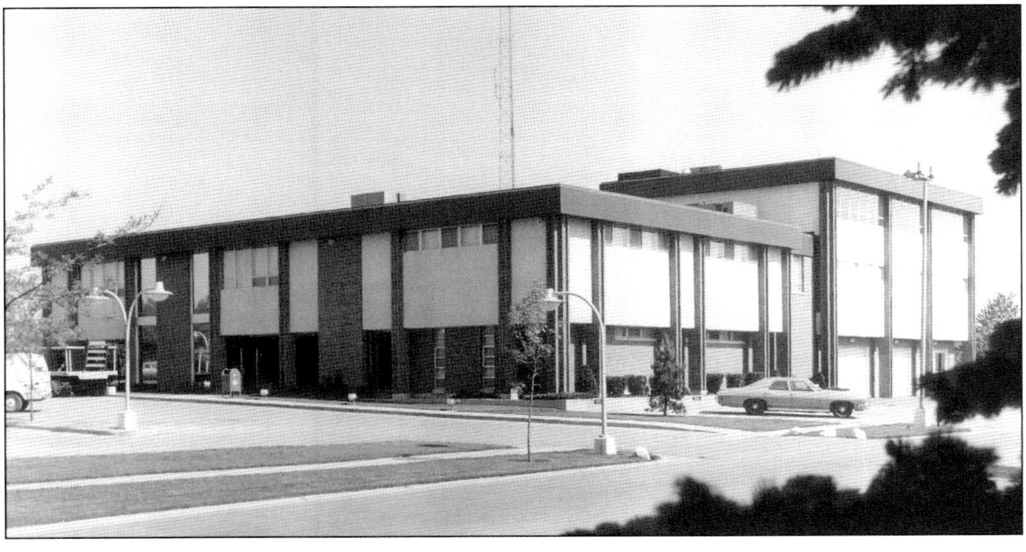

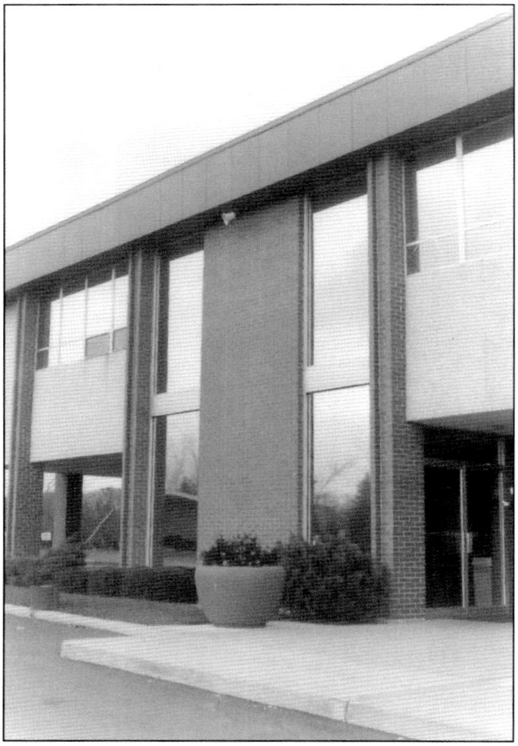

These are two different views of city hall as it appeared in 1978. At left is the south facade of the building that faces Kirchoff Road. Below is the covered entrance to the building, just visible in the lower-right corner of the top photograph as well. The Rolling Meadows Police Department occupied the first floor of city hall, while the city's administrative offices and water department occupied the second floor. Since then, offices and departments have shifted around within the building. The police department moved upstairs, sharing the second floor with the mayor's and city manager's offices and the city meeting hall. (Both courtesy of Esther Perica.)

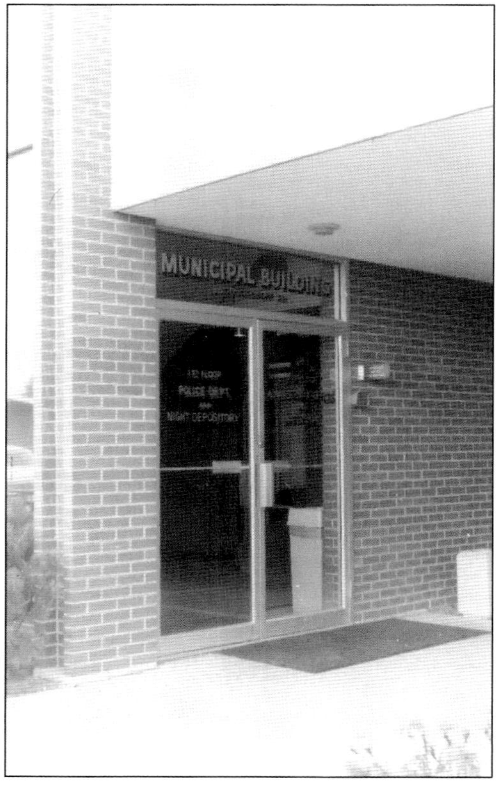

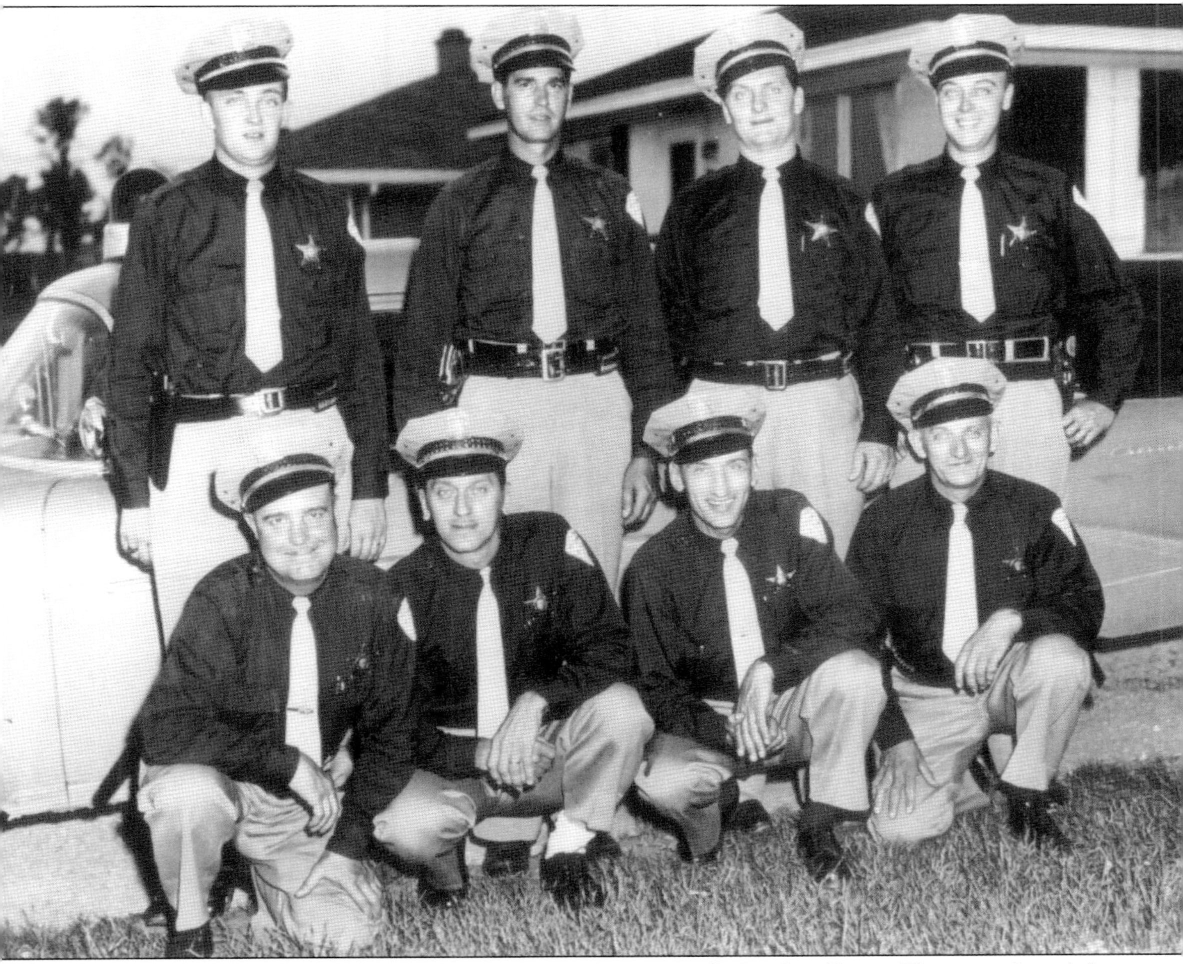

The Rolling Meadows Police Department in 1956 consisted of eight officers. They are, from left to right, (first row) Marvin Browning, Steve Bialo, newly appointed chief of police Cy Campbell, and John Macior; (second row) William Reilly, Ron Johnson, Romain Waymel, and Charles Kramer. Here they pose with the department's first squad car, a Chevrolet. (By Capt. Ralph Evans; courtesy of RML.)

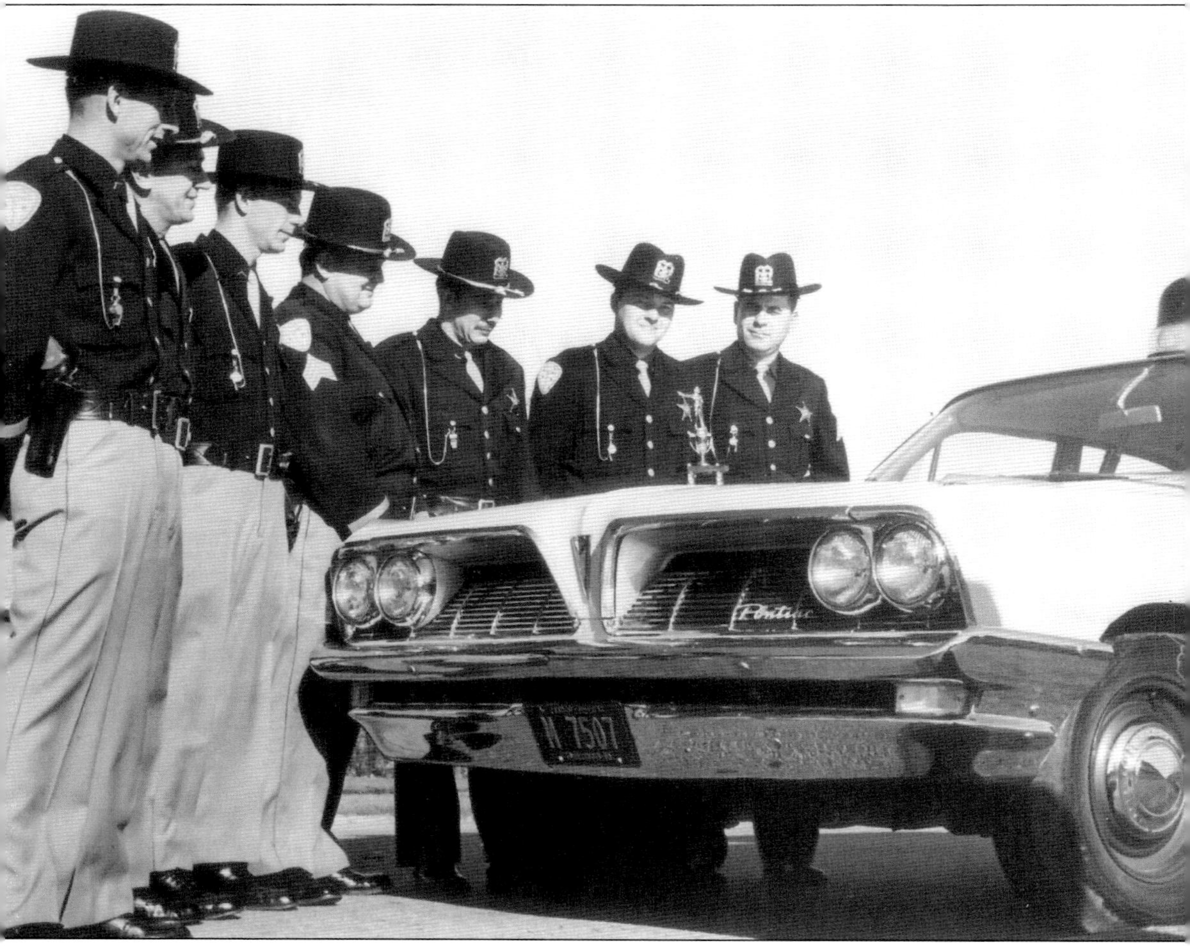

Eight years later, in 1964, the Rolling Meadows Police Department inspects its newest squad car, a Pontiac. From left to right are William Golden, Steve Bialo, Ken Jacobsen, Jim Ruggio, Ralph Evans, Don Allen, and George Gallanis. Missing is Chief of Police Cy Campbell. Chief Campbell resigned just six years later in January 1970 due to health concerns. (By Capt. Ralph Evans; courtesy of RML.)

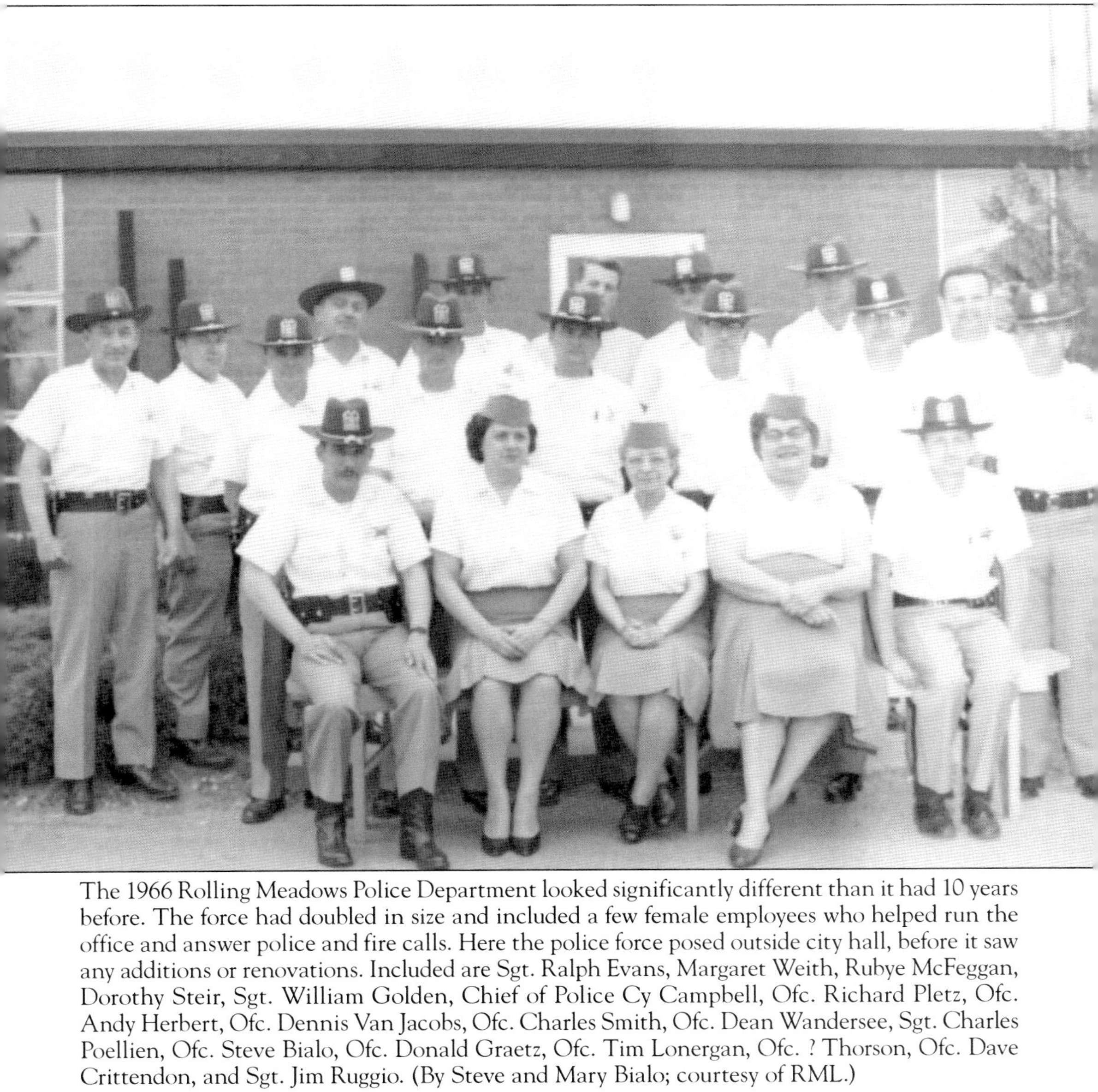

The 1966 Rolling Meadows Police Department looked significantly different than it had 10 years before. The force had doubled in size and included a few female employees who helped run the office and answer police and fire calls. Here the police force posed outside city hall, before it saw any additions or renovations. Included are Sgt. Ralph Evans, Margaret Weith, Rubye McFeggan, Dorothy Steir, Sgt. William Golden, Chief of Police Cy Campbell, Ofc. Richard Pletz, Ofc. Andy Herbert, Ofc. Dennis Van Jacobs, Ofc. Charles Smith, Ofc. Dean Wandersee, Sgt. Charles Poellien, Ofc. Steve Bialo, Ofc. Donald Graetz, Ofc. Tim Lonergan, Ofc. ? Thorson, Ofc. Dave Crittendon, and Sgt. Jim Ruggio. (By Steve and Mary Bialo; courtesy of RML.)

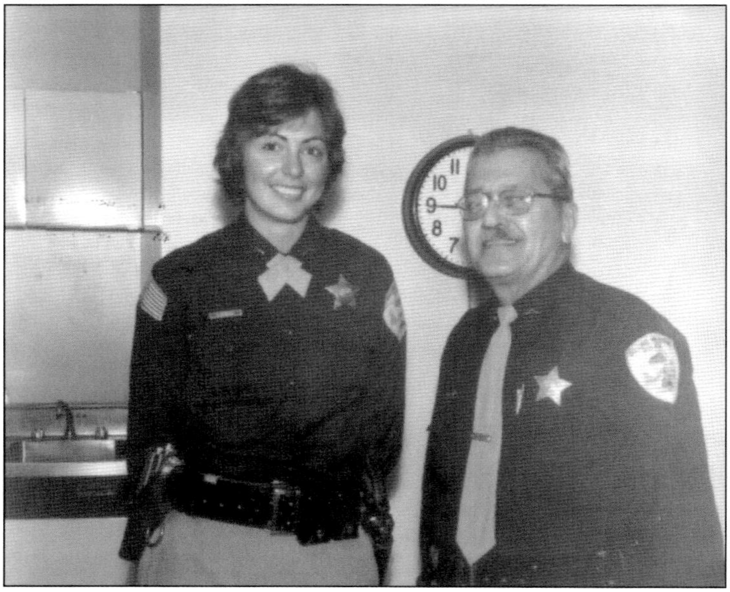

Sharon Ulrich was the first female police officer in the Rolling Meadows Police Department. Meeting the department's height and weight requirements, she submitted her application on a dare. She remained on the force for two years. Here she is joined by Ofc. Steve Bialo in 1975 on the day of his retirement. Bialo served 20 years as a Rolling Meadows police officer. (By Charles Poellien; courtesy of RML.)

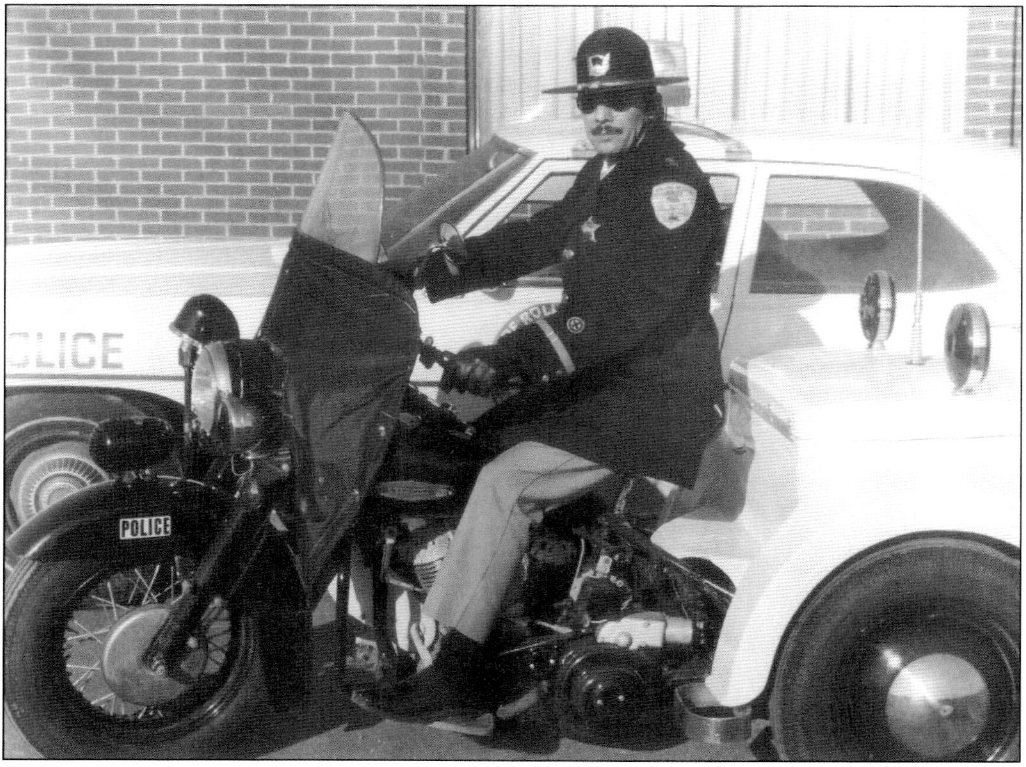

In this photograph taken in 1974, Capt. Ralph Evans rides the department's first motorcycle, which was used to easily patrol the public parks and shopping center. Evans, a member of the police force since 1957, was originally the only officer who had a motorcycle license. Because of that, he was the only person who could drive it back from where it was purchased in Evanston, Illinois. (By Capt. Ralph Evans; courtesy of RML.)

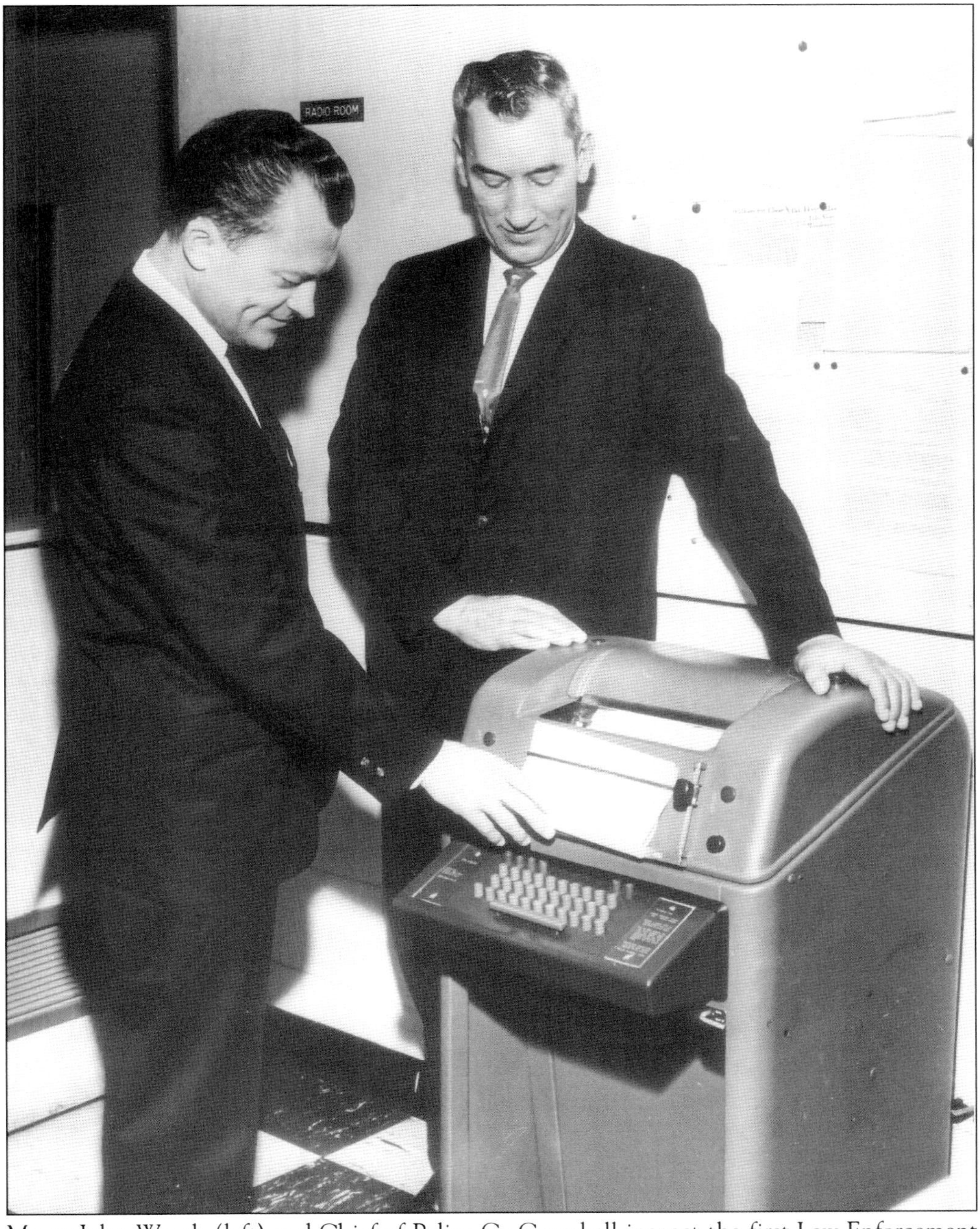

Mayor John Woods (left) and Chief of Police Cy Campbell inspect the first Law Enforcement Agency Data System or LEADS. This computer linkup system was used in investigations. Mayor Woods was known for the harmonious way he brought together all civic departments and districts, the schools, and the community. He worked closely with members of all areas of official city business. (By Capt. Ralph Evans; courtesy of RML.)

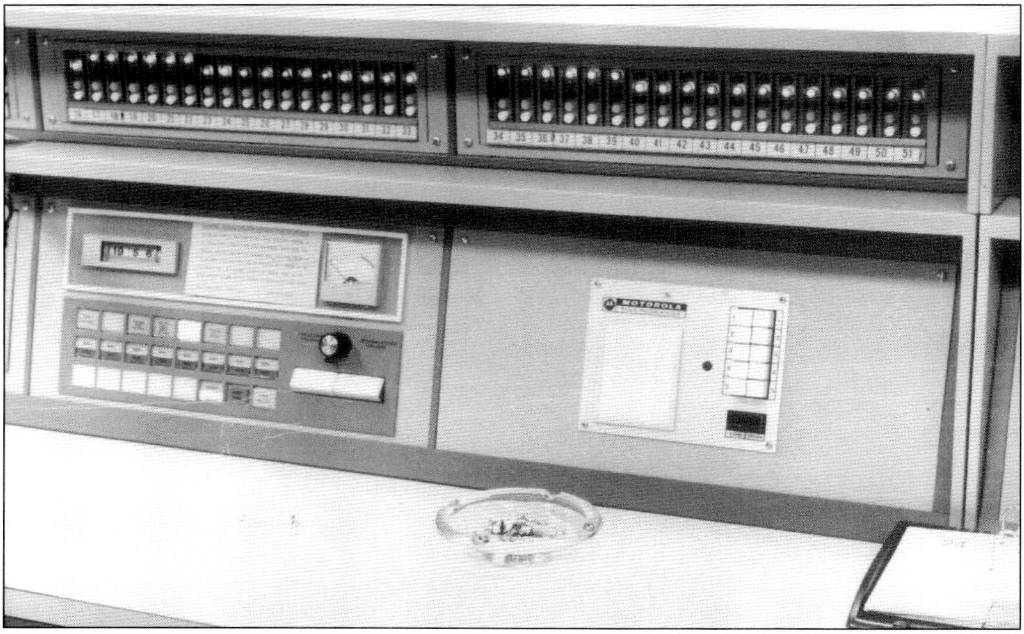

The Rolling Meadows Police Department was established in a time when technology was really blossoming. Chief of Police Cy Campbell made sure that the city was one of the first 10 communities in the area to join a radio emergency network, the Illinois State Police Radio Network (ISPERN). Above, the police force utilized a large radio communication console, modern technology for the time. Below is a rare look inside the Catastrophe Room, which contained the first radio console at city hall in 1964. (Above by Charles Poellien, below by Capt. Ralph Evans; both courtesy of RML.)

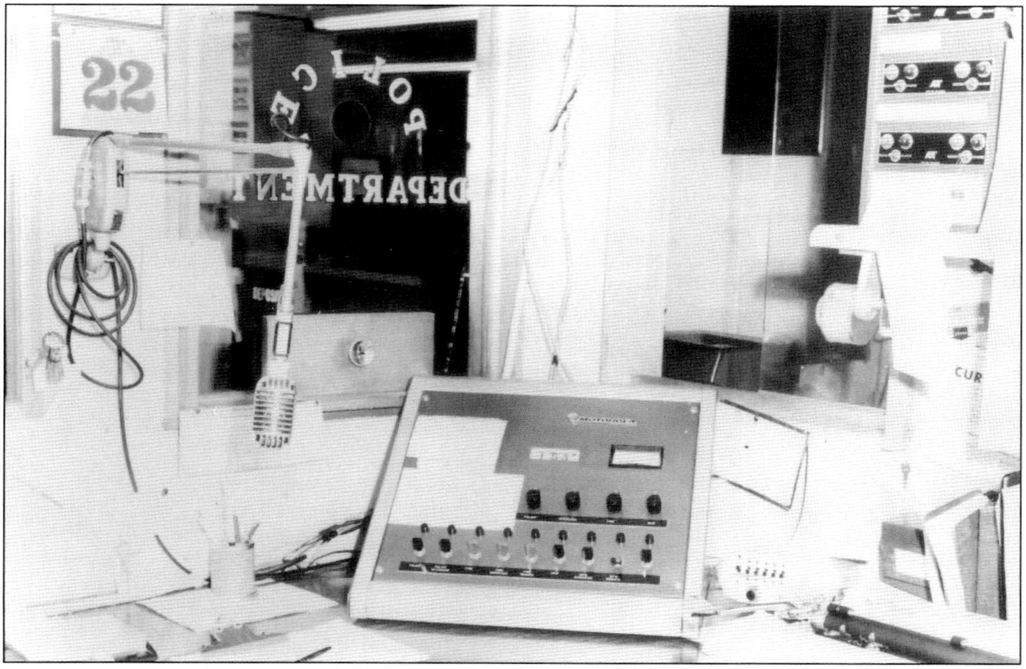

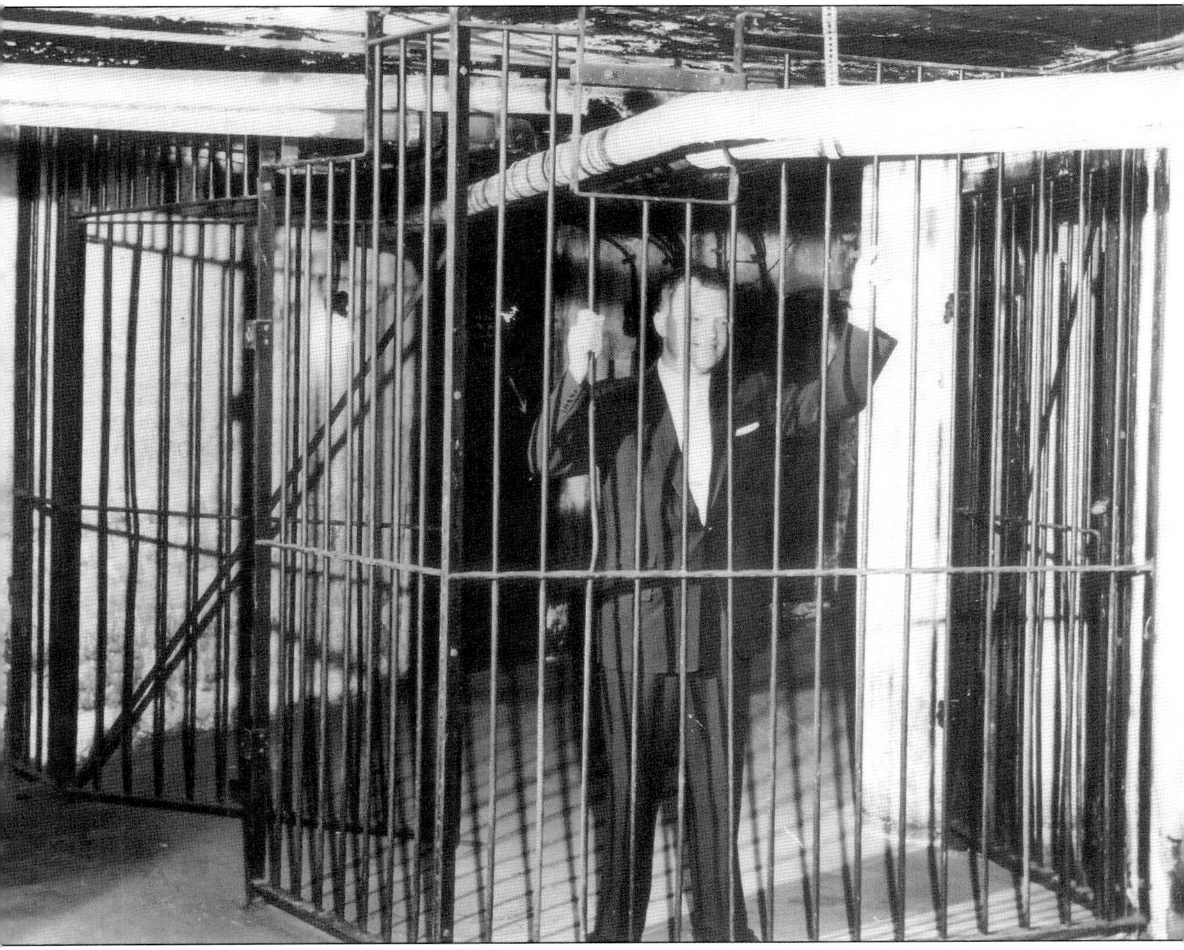

After the new Rolling Meadows City Hall building opened in 1961, the city did not have any jail cells. Any person taken into custody was locked up in the Palatine jail. Mayor John Woods discovered that the Illinois Bell Telephone Company, which had moved into the City of Chicago's old municipal building, had a jail cell it was giving away. Here, Mayor Woods tests out the cell in the Illinois Bell Telephone building before it was relocated to Rolling Meadows City Hall. (By Capt. Ralph Evans; courtesy of RML.)

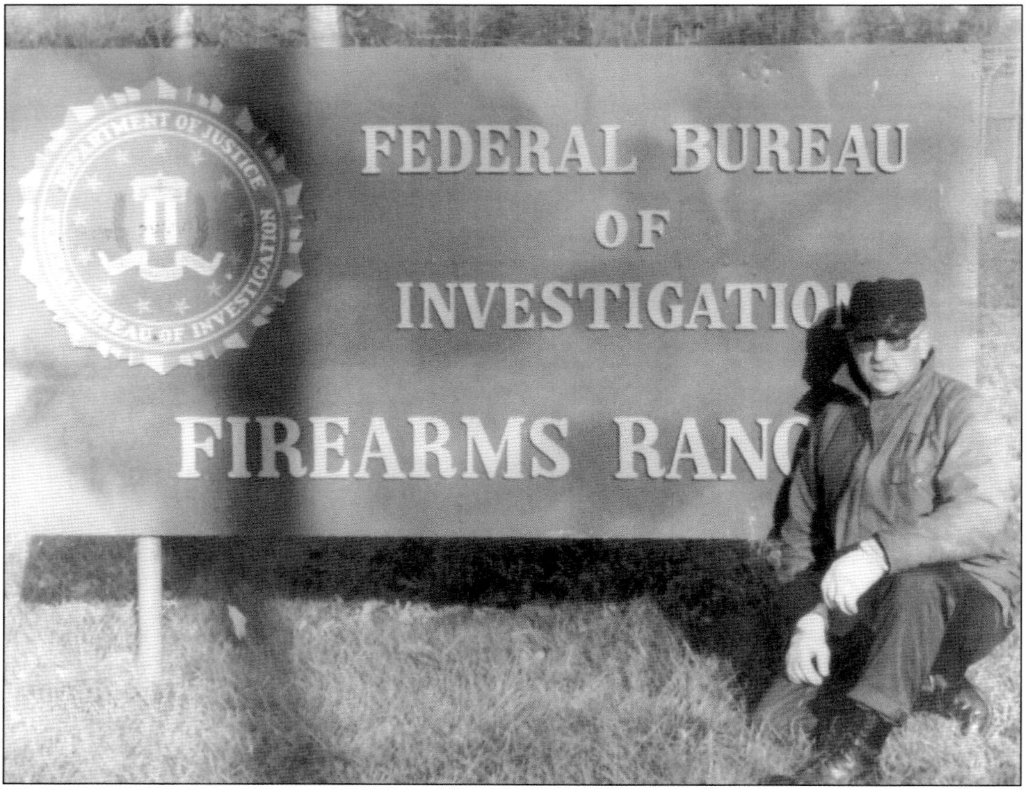

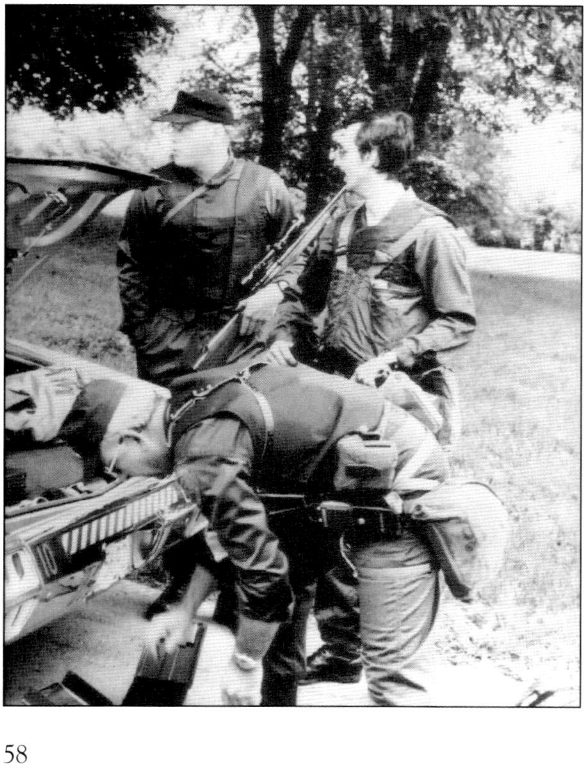

Members of the Rolling Meadows SWAT team received training at the Federal Bureau of Investigation Firearms Range. Above, Sgt. Charles Poellien crouches next to the firearms range sign in December 1975. Left, Rolling Meadows SWAT team members appear in their full gear in 1976. The city's SWAT team members would be called on for various crises, such as hostage situations, and were available to help both city and neighboring police forces if such emergencies arose. Pictured are, from left to right, Charles Poellien (front), Marv Hamann, and Dan Waligurski. (Both by Charles Poellien; courtesy of RML.)

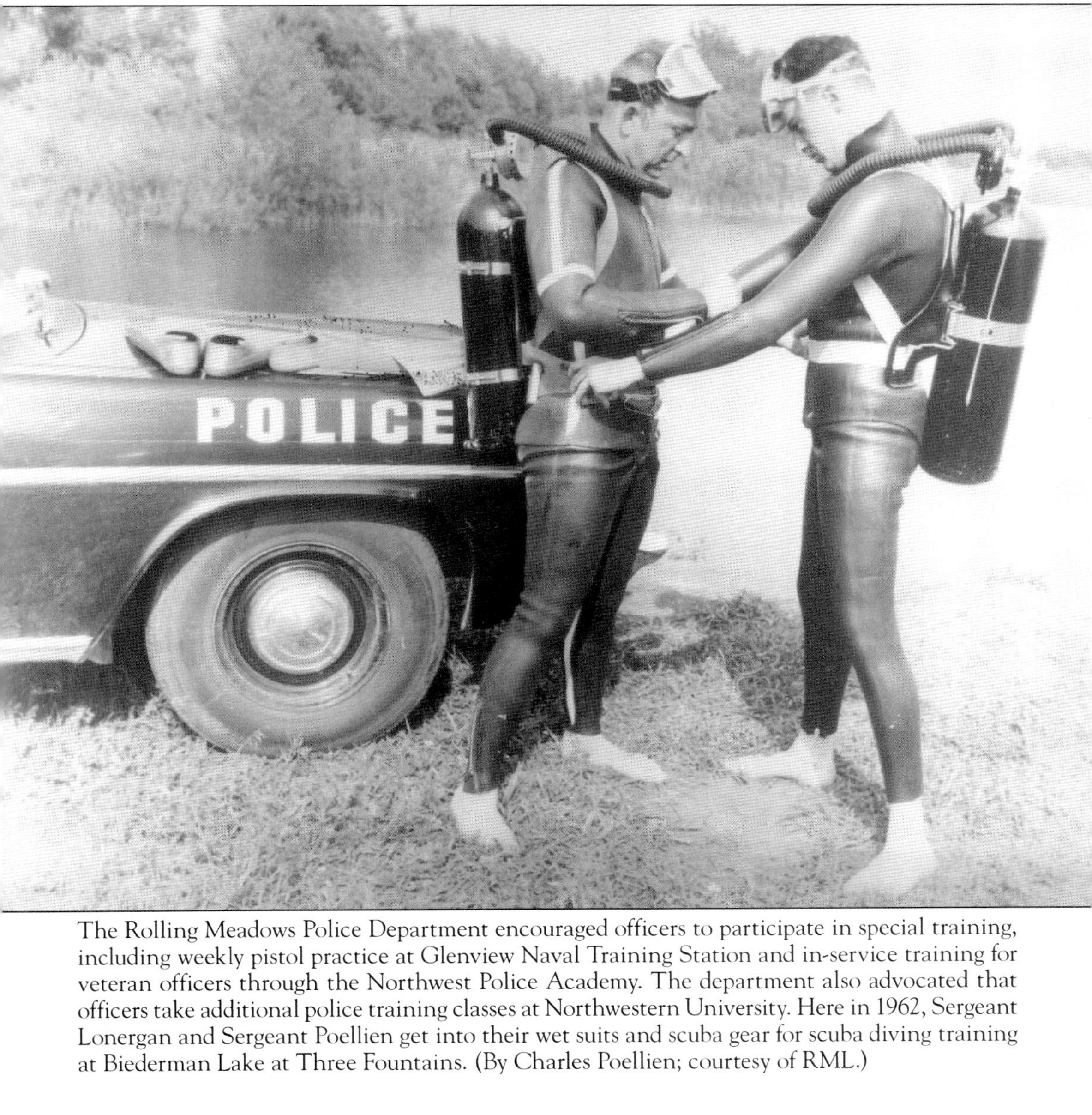

The Rolling Meadows Police Department encouraged officers to participate in special training, including weekly pistol practice at Glenview Naval Training Station and in-service training for veteran officers through the Northwest Police Academy. The department also advocated that officers take additional police training classes at Northwestern University. Here in 1962, Sergeant Lonergan and Sergeant Poellien get into their wet suits and scuba gear for scuba diving training at Biederman Lake at Three Fountains. (By Charles Poellien; courtesy of RML.)

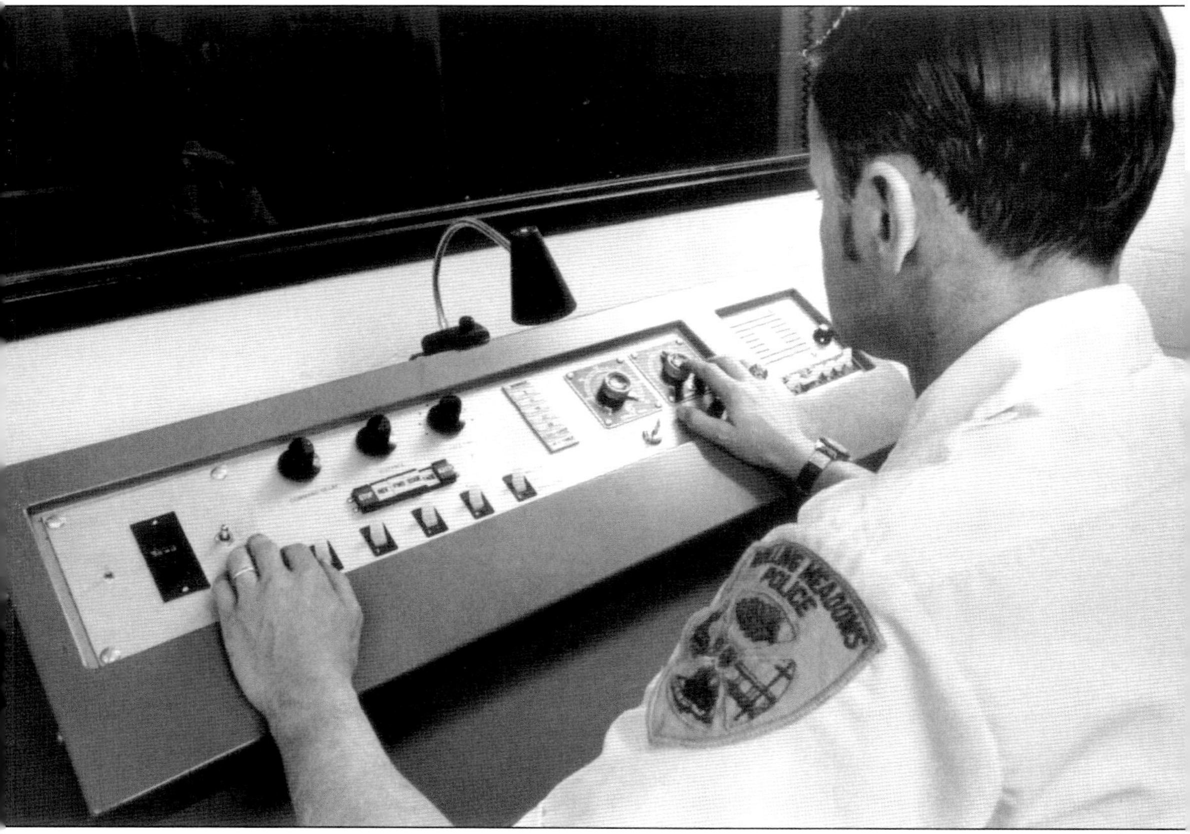

The Rolling Meadows Police Department made a point of offering new training for its officers. In 1963, the department opened its very own pistol range for officers on Central Road next to the city garage, which housed the park district and public works department offices. The pistol range allowed officers to practice their marksmanship. Here an officer watches over the training taking place in the range. (Courtesy of Dom Najolia.)

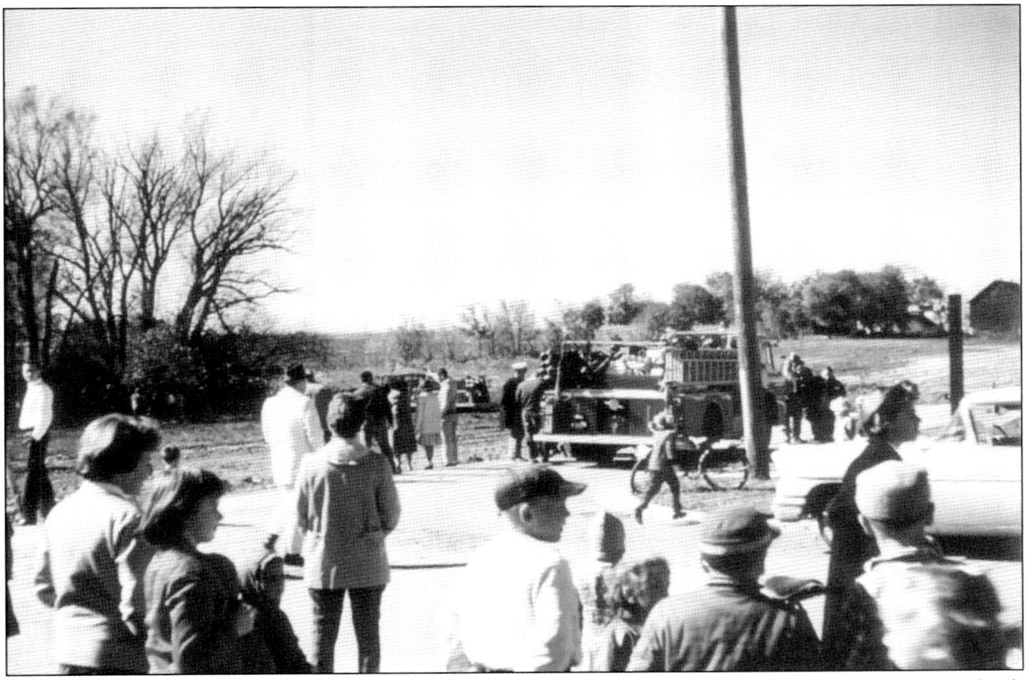

Volunteer firefighters respond to one of the first fires in Rolling Meadows while residents look on at the corner of Central Road and Owl Drive around 1956. Until 1958, these volunteers were part of the Palatine Fire Protection District. In March of that year, Rolling Meadows petitioned to separate from the district to form its own fire district comprised of 37 volunteers. (By Ronald Brightwell; courtesy of RML.)

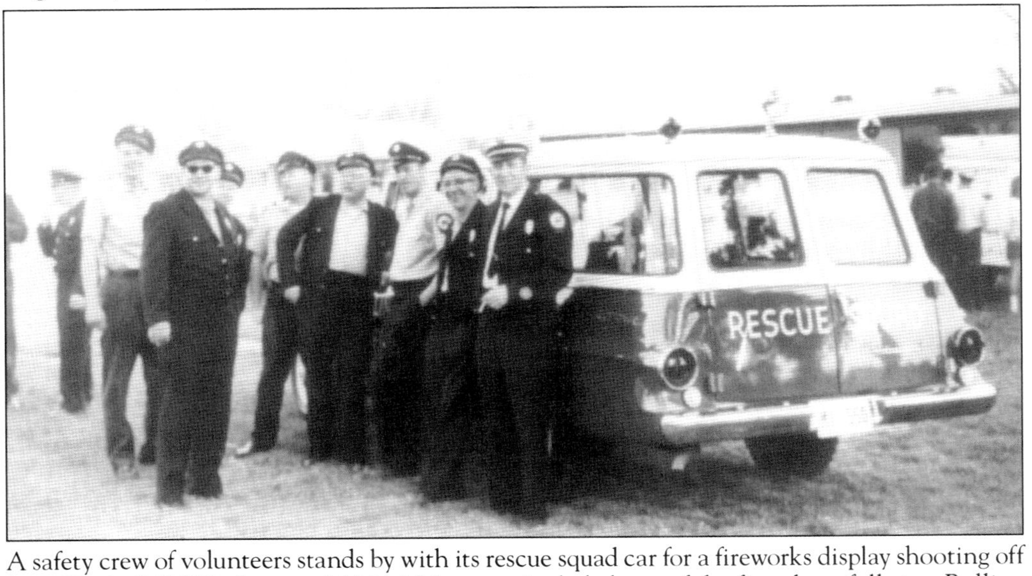

A safety crew of volunteers stands by with its rescue squad car for a fireworks display shooting off from Kimball Hill Park around 1964. Volunteers included two of the first three full-time Rolling Meadows firefighters, Bill Kugelberg and Paul Hoffman. Other volunteers were Jim Polluch, Harold Molm, Don Soderberg, Ron Geske, Bob Swerth, Bill Freeman, Stanley Kotlarz, and Nick Rigilio. (By Thomas Fogarty; courtesy of RML.)

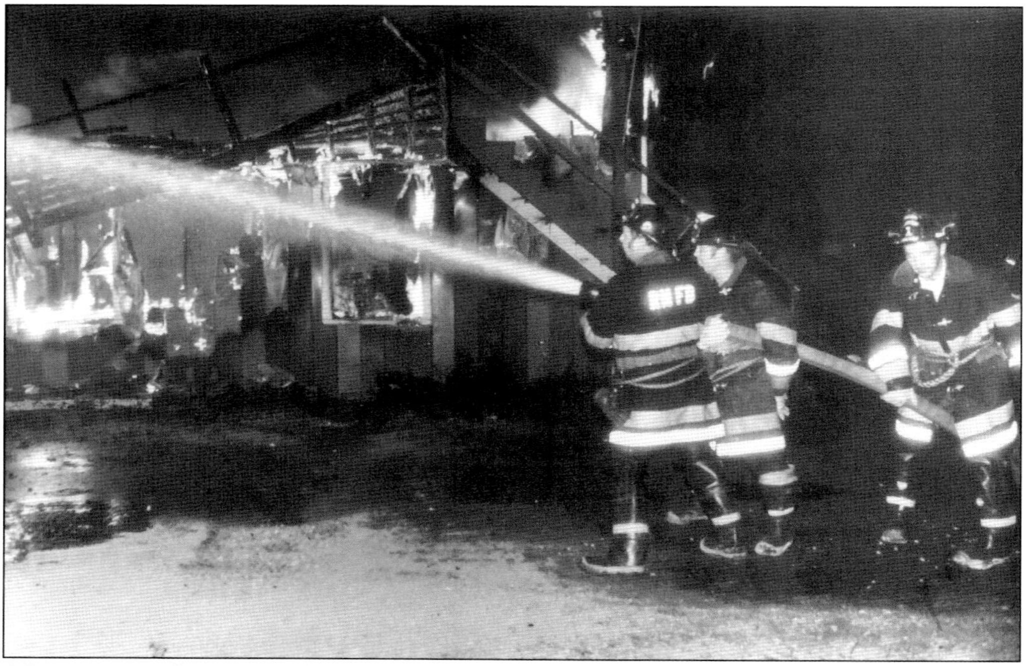

After 10 years of serving as chief of the Rolling Meadows volunteer firefighters, Thomas Fogarty was appointed the first full-time fire chief for the newly formed fire department. Prior to 1973, the city only had a "fire district" comprised of local volunteers who received professional firefighter training but who also had responsibilities to full-time day jobs. In the spring of 1967, the city hired Fogarty, Bill Kugelberg, and Paul Hoffman as the city's first full-time firefighters. Below, volunteer firefighters talk to students during Fire Prevention Week. From left to right are Lt. Nick Rigilio, Jack Fahn, and Les Meyer. Above, a group of firefighters from the new fire department put out a large, destructive fire. (Above by Jean Weber, below by Thomas Fogarty; both courtesy of RML.)

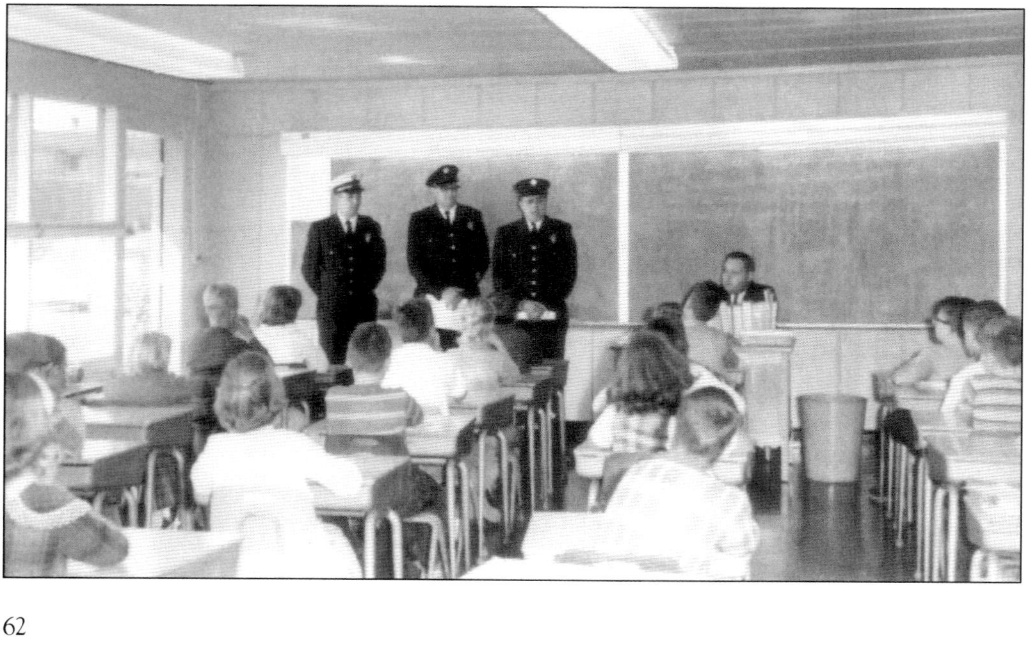

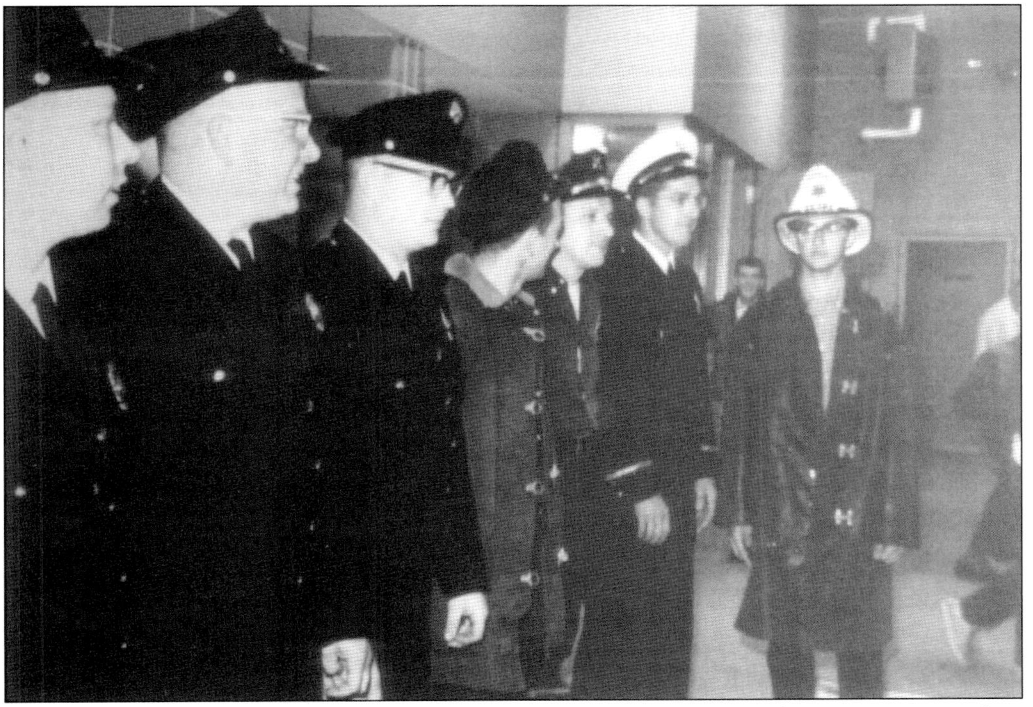

Local youth were encouraged to take part in building and growing their community. One teenager would be appointed the Teen Government fire chief and would spend time with the city's firefighters. Above, in 1965, the second Teen Government fire chief inspects his "troops." The officers pictured are, from left to right, Paul Hoffman (one of the first three full-time firefighters), Bob Swerth, Harold Malm, Don Plant, Bud Broeske, and Ed Vanderweil. Below, the Teen Government fire chief looks at the fire equipment with one of the firefighters. (Both by Thomas Fogarty; courtesy of RML.)

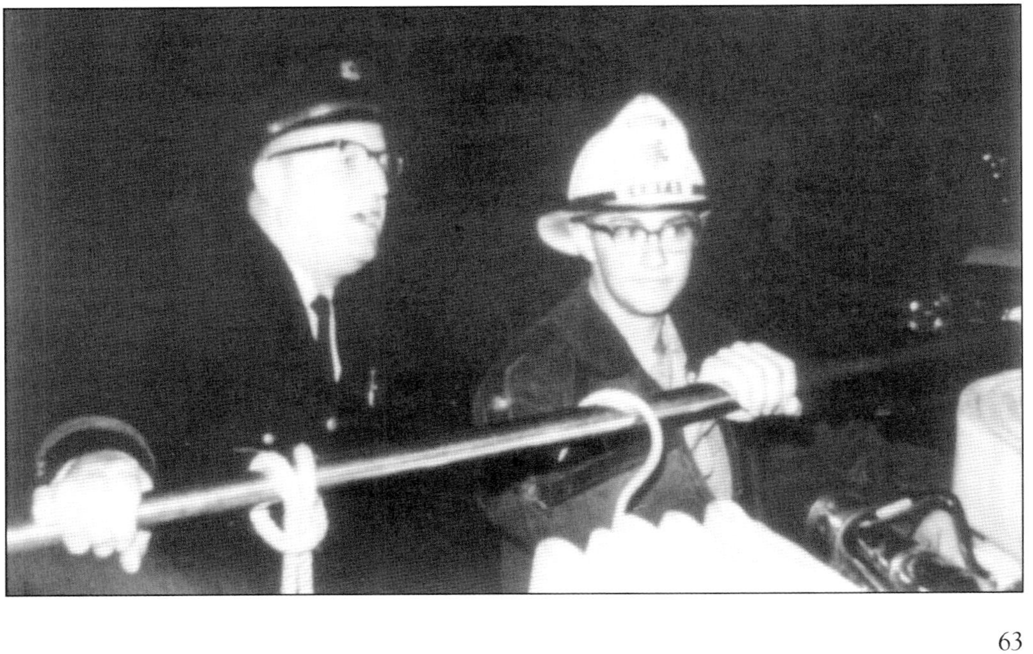

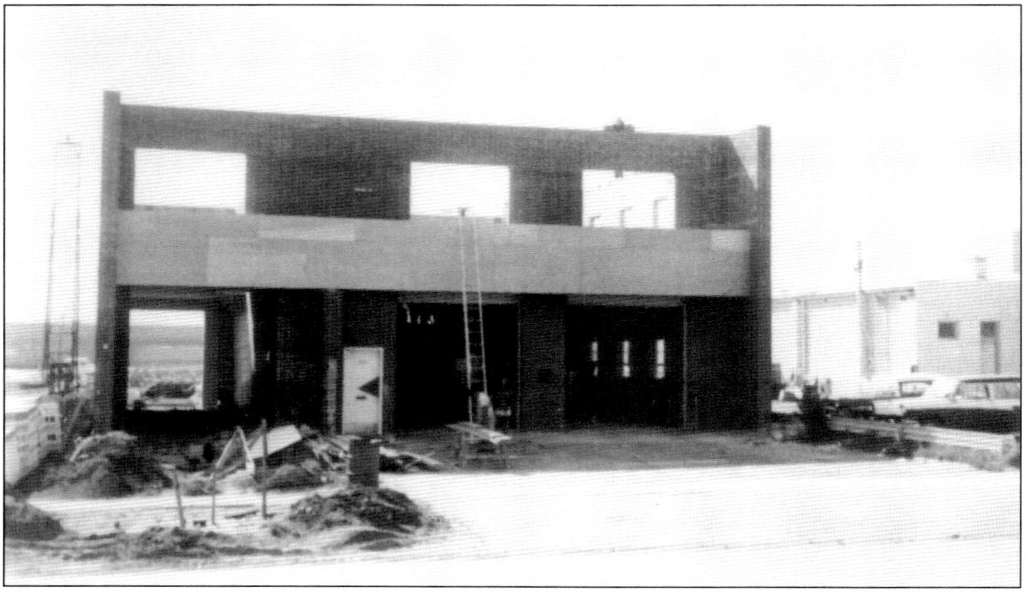

After separating from the Palatine Fire Protection District in April 1958, the Rolling Meadows Fire District started building its first fire station. The land was donated by Kimball Hill, and its location on Meadow Drive was ideal as it was centrally located in the city and allowed firefighters to respond to any call in the city within minutes. In 1963, an addition doubled the size of the station by adding a full second floor complete with sleeping quarters, storage areas, and a meeting room. Construction continued through 1964, when the above photograph was taken, and the station was fully operational the summer of that year. Below is the fire station as it appeared in 1978 and how it has continued to look for several decades. (Above by Thomas Fogarty, courtesy of RML; below courtesy of Esther Perica.)

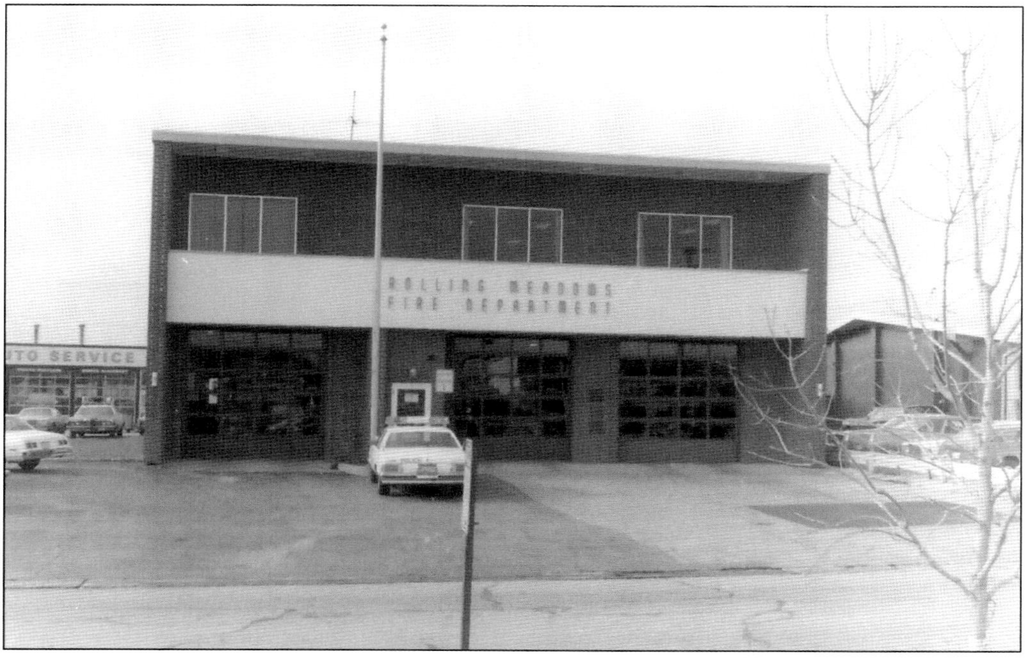

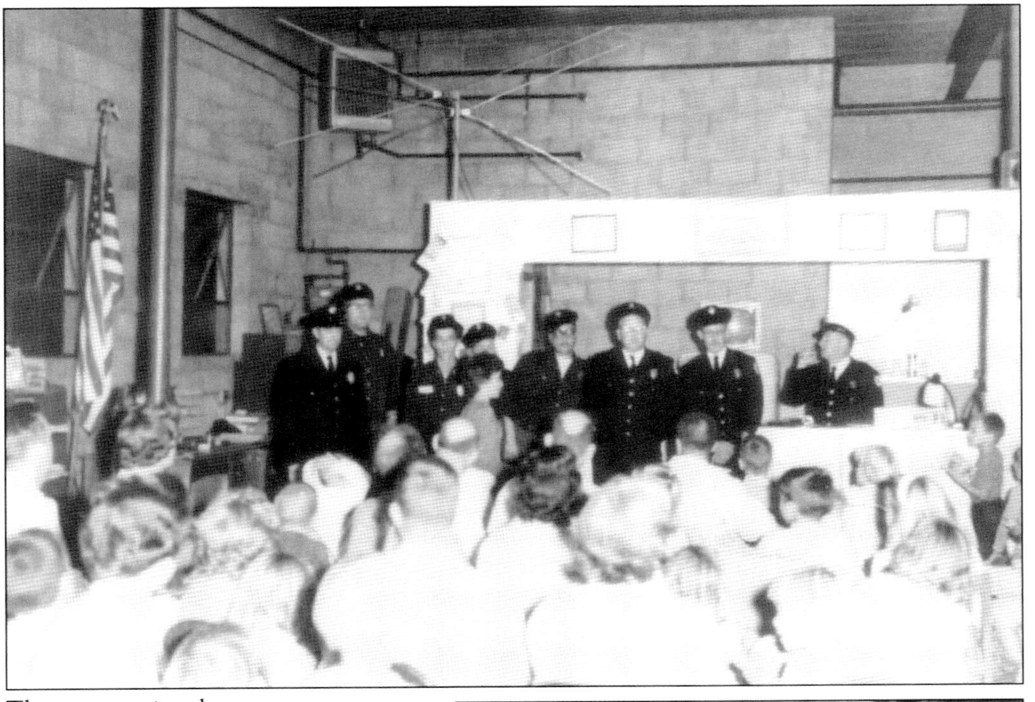

The community always came out for the Fire Prevention Week demonstrations at the firehouse. Volunteers would teach residents about cardiac massage, resuscitation, fire causes, portable power, extinguishers, and more. Here, a crowd gathers in the first firehouse in October 1963. The firefighters pictured are, from left to right, R. Blane, V. Wandersee, N. Rigilio, J. Nauheimer, J. Polluch, R. Suerty, G. ?, and E. Martin. (By Thomas Fogarty; courtesy of RML.)

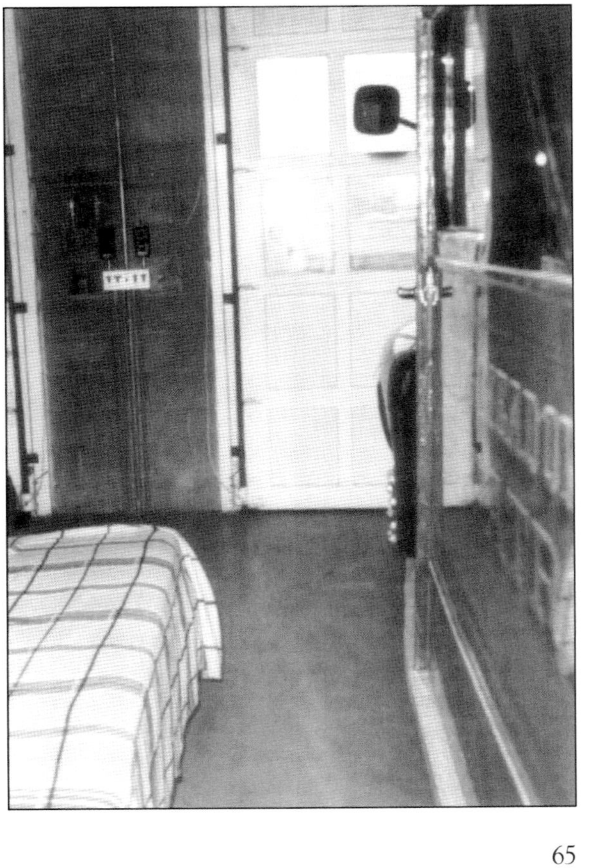

Until 1964, the Rolling Meadows Fire Station was one level. As a result, the volunteer firefighters' sleeping quarters were on the apparatus floor, close to where the fire trucks were parked. To respond to calls during the night, the volunteers started night duty. Fire chief Thomas Fogarty and Jim McFeggan were the first to volunteer for night duty. It was a difficult job to perform, considering the building had no heat and would become very cold during the harsh Midwest winters. (By Thomas Fogarty; courtesy of RML.)

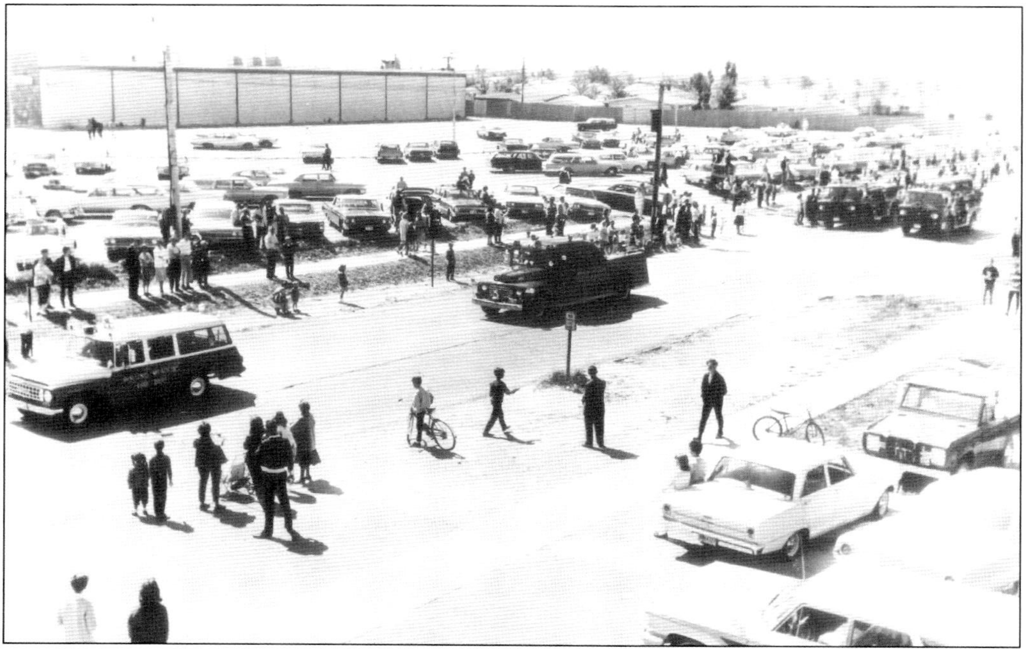

The Memorial Day Parade, although more scaled back than the annual Fourth of July Parade, has been a beloved and important tradition for Rolling Meadows residents for decades. This Memorial Day Parade included the debut of the first ambulance and fire patrol truck that the city purchased from the Chicago Fire Department for a mere $1. (By Capt. Ralph Evans; courtesy of RML.)

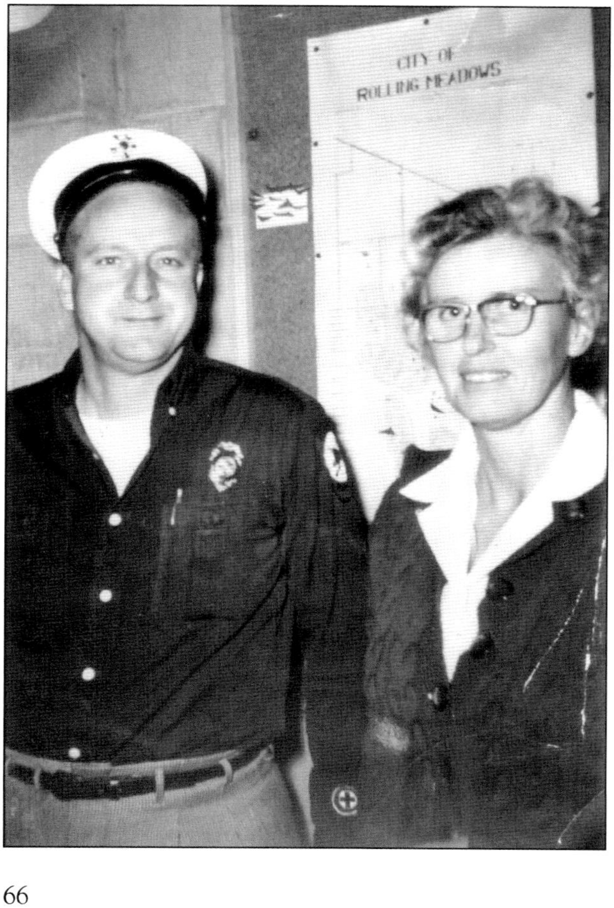

Fire chief Thomas Fogarty poses with Dr. F. Patience Noecker, who became the Rolling Meadows Fire District's doctor in 1960. Dr. Noecker would often work alongside firefighters on emergency calls and instruct them how to respond to injuries. She also labored to update the fire district's first aid procedures. (By Thomas Fogarty; courtesy of RML.)

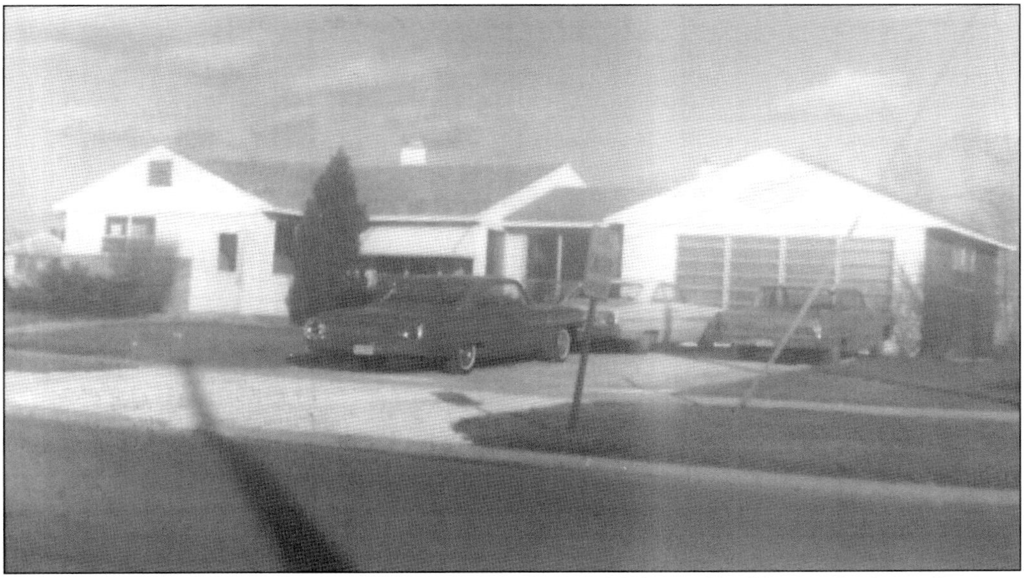

In 1958, Rolling Meadows decided that it was time to establish a public library. Finding a location for this new cultural center was difficult, but Kimball Hill offered his office building on Meadow Drive (one of his original starter homes) to be converted into a library. Residents went door to door with little red wagons collecting both monetary and book donations to fund the library and to create the initial circulating collection. The first library opened on February 29, 1960. Within just a few short years, the building was unable to accommodate the increasing number of patrons, so a new library was built at its current location just down the street on Martin Lane. The new library opened on October 31, 1967. (Below by Phil Niemeyer; both courtesy of RML.)

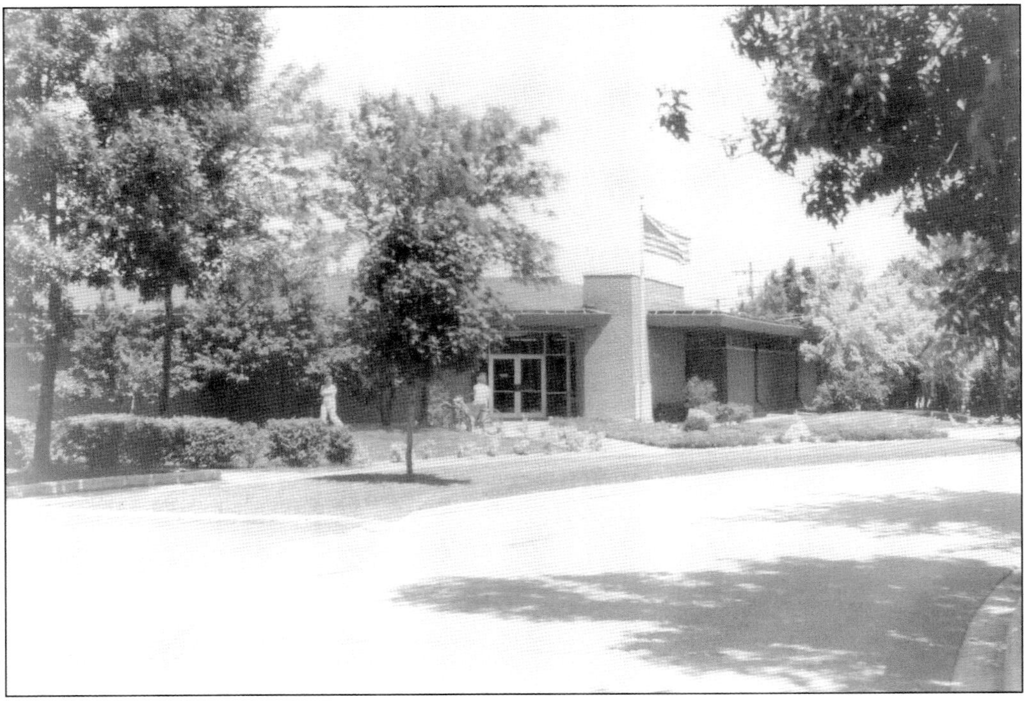

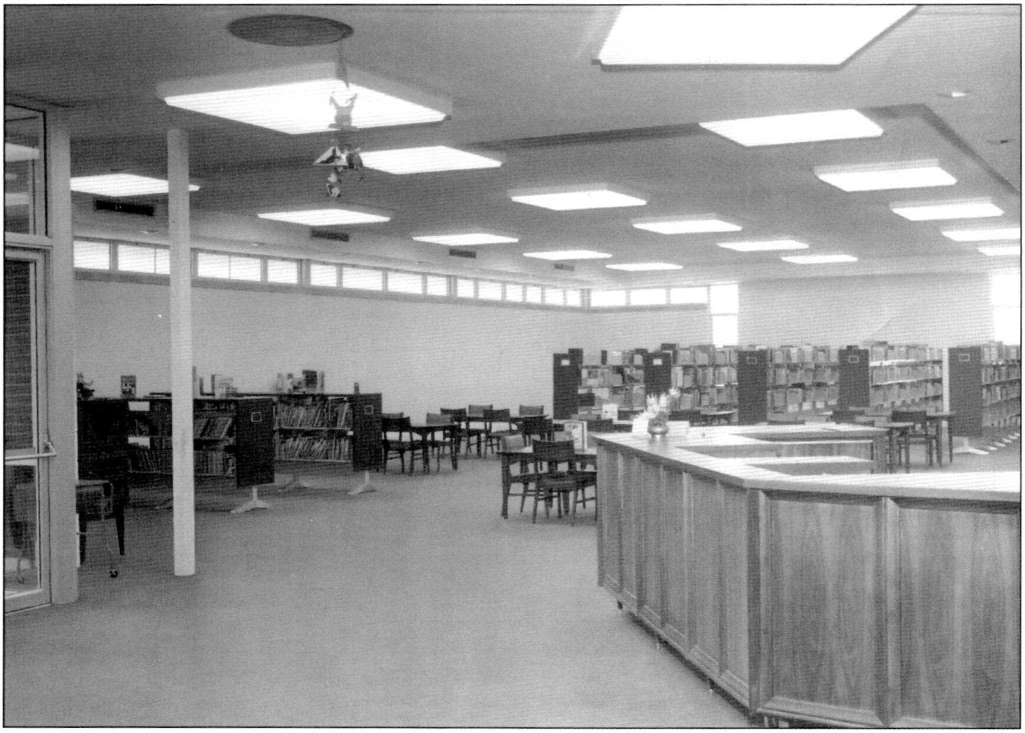

The new Martin Lane library building was constructed to meet the needs of the Rolling Meadows Library's patrons. The library now had more space to expand its collection in order to provide more comprehensive information to the public. The open layout of the new library and the increased amount of light fixtures promoted more quality use of library services. The card catalog, the predecessor to the library's electronic database of its materials, now was in a prominent and easily accessible place. Several years after these photographs were taken, the library was completely remodeled and gained a lower level, designated for the children's collection as well as youth programs. The renovations further increased the amount of usable library space, thus allowing for a larger collection and even better service to patrons. (Both courtesy of RML.)

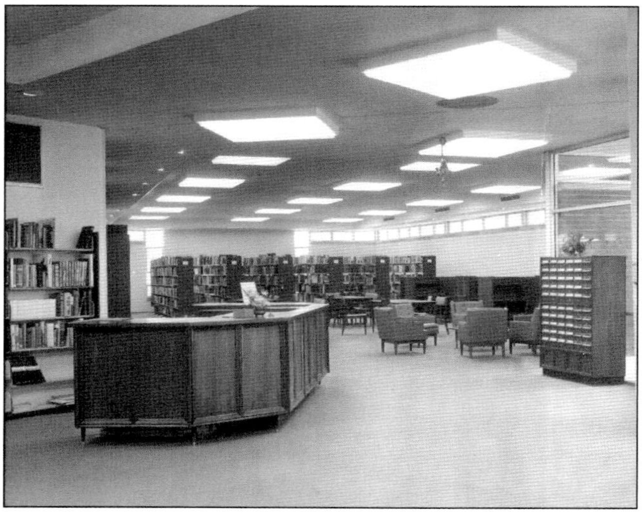

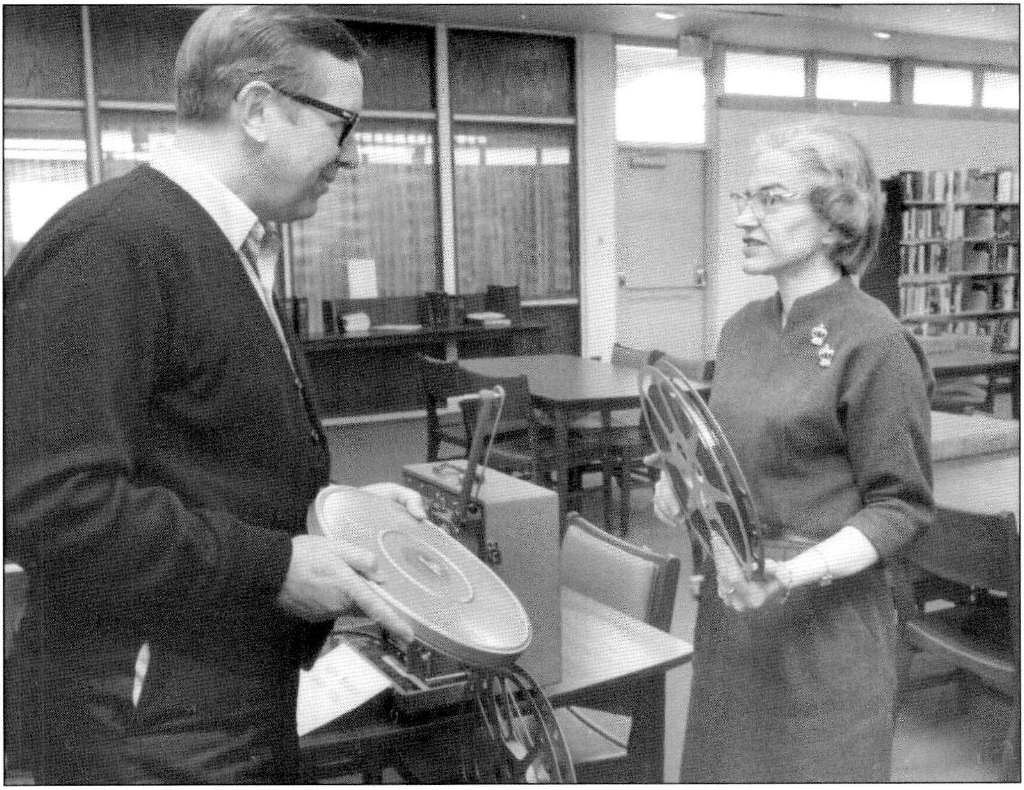

The Rolling Meadows Library joined the North Suburban Library System (NSLS), which provided an interlibrary loan service to its member libraries. Through this NSLS service, a patron of one member library could check out materials from another member library that the patron's home library did not have, and the materials would be shipped directly to the patron's home library. In 1970, the Rolling Meadows Library joined 14 other local libraries in a reciprocal borrowing program that allowed a patron of one library to register his or her library card at other participating libraries to personally access and check out their collections. Another benefit of NSLS membership was that the Rolling Meadows Library had access to several hundred 16mm films. Above, Mary Ann Strebler from the library talks with an NSLS representative about the films. Left, they pose to celebrate this new lending program. (Both courtesy of RML.)

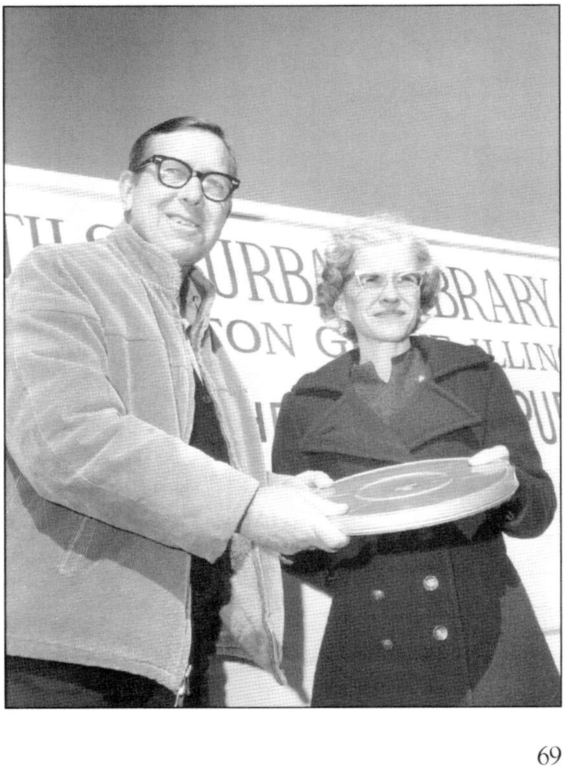

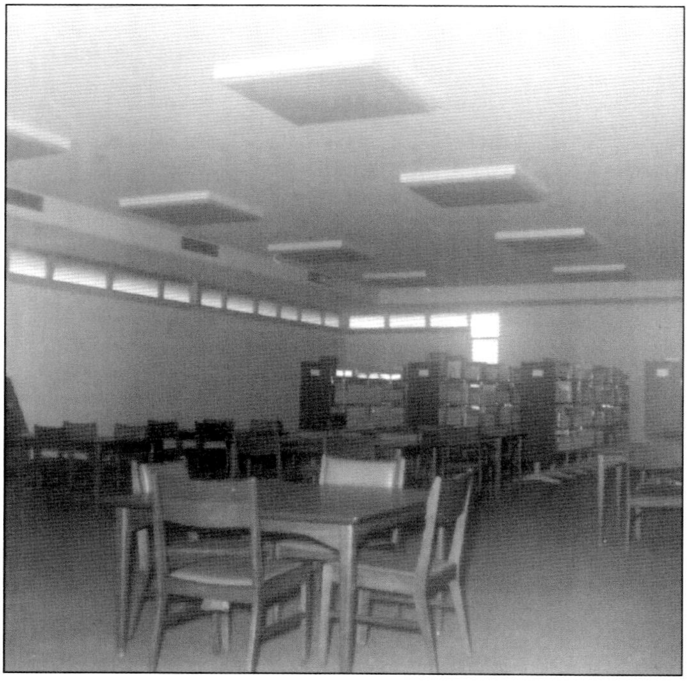

In the first library building on Meadow Drive, which was an original Kimball Hill home, there was not enough space for many patrons to browse the collection or sit and read at the same time. The library used the house's bedrooms for processing and storage, which left only the kitchen for the children's section and the garage for the main collection. In the new library building on Martin Lane, over 100 patrons could sit and read simultaneously, compared to only 24 in the Meadow Drive building. The library utilized both study tables and chairs, left, and lounge chairs, below. (Both courtesy of RML.)

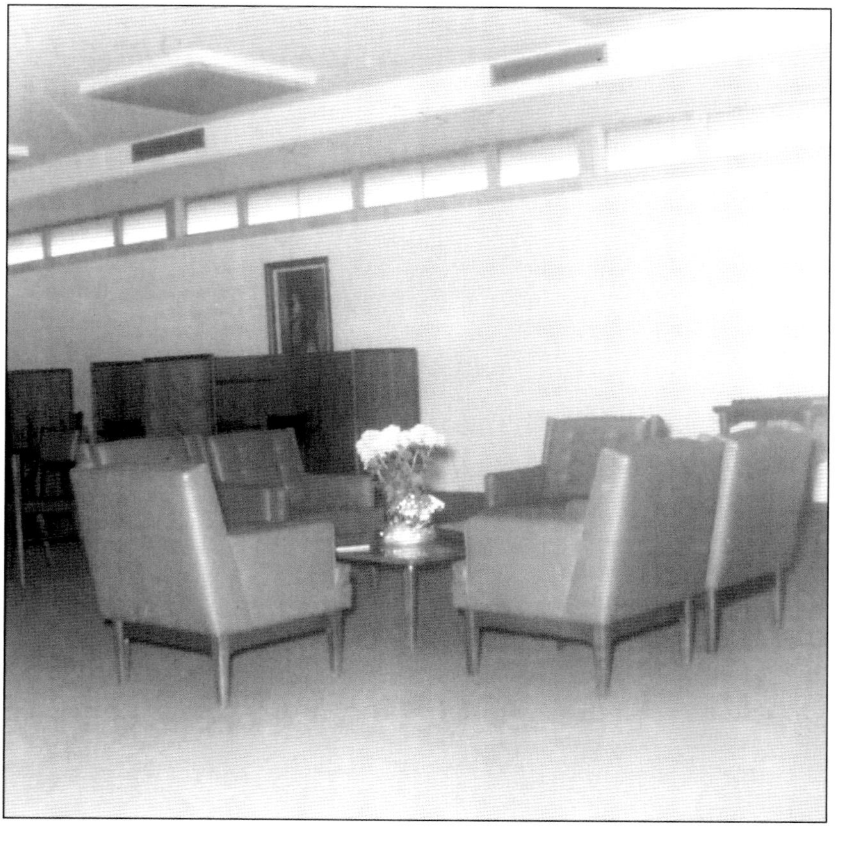

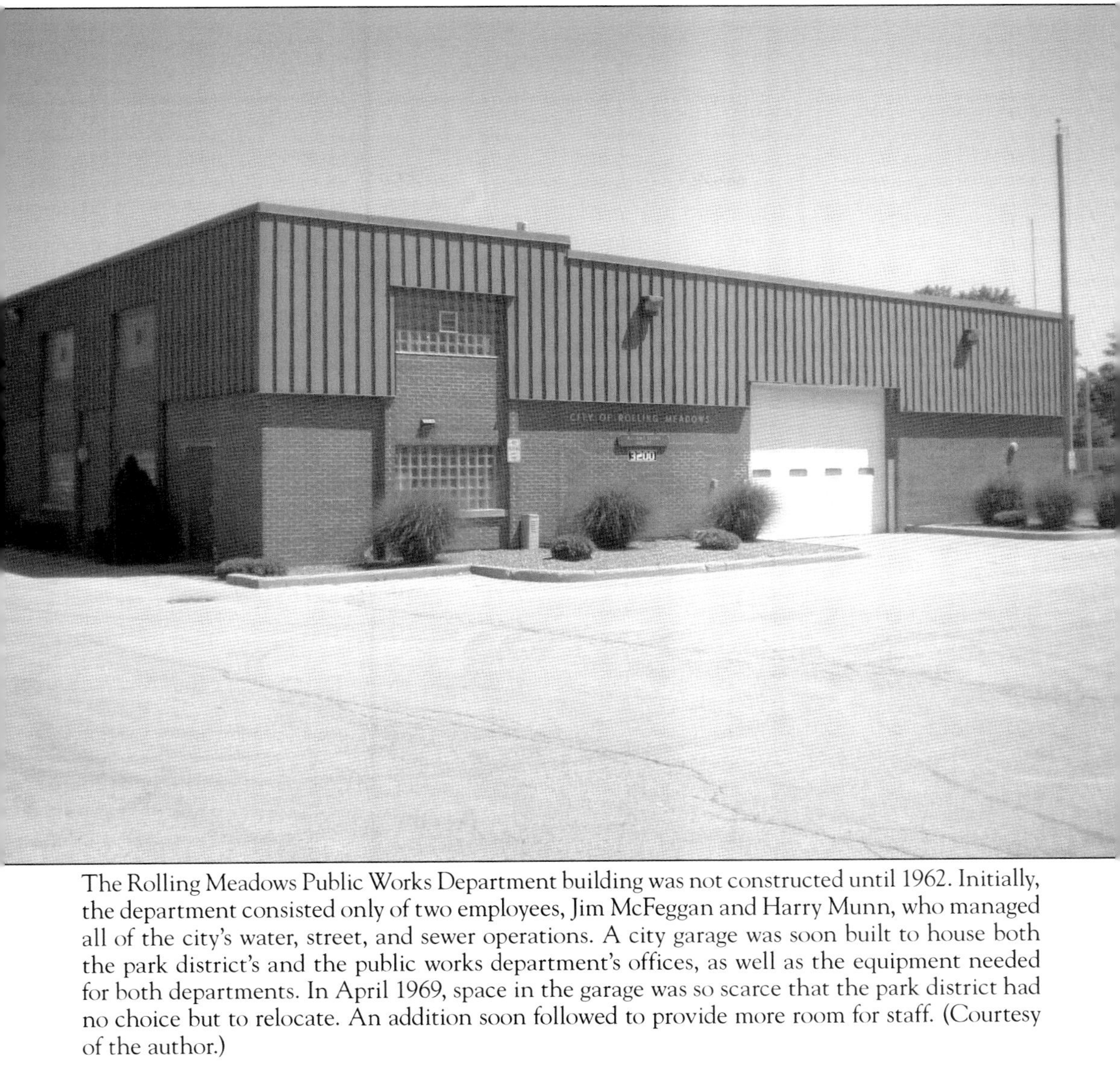

The Rolling Meadows Public Works Department building was not constructed until 1962. Initially, the department consisted only of two employees, Jim McFeggan and Harry Munn, who managed all of the city's water, street, and sewer operations. A city garage was soon built to house both the park district's and the public works department's offices, as well as the equipment needed for both departments. In April 1969, space in the garage was so scarce that the park district had no choice but to relocate. An addition soon followed to provide more room for staff. (Courtesy of the author.)

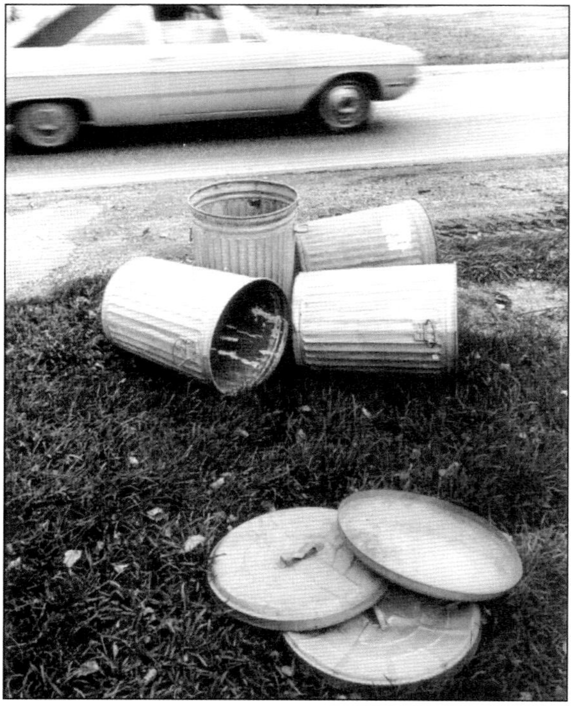

In 1967, public works employee Jim McFeggan started an experiment to substitute metal trash cans with disposable paper trash bags. He found that the bags required less storage space and were more sanitary than trash cans. By 1969, Mayor Roland Meyer proposed that the entire city switch over to the new paper trash bags. During the 1960s, most of Rolling Meadows' neighboring communities utilized private companies for garbage collection. The city, hoping to lower costs for such services, decided to offer its own garbage collection service and purchased three Mercedes-Benz trucks. Combined with the new disposable paper trash bags, these efficient "luxury" garbage trucks allowed garbage pickup to be as much as 50 percent faster than was possible with privately owned garbage trucks and the old metal trash cans. (Both courtesy of Dom Najolia.)

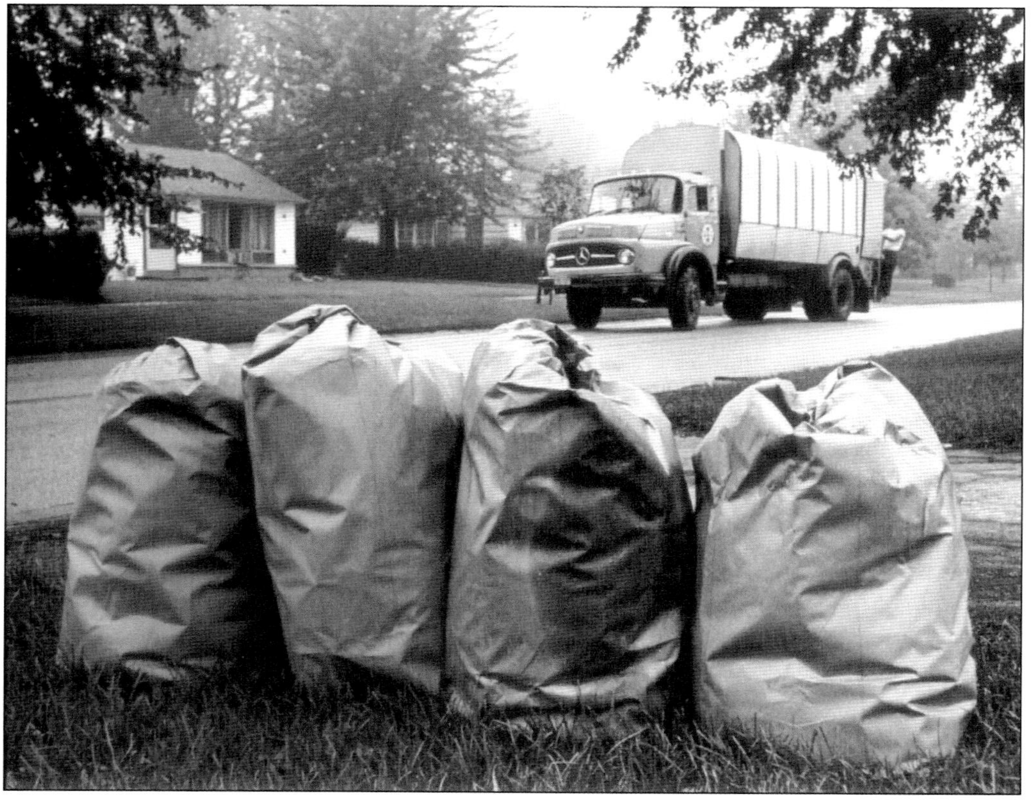

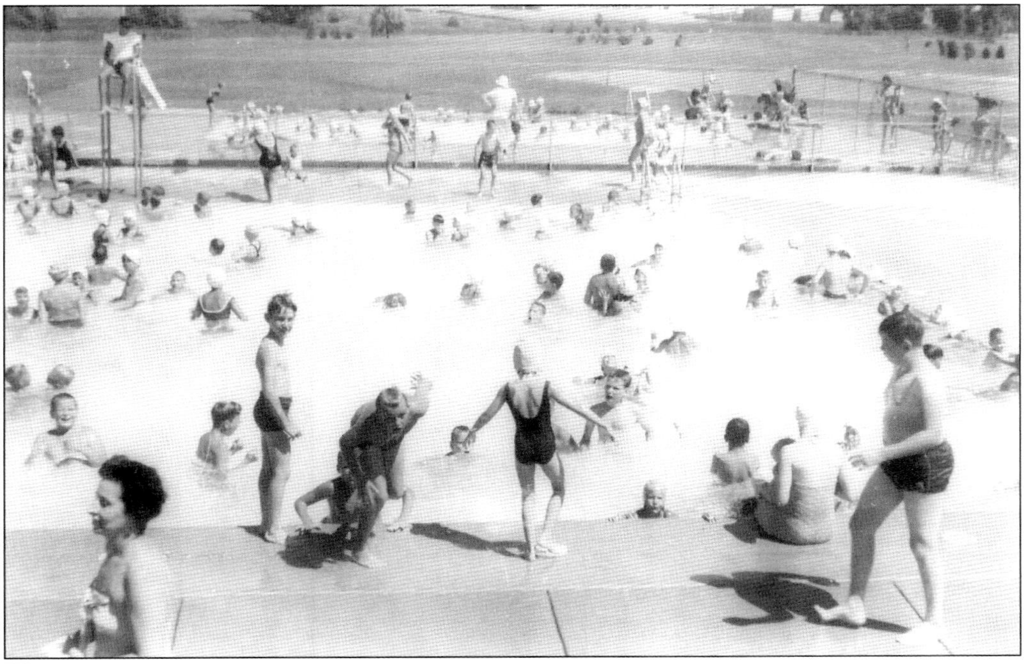

The Rolling Meadows Park District's Olympic Pool opened on July 18, 1962. In the first two weeks, the pool welcomed almost 12,000 people who wanted to test out its cool waters. For some time, the pool was so crowded that swimming laps in this Olympic-sized pool was completely impossible. Above, four years after the facility opened, the pool would still become crowded with residents wishing to cool off from Chicagoland's toasty summers. Below, an adventuresome youth jumps off the new diving board into the 12-foot deep end. (Both by Emily Berglund; courtesy of RML.)

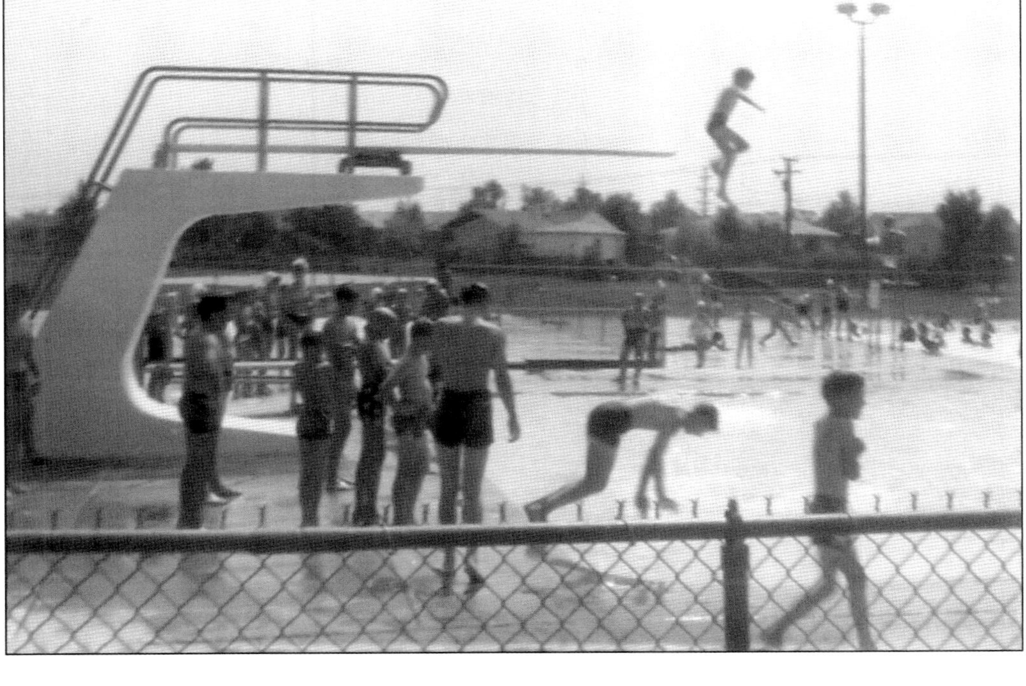

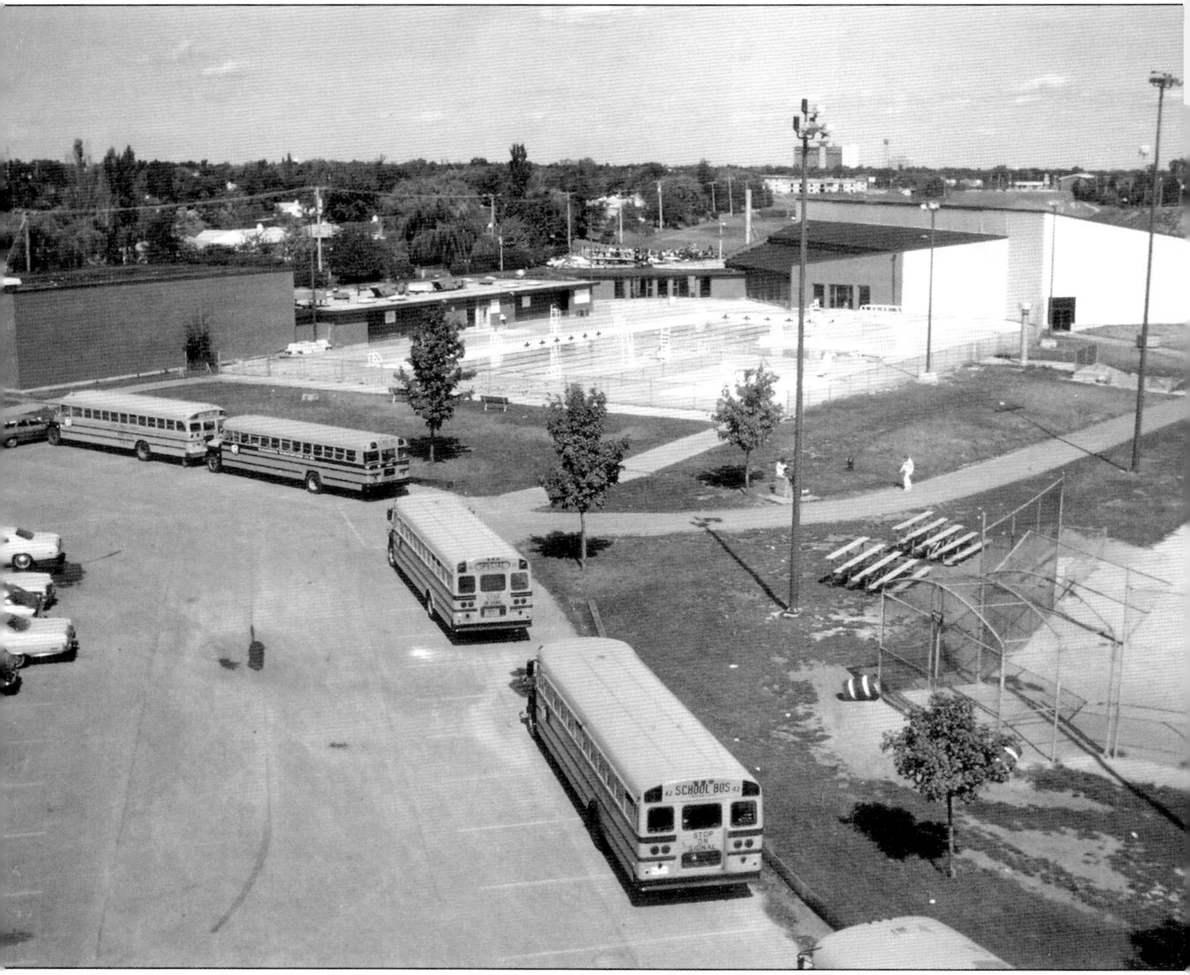

The Rolling Meadows Sports Complex opened on October 12, 1970. The pool area included swimming lanes, a deep end with a diving board (since replaced), and a small kiddie pool with a child-sized slide. In addition to housing the existing Olympic Pool, the complex offered a gymnasium (tailored for gymnastics, far left) and an ice arena that opened a few months after the rest of the complex (upper right). Located just down the creek from park district recreational land and the new Rolling Meadows Library building, the newly formed Sports Complex became an important center for this maturing city. (Courtesy of Dom Najolia.)

Three

Schools and Churches Blossom

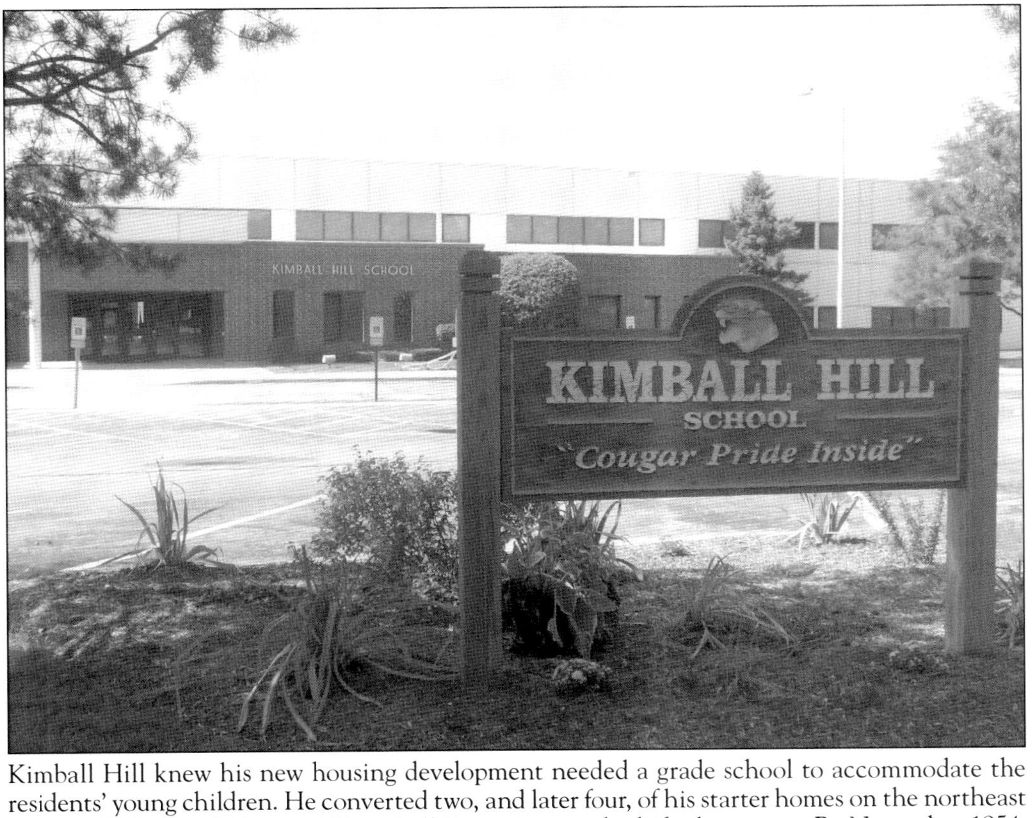

Kimball Hill knew his new housing development needed a grade school to accommodate the residents' young children. He converted two, and later four, of his starter homes on the northeast corner of Meadow Drive and Campbell Street into makeshift classrooms. By November 1954, a permanent building was constructed and was named after Hill. In 1955, Joseph Kiszka was appointed principal. The school serves the children in the north and northeast portions of Rolling Meadows. (Courtesy of the author.)

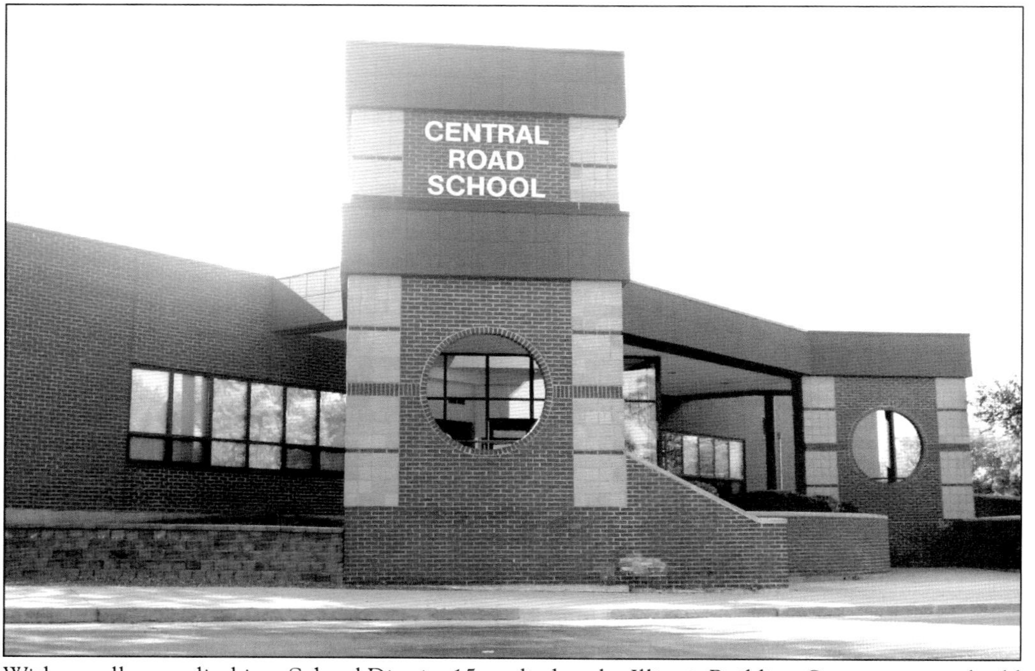

With enrollment climbing, School District 15 applied to the Illinois Building Commission to build another school. Just after Thanksgiving 1960, Central Road School opened with 12 classrooms and Marion Omiatek as principal. Just six years later, the board of education added 14 more classrooms to Central Road School to keep up with student enrollment. "Central," as it was nicknamed, serves the children from the west end of the city. (Courtesy of the author.)

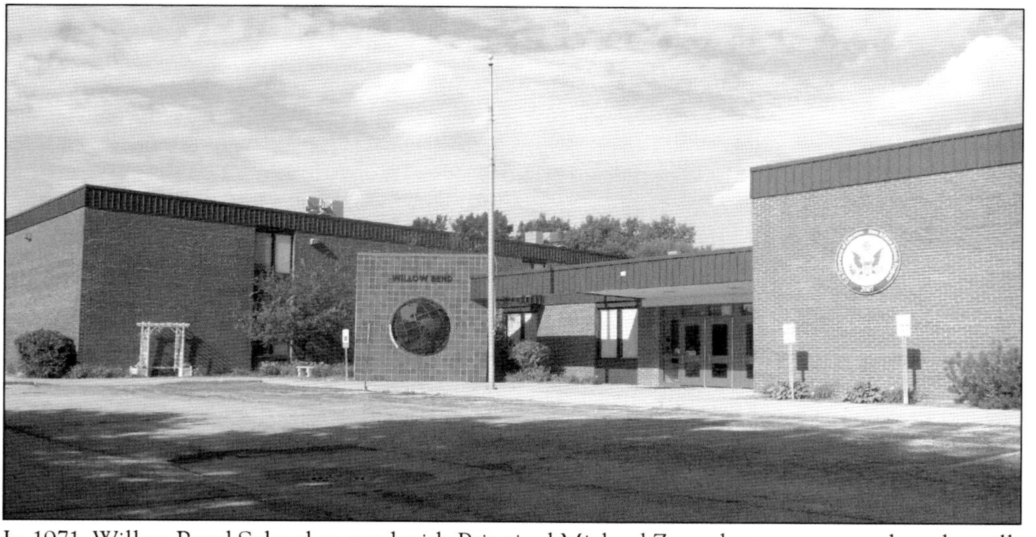

In 1971, Willow Bend School opened with Principal Michael Zawacke to accommodate the still-increasing enrollment of elementary school–aged children in Rolling Meadows, serving children in the southern portion of the city. However, by 1972, enrollment peaked and started to decline. The two elementary schools built in the late 1950s, Jonas Salk and Cardinal Drive, were closed. Kimball Hill, Central Road, and Willow Bend Schools remain the only elementary schools in Rolling Meadows. (Courtesy of the author.)

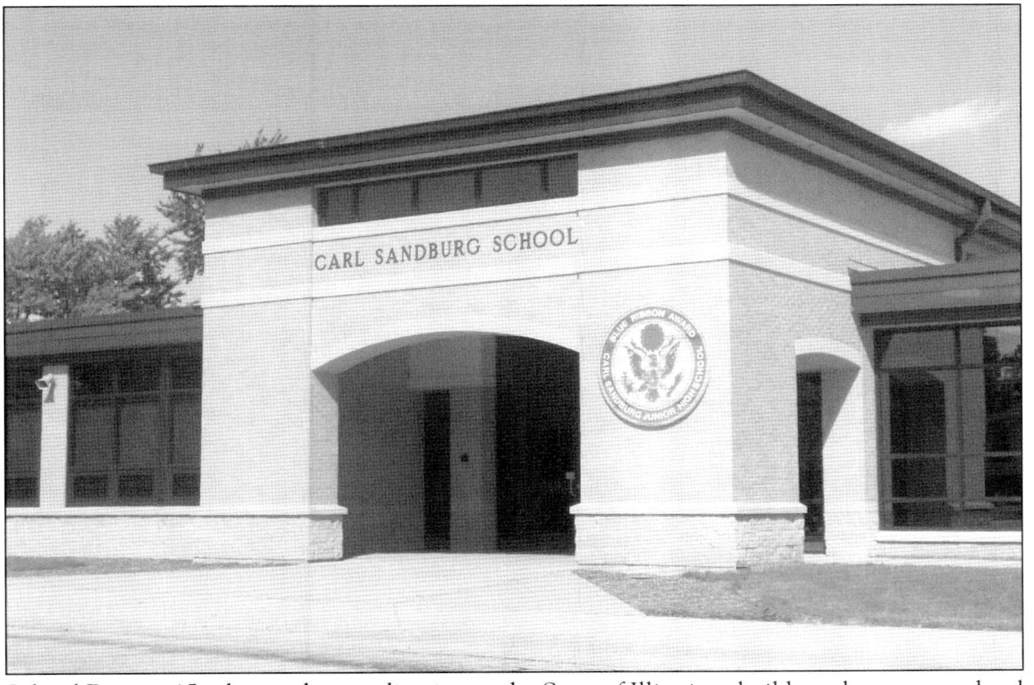

School District 15 submitted an application to the State of Illinois to build an elementary school in the east end of Rolling Meadows. The opened in September 1961 and was named after Carl Sandburg, the famous Illinois poet. Joseph Kiszka, the previous principal of both Kimball Hill and Jonas Salk Schools, became the principal of Carl Sandburg School. Many years later, the school was entirely converted into a junior high school. (Courtesy of the author.)

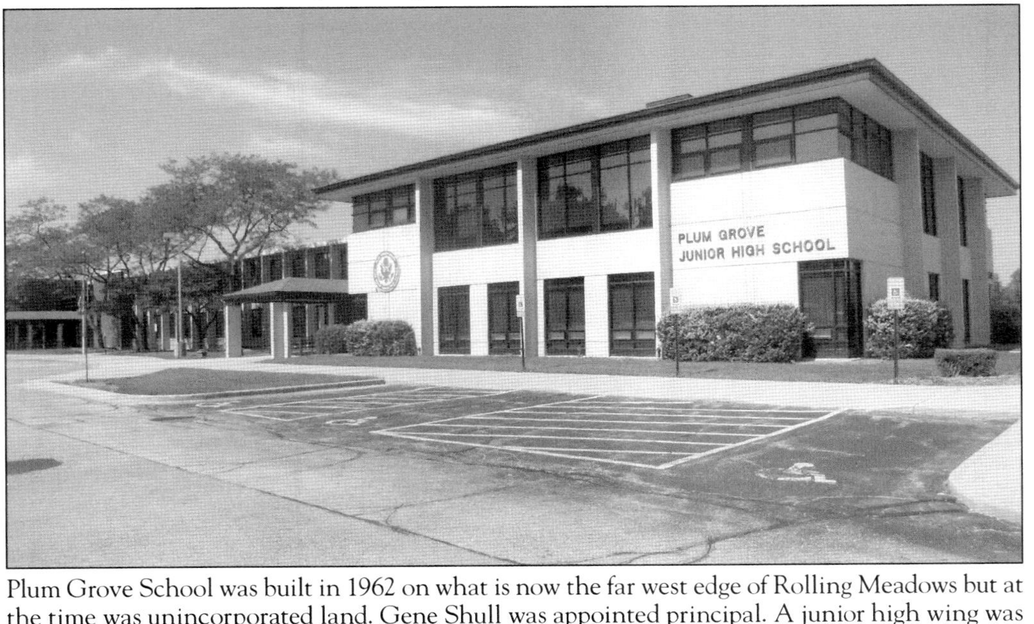

Plum Grove School was built in 1962 on what is now the far west edge of Rolling Meadows but at the time was unincorporated land. Gene Shull was appointed principal. A junior high wing was soon built, and on March 1 of the same year, seventh- and eighth-graders at Jonas Salk School were transferred to Plum Grove Junior High School. (Courtesy of the Fred Schroeder.)

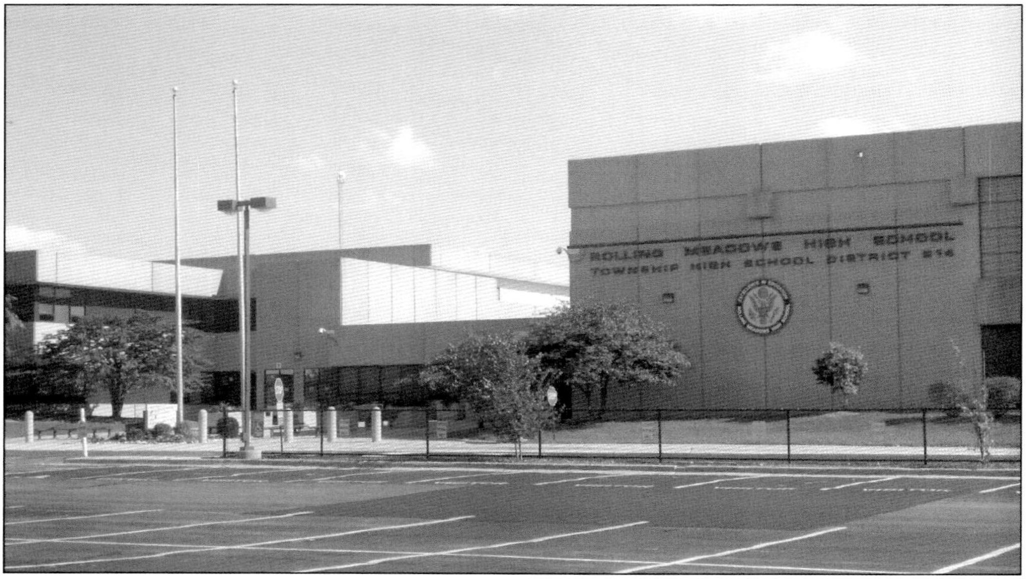

Enrollment projections in the High School District 214 area indicated that the district would have to build a new high school and have it operational by the start of term in 1971. Because enrollment was booming in Rolling Meadows, the district ultimately chose this location for its seventh high school. Construction began on Rolling Meadows High School on December 1, 1969. The school opened in 1971 with Robert Hoese as the principal. The exterior of the building has only undergone minor adjustments to accommodate its students. Below, one such change is a plaque and small garden given to the school by the Class of 1984. (Both courtesy of the author.)

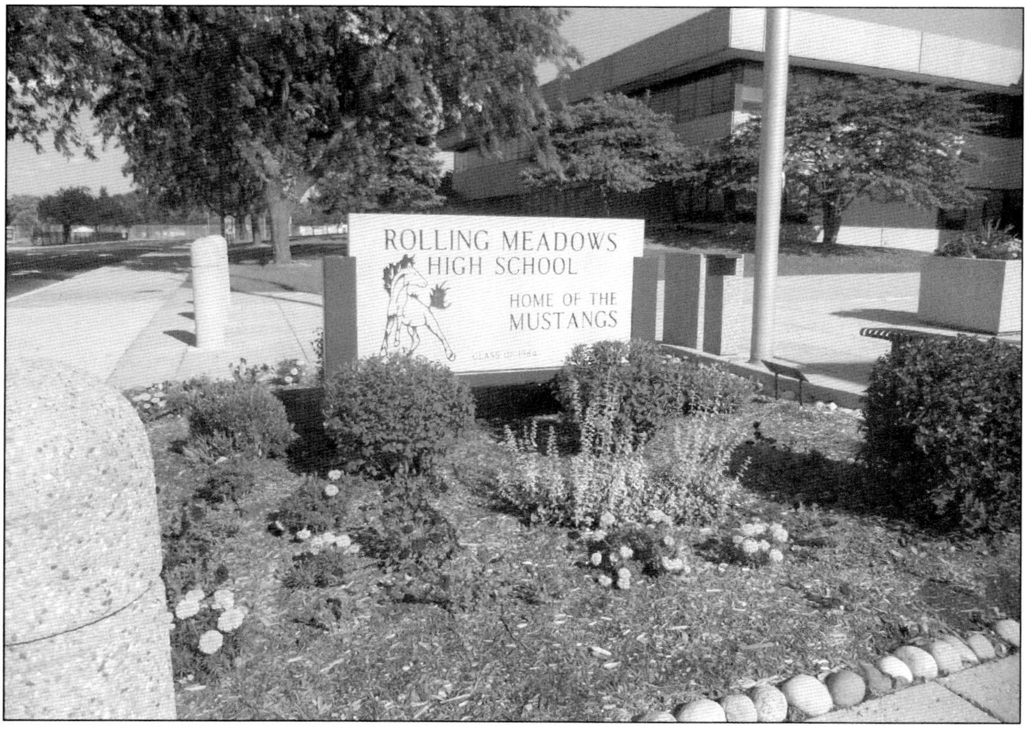

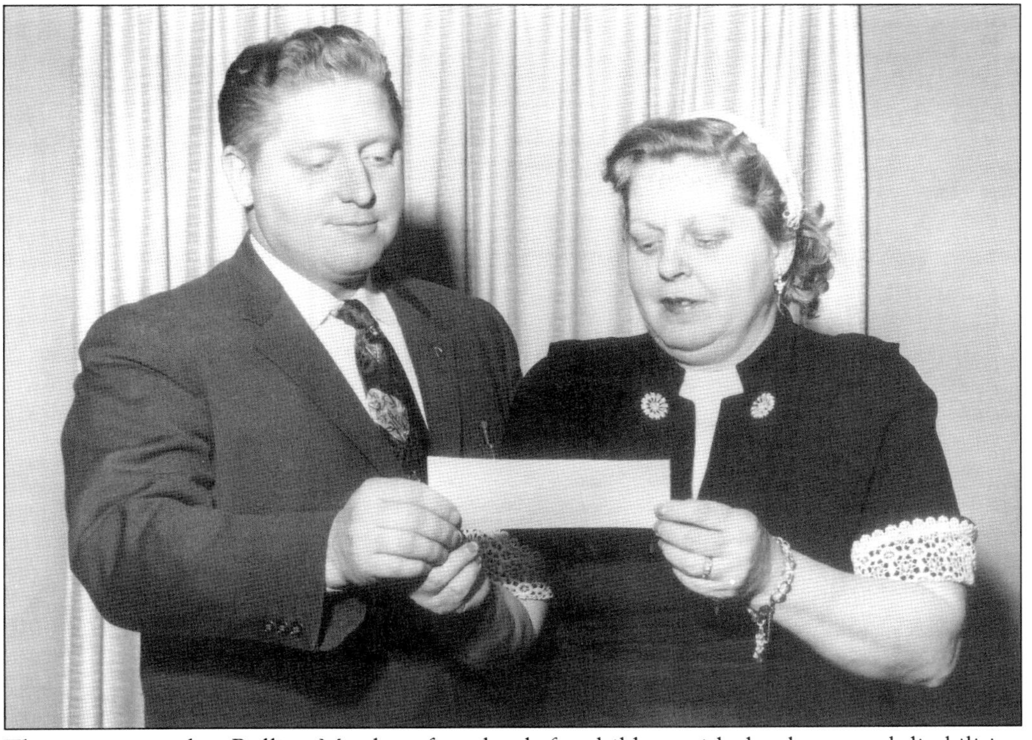

There was a need in Rolling Meadows for schools for children with developmental disabilities. Audrey Krause (above right) started a Sunday school class at the Community Church of Rolling Meadows specifically for special needs children. The class was designed to help each child develop his or her physical potential. From that Sunday school class, the idea for Clearbrook School was born. Above, in 1956, the president of the Rolling Meadows Jaycees, Frank Knudsen, presents Krause with a check from a Jaycees event benefitting Clearbrook. In 1966, Clearbrook moved into its current location on Campbell Street, below. Clearbrook has evolved into the largest provider in Illinois of programs, services, and support for children and adults with developmental disabilities. Clearbrook offers vocational training, workshops, housing, and much more for special needs people living in Illinois, not just in Rolling Meadows. (Above by Frank Knudsen, courtesy of RML; below courtesy of the author.)

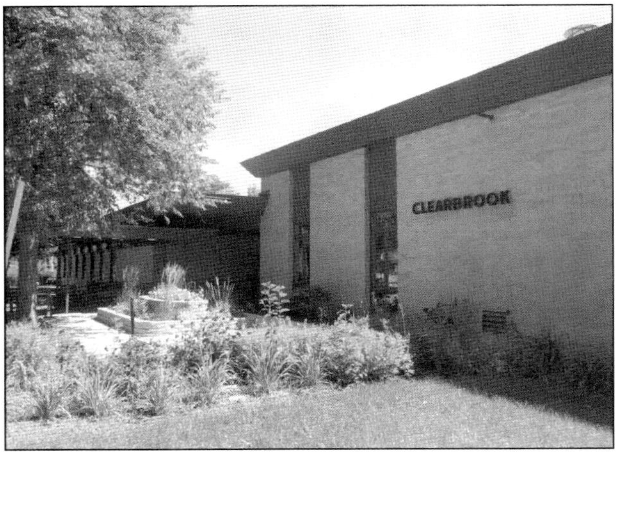

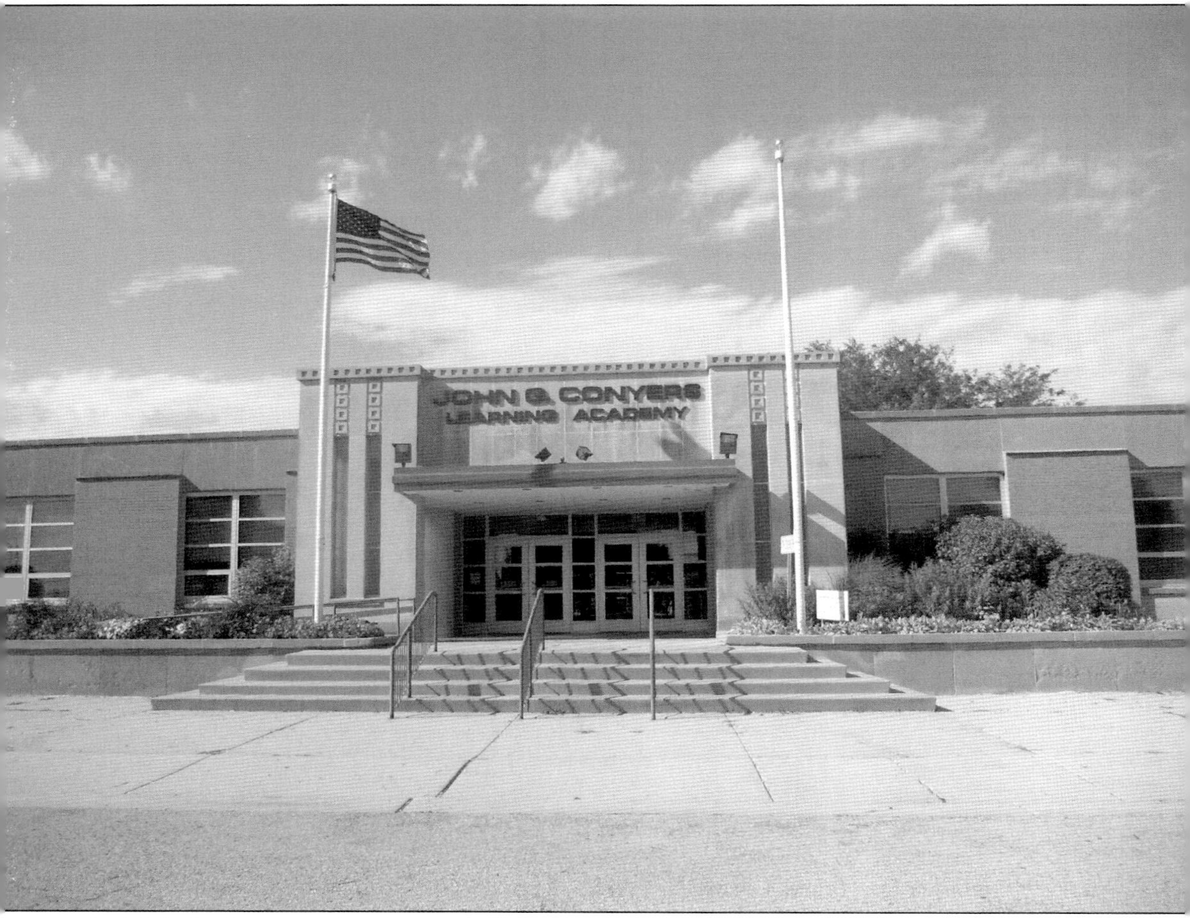

In 1995, the Learning Academy opened its doors to young children with developmental delays or disabilities. The school, part of Community Consolidated School District 15, creates an individualized educational plan for each student. School specialists and parents of students work together to help each child reach his or her personal objectives. The school also offers a pre-school integration program that blends children with disabilities and children without disabilities in the same classroom to promote play, learning, and development of social skills for all students. The school was renamed John G. Conyers years later to honor the superintendent of School District 15, who was retiring after holding the position for almost two decades. Conyers Learning Academy is located on Central Road, just across the street from Rolling Meadows High School. (Courtesy of the author.)

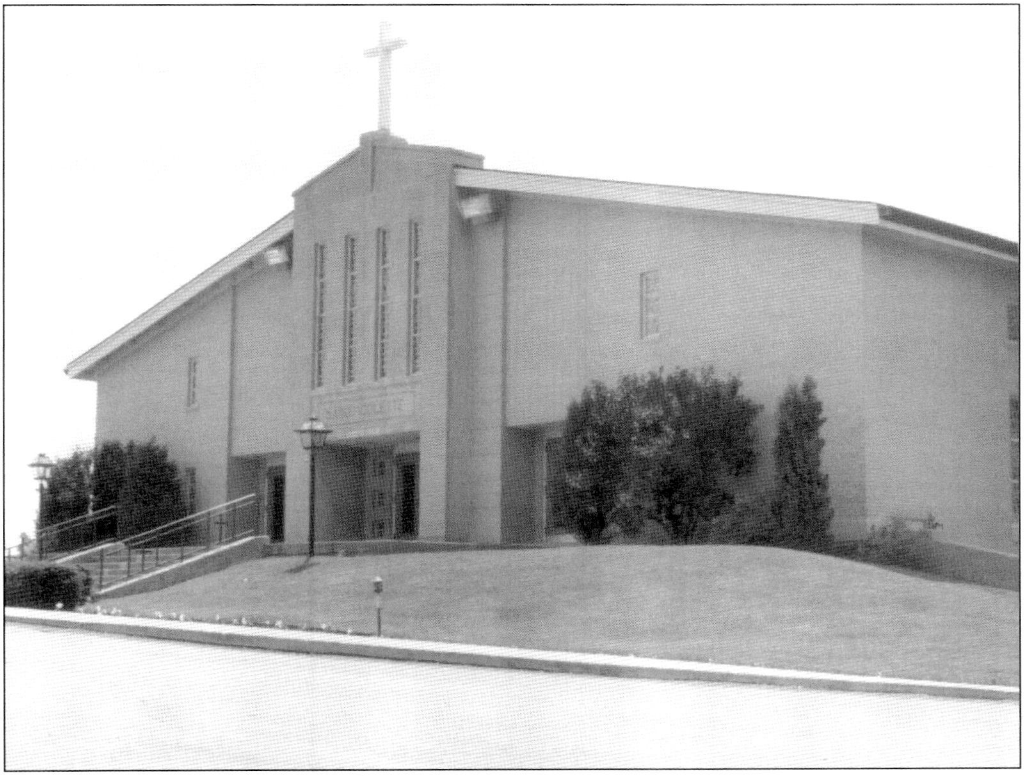

The Chicago Archdiocese owned 40 acres of land in Rolling Meadows that it planned to use for a new Catholic church. In 1957, Fr. James F. Halpin was appointed to organize the new parish. He said mass in the gymnasium at the nearby Jonas Salk School until church construction was finished. For a while the church was simply called "the Catholic Church," but ultimately Cardinal Samuel Stritch approved the name "St. Colette." St. Colette is the patron saint of children and large families, which is fitting for a church located in a city such as Rolling Meadows that has a focus on families. Right, a statue of St. Colette stands in a small garden facing the doors into the church. (Above by Rick Sutton, courtesy of RML; right courtesy of the author.)

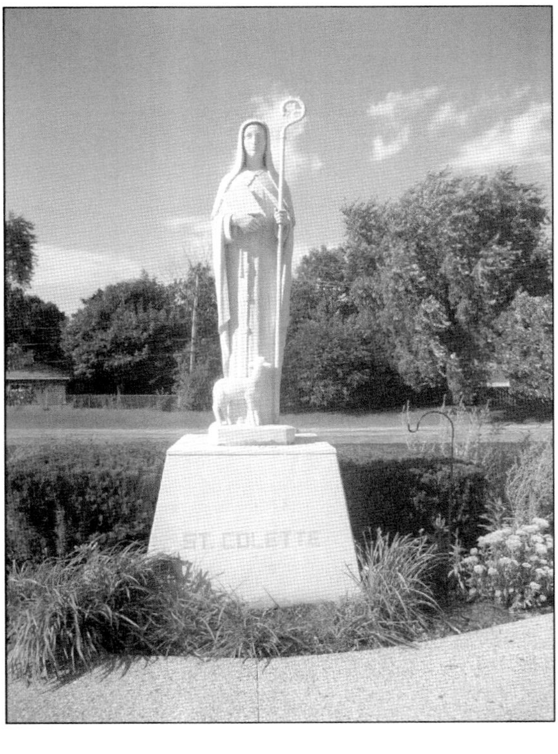

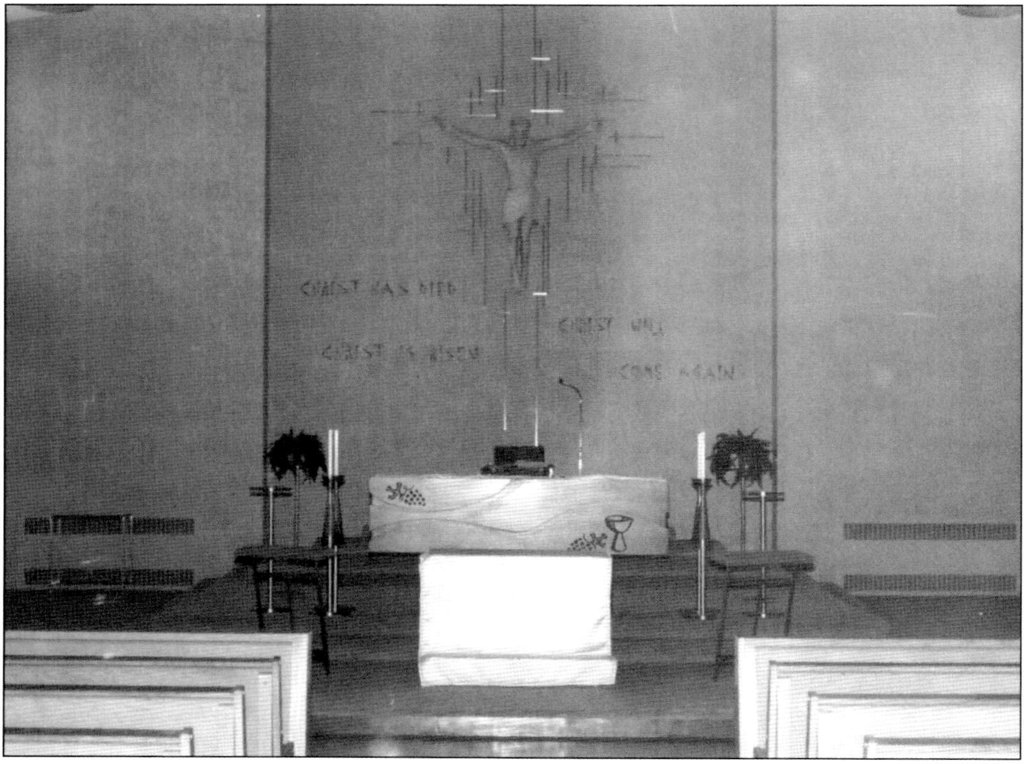

These photographs show the interior of St. Colette's sanctuary, where the many Catholic families in Rolling Meadows gather. The first mass in this church building was held on December 22, 1959. At the time, St. Colette was the largest church in Chicago's northwest suburbs, able to accommodate over 1,000 people. This church remains the only Catholic church in Rolling Meadows. St. Colette has always offered mass in English, and it recently began offering mass entirely in Spanish for the growing Spanish-speaking population in Rolling Meadows. (Both by Rick Sutton; courtesy of RML.)

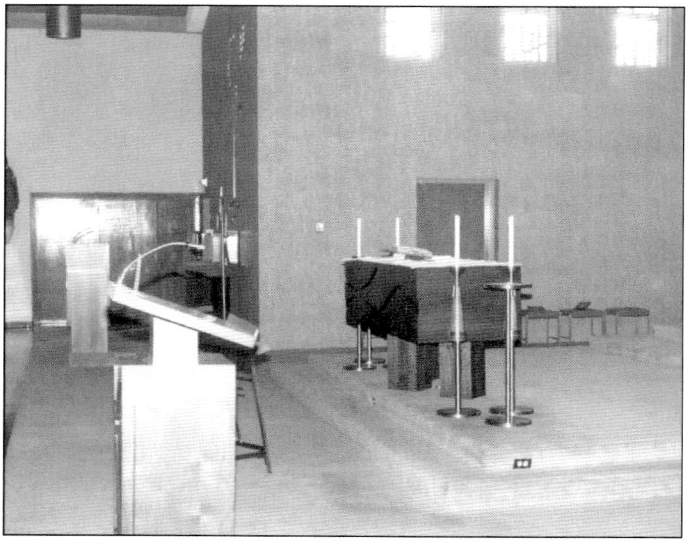

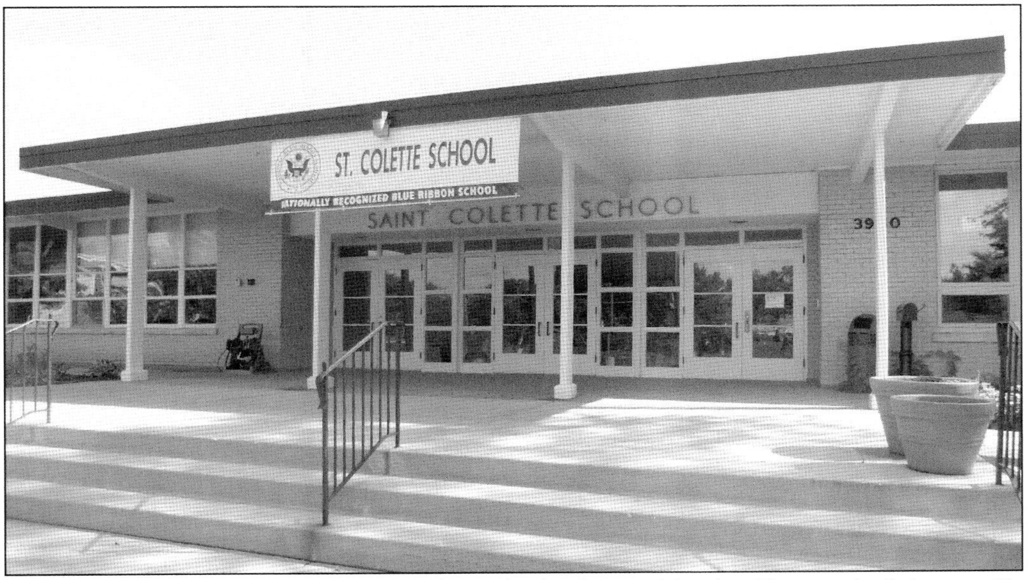

In addition to creating a Catholic church on the land owned by the Chicago Archdiocese, Fr. James F. Halpin wished to establish an educational facility on the property. A few years after the church had moved into its new building, the sisters from Sacred Heart of Mary, who came to Illinois from New York, started a grade school on St. Colette's property. Very quickly, enrollment was up to 750 students, and the school has continued to thrive ever since. These sisters went on to found Sacred Heart of Mary High School for girls not too far from St. Colette Catholic Church and School. Father Halpin later retired as the active pastor of St. Colette and was appointed pastor emeritus but chose to stay in St. Colette's rectory. (Courtesy of the author.)

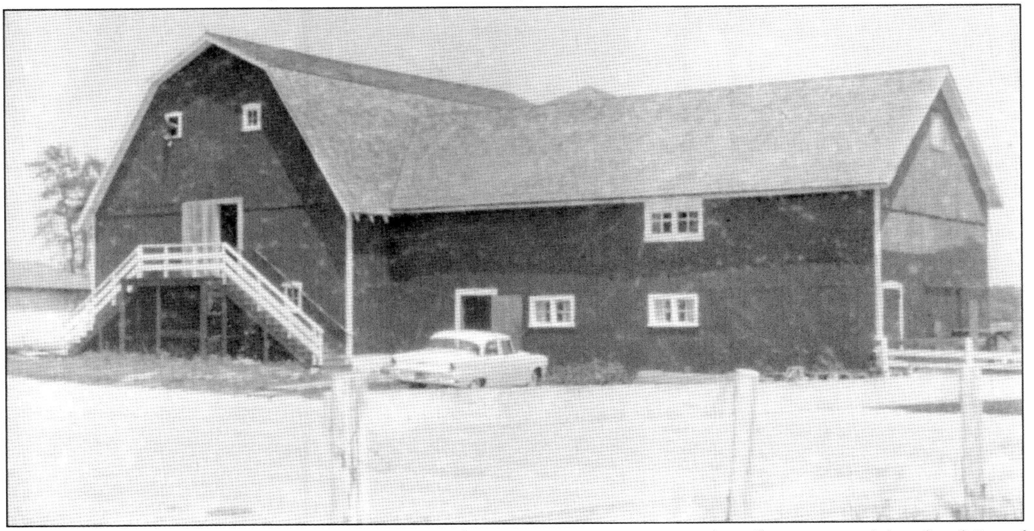

The Community Church of Rolling Meadows' congregation, under the pastoral leadership of Rev. Nelson Ringsmuth, outgrew its temporary worship space and moved into an old barn. This barn, located on Kirchoff Road, was donated by Kimball Hill. It had once been a part of William Kirchhoff's farm before the land was subdivided and ultimately sold to Hill. Kimball Hill further contributed to the Community Church by underwriting renovation costs. (By E. Singleton; courtesy of RML.)

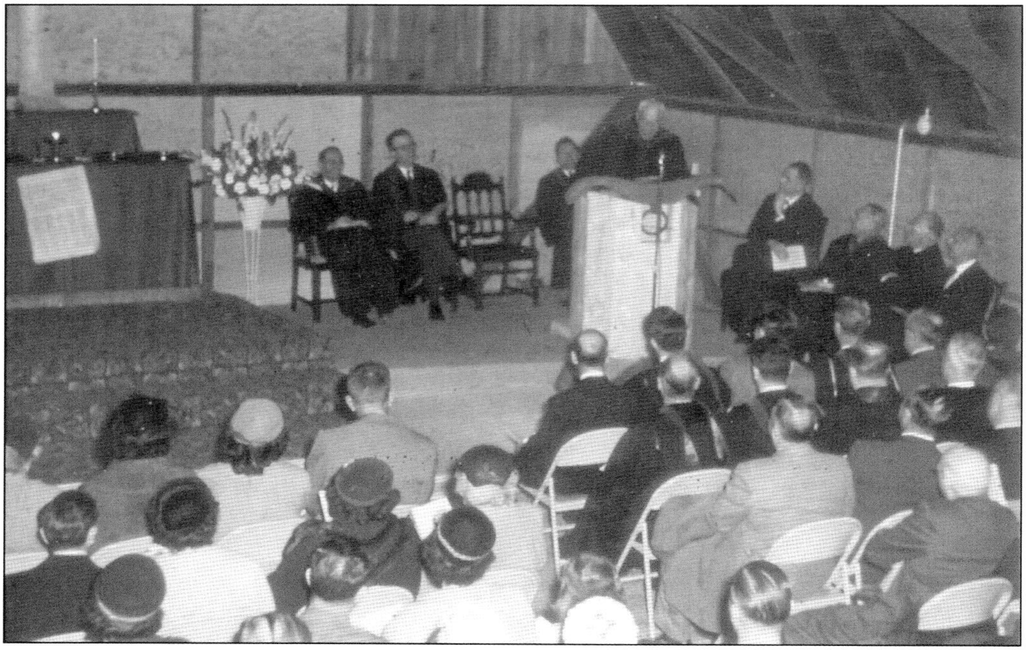

Volunteers spent over 8,000 hours converting an old barn donated by Kimball Hill into a permanent worship space for the Community Church of Rolling Meadows. The church retained some of its rustic charm with exposed rafters and the pulpit, which was made out of an old yoke, above. The congregation sat on folding chairs instead of traditional pews. Below, the new sanctuary on the corner of Kirchoff Road and Meadow Drive appears much less rustic and more polished than its predecessor. However, it does slightly echo the old barn sanctuary with the exposed rafters that come to a peak. (Above by Emily Berglund, below by Rick Sutton; both courtesy of RML.)

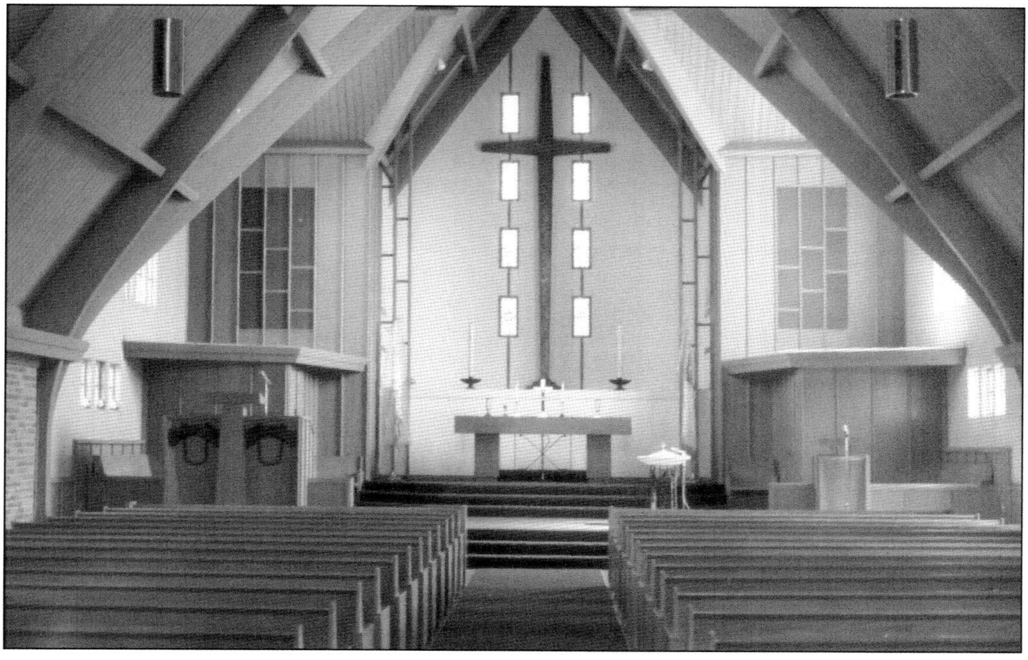

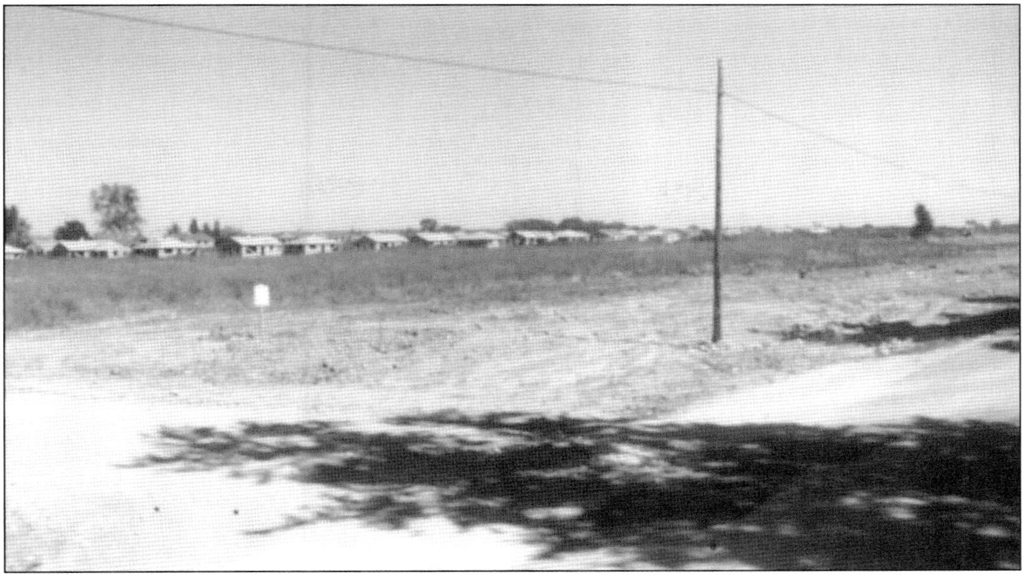

This is a rare photograph of the corner of Kirchoff Road and Meadow Drive before the Community Church of Rolling Meadows relocated from the renovated barn to this site, centrally located in the city. The church's educational building was built first, followed by a new sanctuary. (By Emily Berglund; courtesy of RML.)

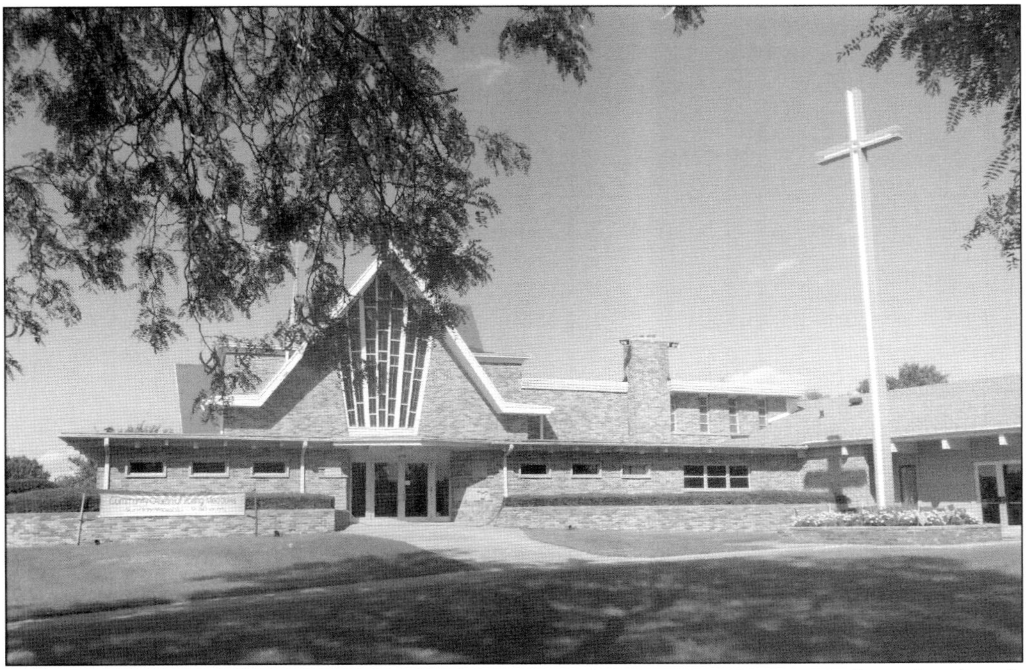

The last service held in the church barn was on October 5, 1958. The year before, the church had built an educational building on the corner of Kirchoff Road and Meadow Drive. Services moved into that building after the barn was demolished to make room for the Rolling Meadows Bowl. Years later, construction began to add a sanctuary on the corner of the property. (Courtesy of the author.)

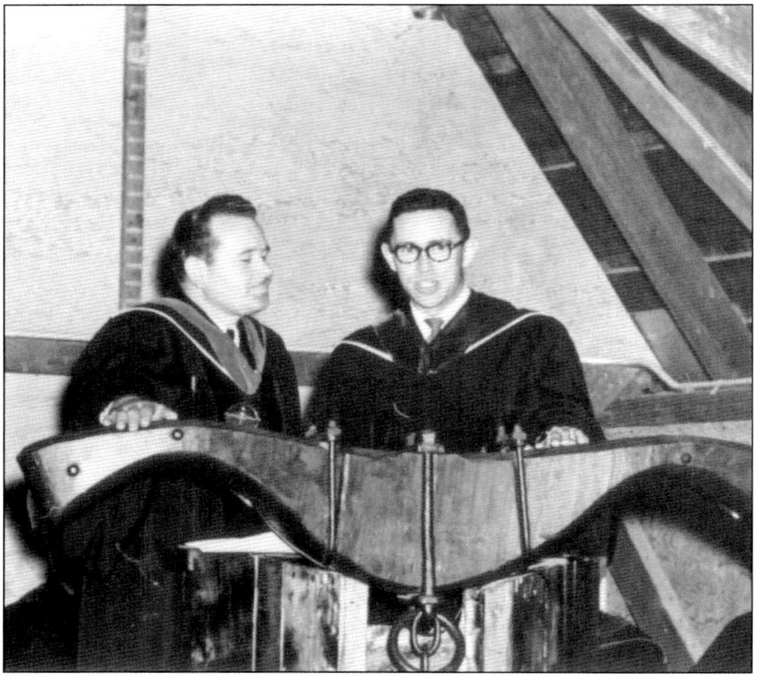

Rev. Nelson Ringsmuth was a local man who specialized in founding churches. Without him, the Community Church of Rolling Meadows might not have developed as quickly and as fruitfully as it did. Here Reverend Ringsmuth (left) stands at the pulpit in the church's new sanctuary in the remodeled barn at a Sunday service in February 1955. Next to him is associate pastor Clyde Dodder. (By Art Nyblin; courtesy of RML.)

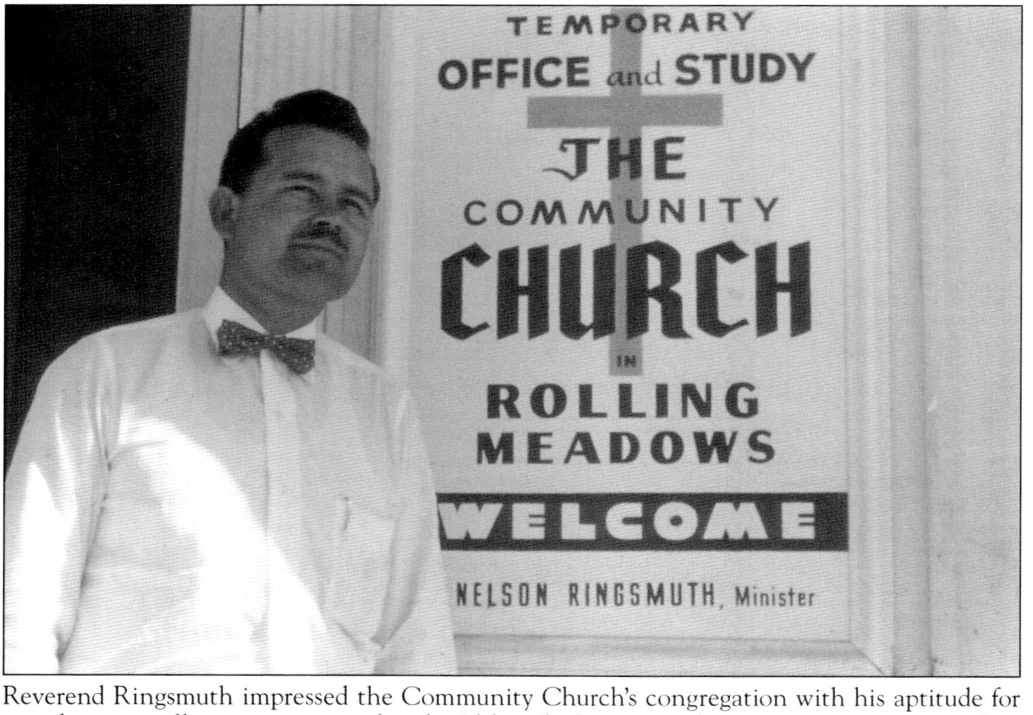

Reverend Ringsmuth impressed the Community Church's congregation with his aptitude for preaching as well as organizing a church. Although the reverend was experienced in founding churches, as opposed to serving as a single church's minister, he remained the Community Church's pastor until 1960. In this photograph, he stands outside of the office for the church he helped create. (By Emily Berglund; courtesy of RML.)

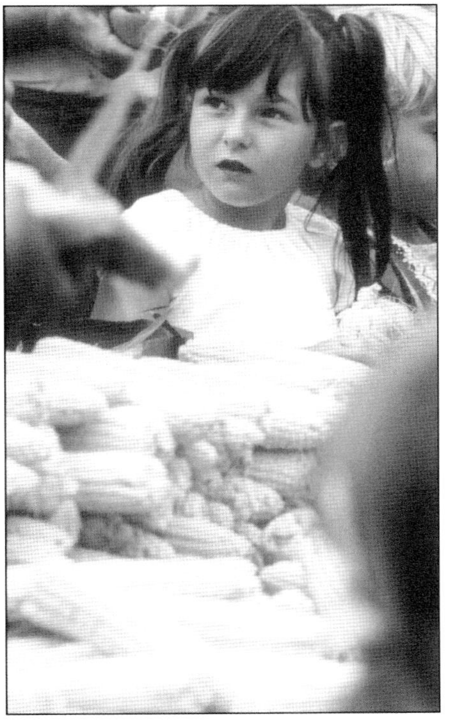

The Community Church of Rolling Meadows has always been well known for its community outreach. In fact, its location on Kirchoff Road and Meadow Drive has made it an important "center" in the city. Every summer since 1957, the church has hosted Corn Fest, a fundraiser on the church's front and back lawns where Rolling Meadows residents can come, talk, and enjoy all-you-can-eat fresh corn, as the young girl is about to do at right. Below, children come prepared to the church with empty baskets for the 1957 annual Easter Egg Hunt. (Right courtesy of Dom Najolia; below by Art Nyblin, courtesy of RML.)

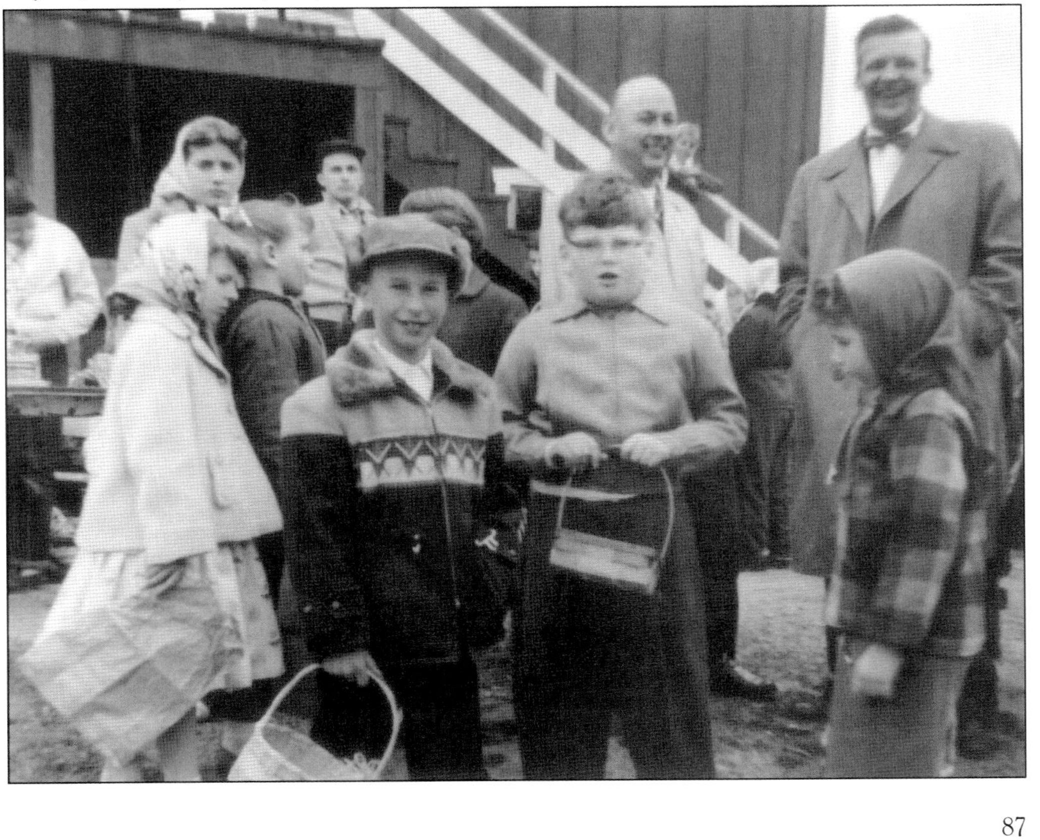

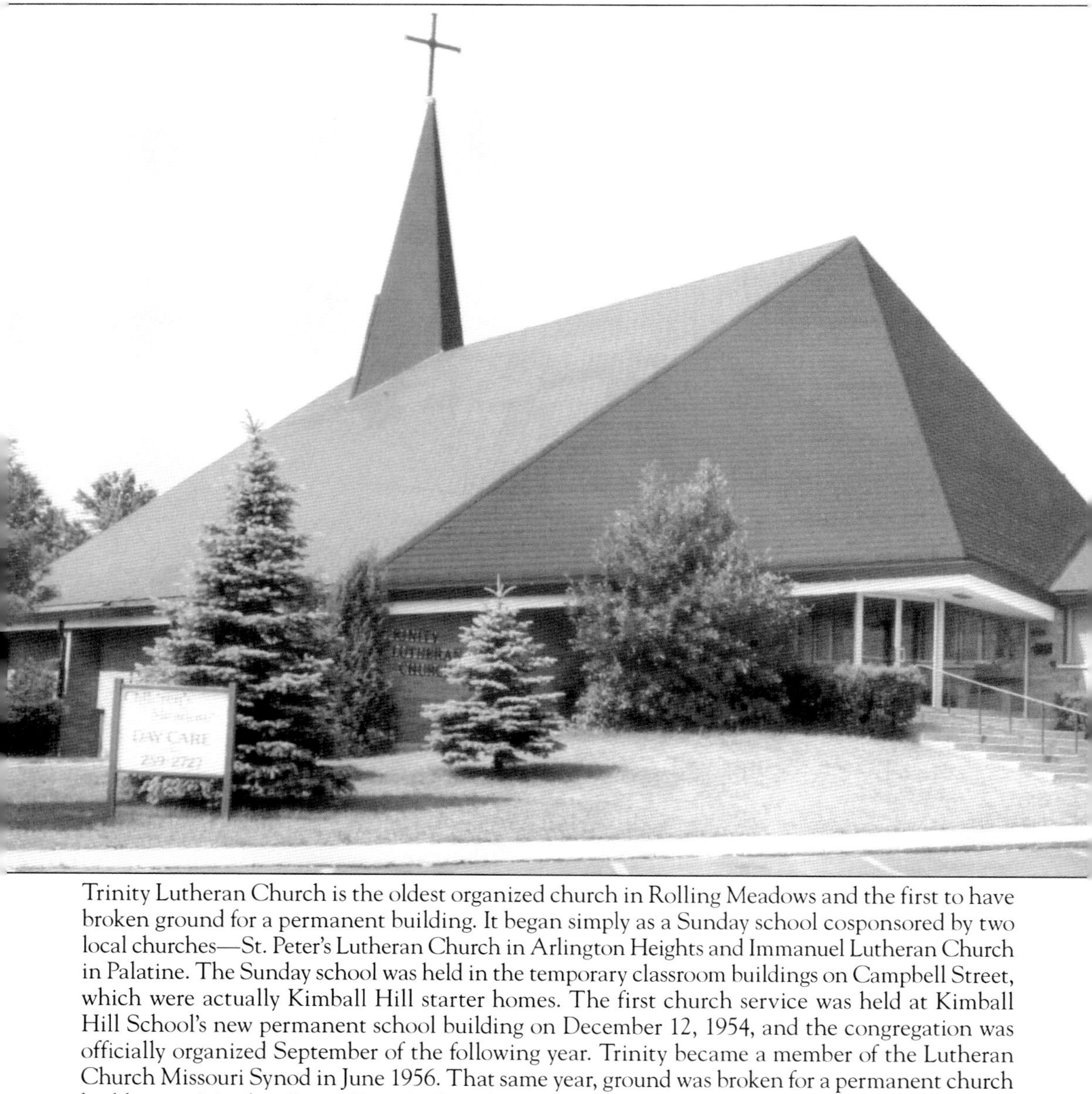

Trinity Lutheran Church is the oldest organized church in Rolling Meadows and the first to have broken ground for a permanent building. It began simply as a Sunday school cosponsored by two local churches—St. Peter's Lutheran Church in Arlington Heights and Immanuel Lutheran Church in Palatine. The Sunday school was held in the temporary classroom buildings on Campbell Street, which were actually Kimball Hill starter homes. The first church service was held at Kimball Hill School's new permanent school building on December 12, 1954, and the congregation was officially organized September of the following year. Trinity became a member of the Lutheran Church Missouri Synod in June 1956. That same year, ground was broken for a permanent church building on Meadow Drive. Rev. Carl F. Thrun became pastor in 1962, and with him the church expanded to hold a congregation of 1,200. (By Rick Sutton; courtesy of RML.)

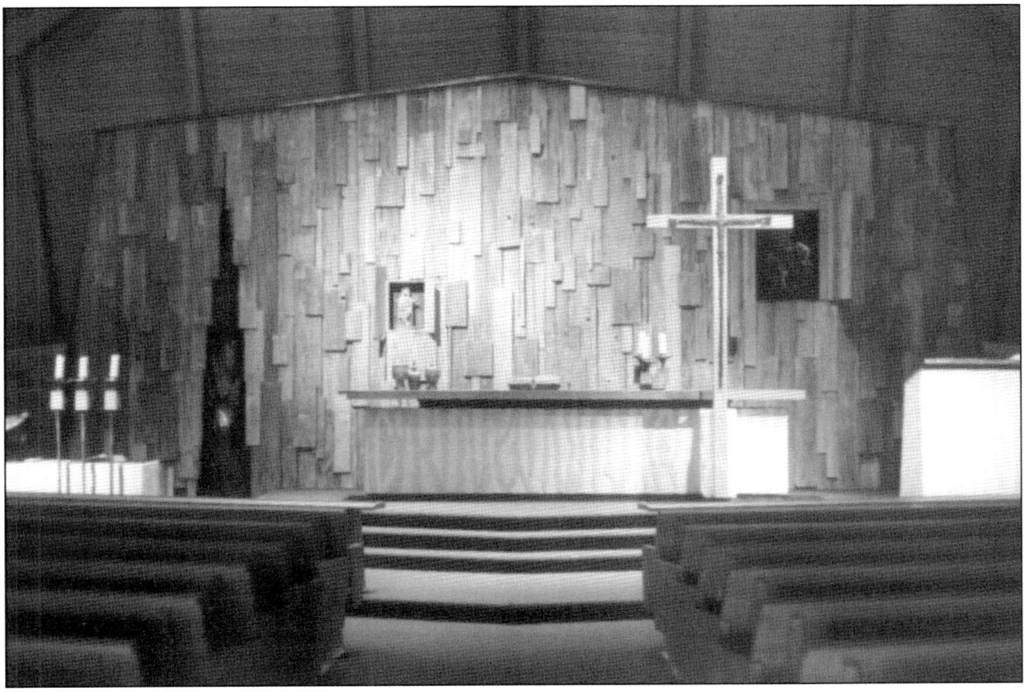

At first, Trinity's pastors were Reverend Stephan of St. Peter's Lutheran Church in Arlington Heights and Rev. Hilmar Rosenberg of Immanuel Lutheran Church in Palatine, the two churches that had originally sponsored Trinity's Sunday school. On September 7, 1957, Rev. Channing E. Miller was installed as Trinity's permanent minister. Five years later, Rev. Carl F. Thrun assumed the role as pastor. Above is a view of the sanctuary of the completed church building. Below, in 1978, the church's marquee alerts passersby to the schedule of church services. The pastor at the time was still Reverend Thrun. (Above by Rick Sutton, courtesy of RML; below courtesy of Esther Perica.)

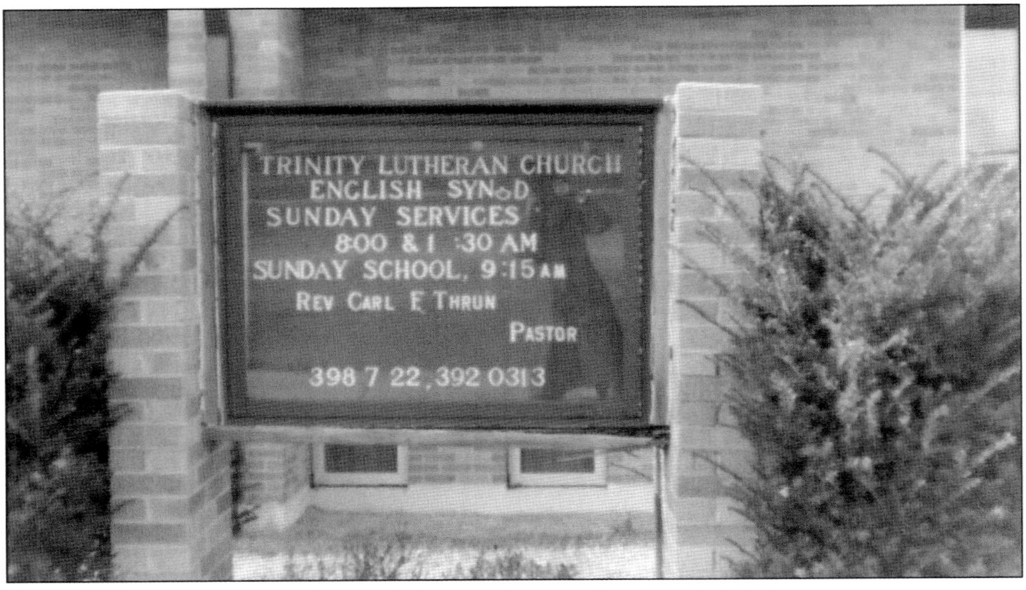

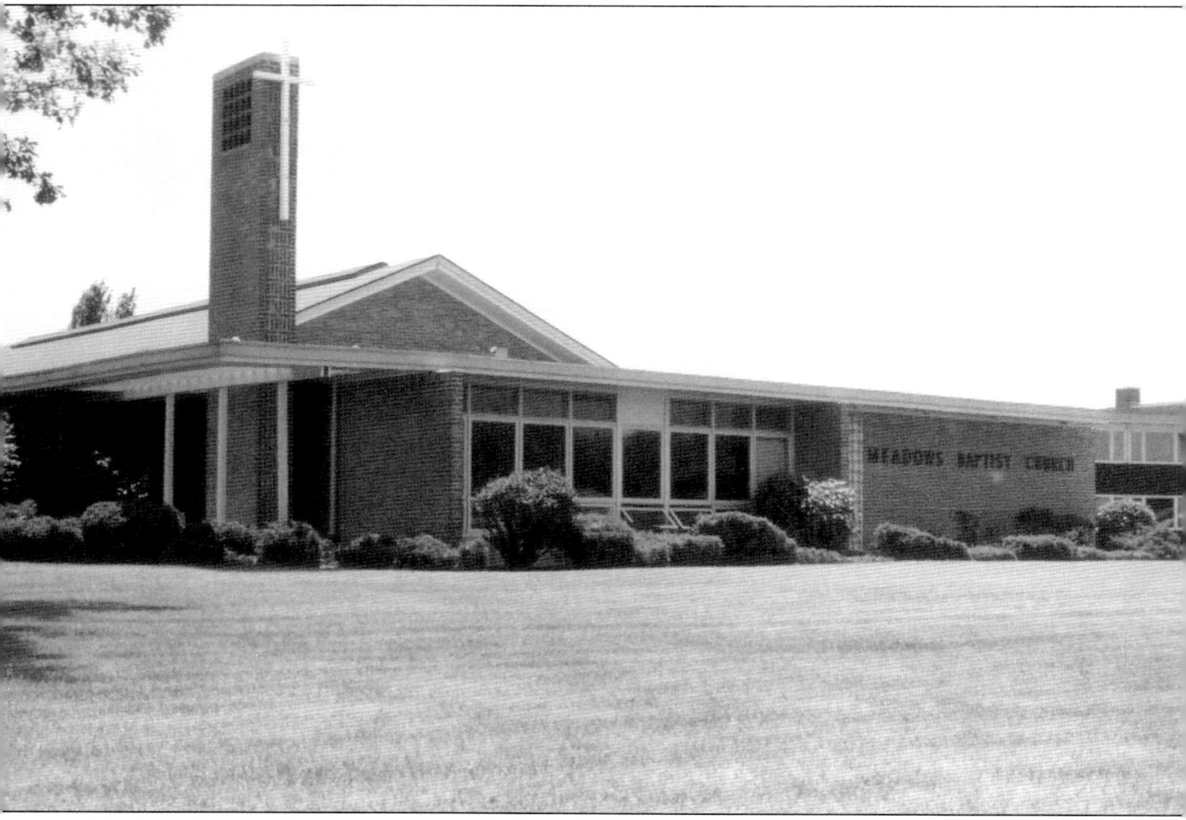

Meadows Baptist Church was once called Meadows Gospel Church and began in resident Gordon Hultgren's South Street home. Michael Green served as the first minister of the new church, which held services for its growing congregation in Kimball Hill School. In July 1957, the church started proceedings to join the Baptist General Conference. Land was purchased close to where Carl Sandburg School was later built, but a land swap with School District 15 shifted Meadows Baptist Church to its current location on the corner of Kirchoff Road and Oriole Lane. Ground was broken on April 24, 1960, for the church complex. More than 60 congregation members personally aided with the construction to help save money. The church prides itself on an international outlook, and missionary work was an early part of the church's mission. (By Rick Sutton; courtesy of RML.)

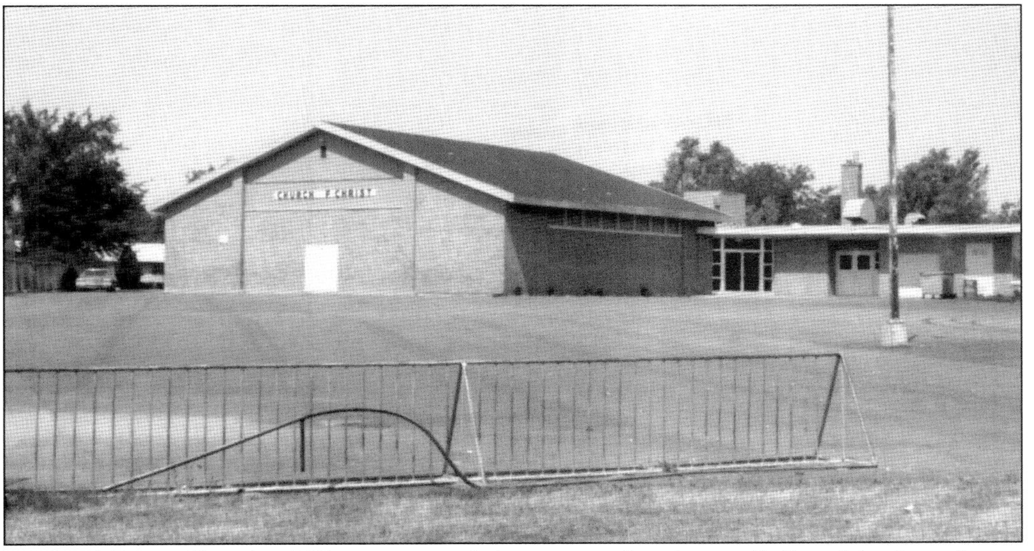

Cardinal Drive Church of Christ is one of the newest churches in Rolling Meadows. It was originally located in Des Plaines, but much of the church's congregation was located in Rolling Meadows. The church decided to find a location closer to the congregation and purchased the then-unused Cardinal Drive School building to repurpose into a church. Pictured is the outside of the church's sanctuary. (By Rick Sutton; courtesy of RML.)

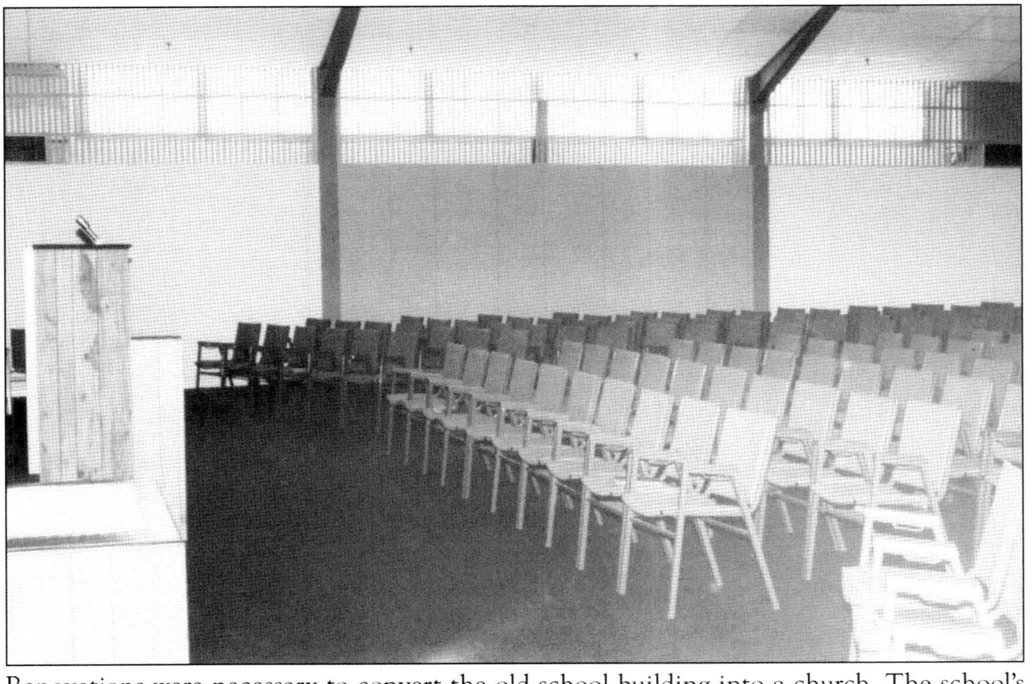

Renovations were necessary to convert the old school building into a church. The school's gymnasium received panels and carpeting and became the sanctuary, as pictured. Classrooms were converted into a fellowship hall, a kitchen, and Sunday school rooms. The church focused on special programs geared towards the youth of the community, including summer camp and vacation Bible school. (By Rick Sutton; courtesy of RML.)

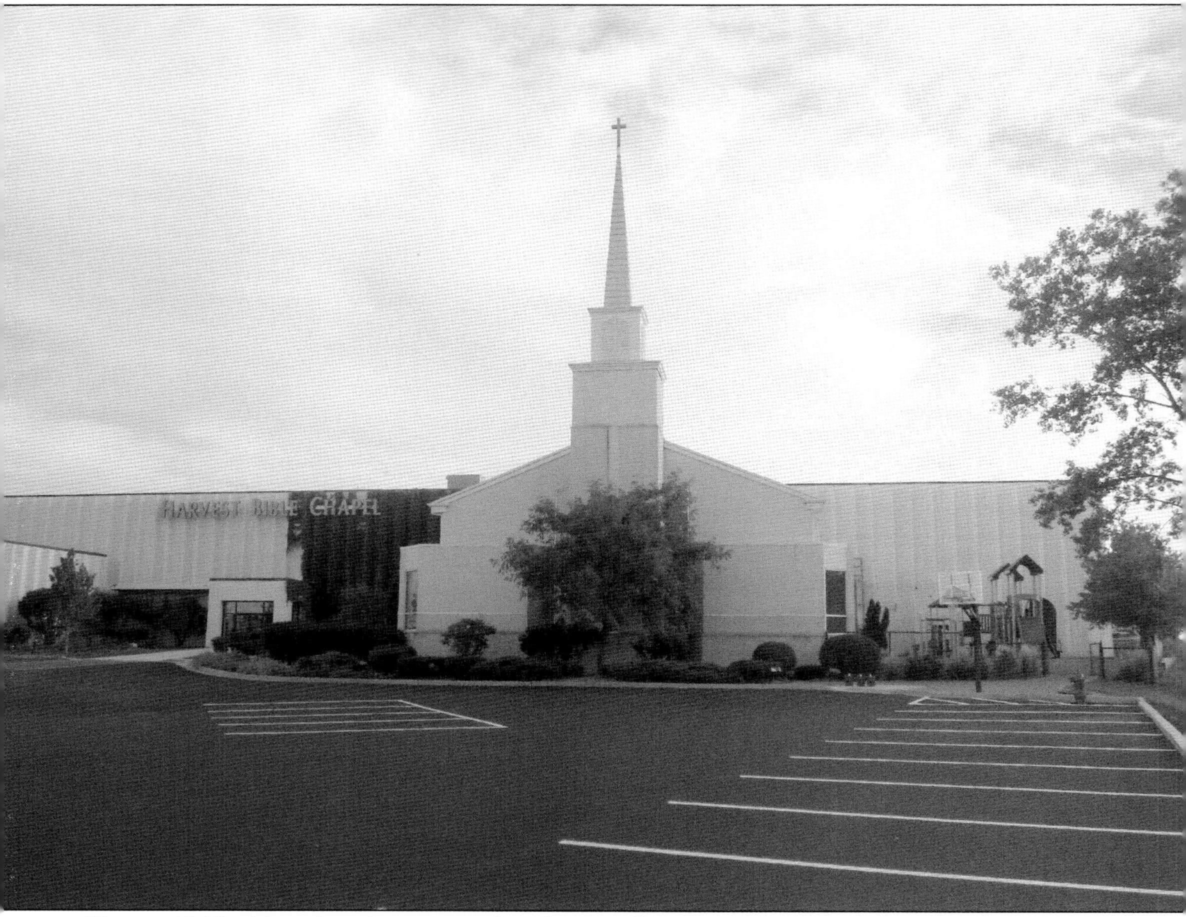

Harvest Bible Chapel is the newest church in Rolling Meadows. It is located west of Illinois Route 53 and Arlington Park Racetrack. This church, founded in September 1988, moved into this building seven years later. Dr. James MacDonald started as the church's senior pastor and has continued to serve in that position ever since. Harvest has a real focus on deepening the congregation's spirituality and relationships with others. The building's metal siding reveals that it once served as a warehouse in its earlier days. The interior, however, has been completely revamped into a modern facility with one of the largest congregations in the area. Harvest Bible Chapel has grown to be a single church located on six campuses. This location is the original campus. (Courtesy of Fred Schroeder.)

Four

The Community in Action

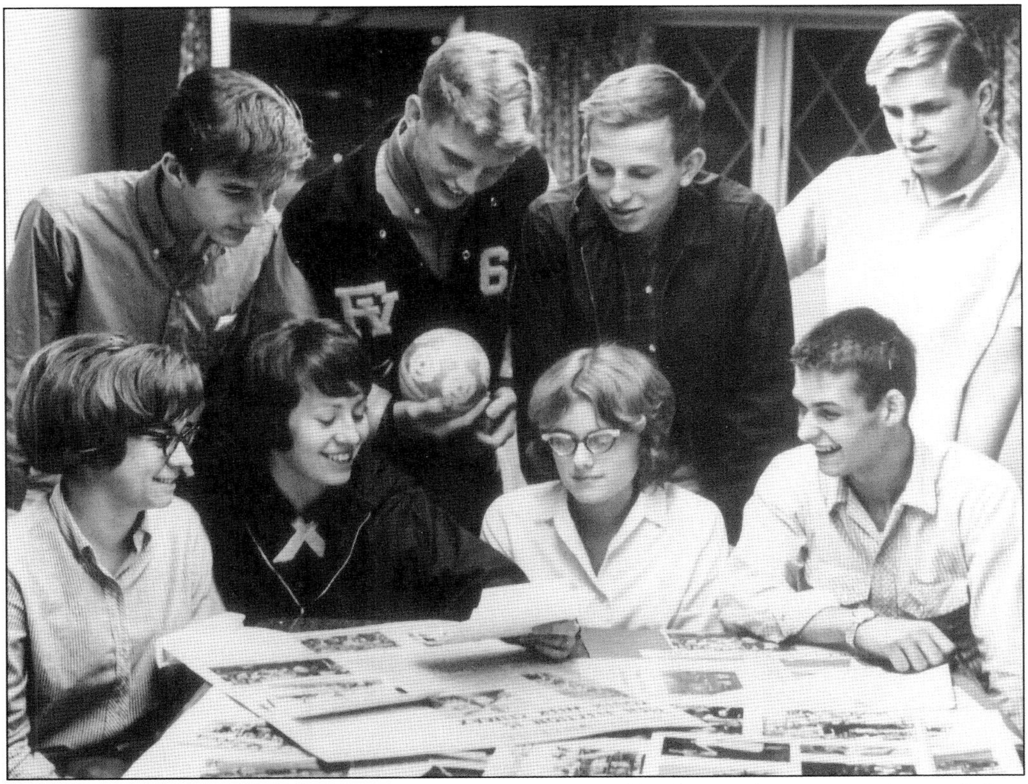

As children in Rolling Meadows grew into teenagers, city officials noted an increase in vandalism and crime. To prevent future incidents, the city worked to involve teenagers in civic affairs to further promote better, safer choices. Pictured here is one such group of teenagers, the 1965 Police Juvenile Advisory Committee (Third Group). From left to right are (first row) Linda Eberhardt, Pat Hester, Pat Bochte, and George Smith; (second row) Keith Kutch, Jim Buckholz, Bill Widinski, and Bryon Bargardt. (By Margaret Hester; courtesy of RML.)

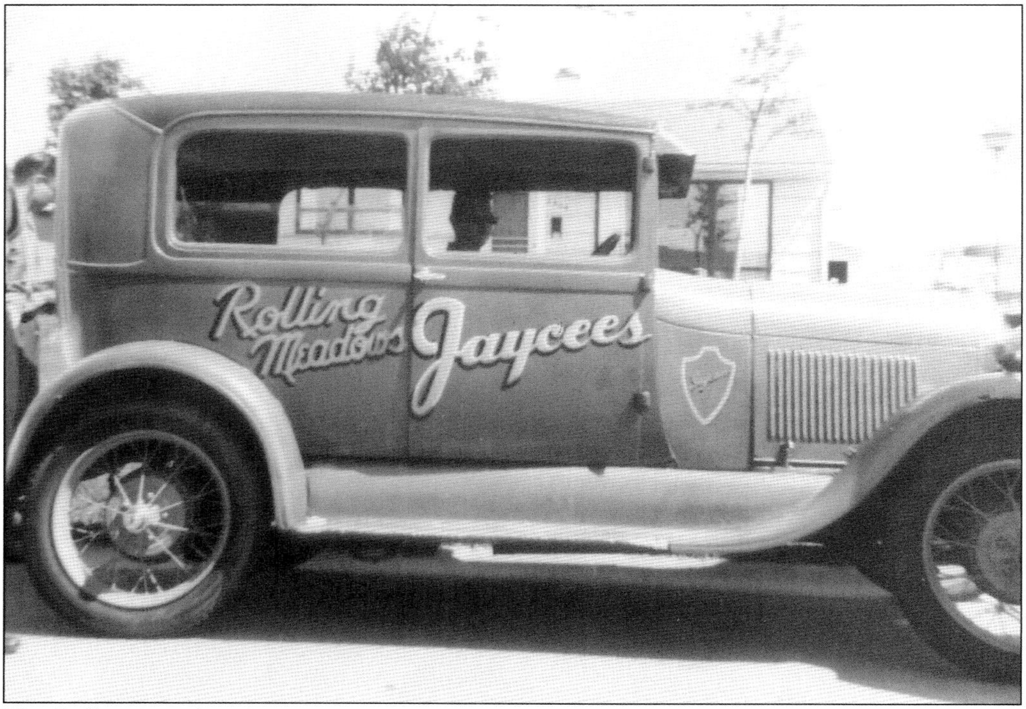

The Rolling Meadows Jaycees were an incredibly significant volunteer group in the early years of the city. Members donated countless hours to fundraisers, collecting money that they gave to help support community programs and groups. They appeared in the city's parades, including this Memorial Day Parade in 1960, with their Ford Model A. (By Frank Knudsen; courtesy of RML.)

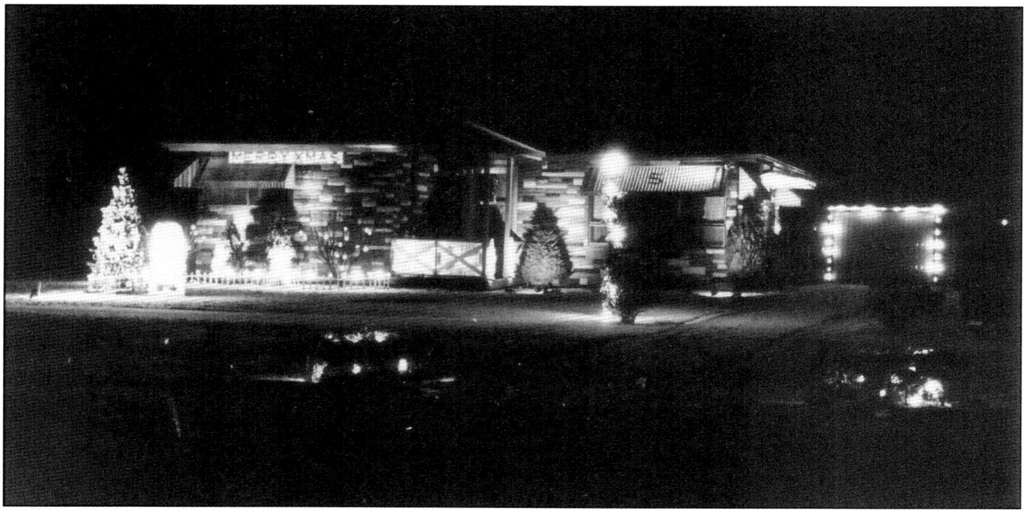

The first holiday season that Rolling Meadows became incorporated, the Rolling Meadows Jaycees sponsored a Christmas (House) Lighting Contest. The winning house from this contest, owned by Bert and Eleanor Splichal, is pictured here. With the amount of pride the city's residents felt in their brand new homes and community, it is no wonder why this contest was so popular throughout Rolling Meadows. (By Bert Splichal; courtesy of RML.)

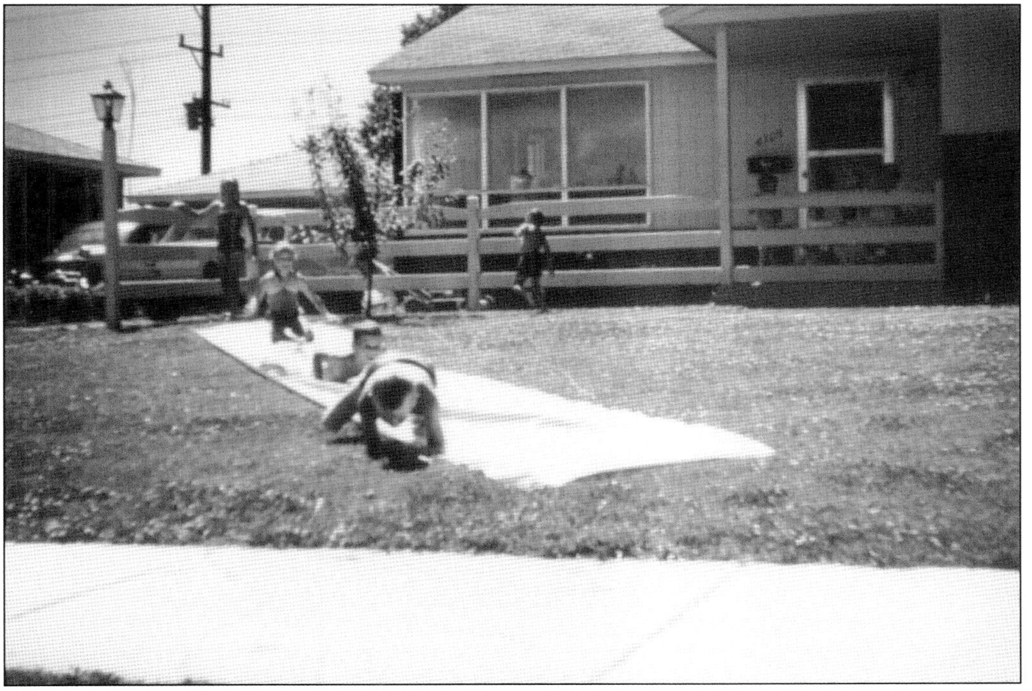

One thing that the residents of Rolling Meadows excelled at was improvising. While the housing development was still growing and in the years that followed, residents took recreational matters into their own hands. Before the park district's Olympic Pool was built, Rolling Meadows children would cool off in their own yards, often using water hoses, sprinklers, or homemade "slides" (wet plastic sheets) to have fun. In the winter, without a proper ice rink, children would skate on temporary outdoor rinks, courtesy of the cold Midwest winter weather. (Both by Ronald Brightwell; courtesy of RML.)

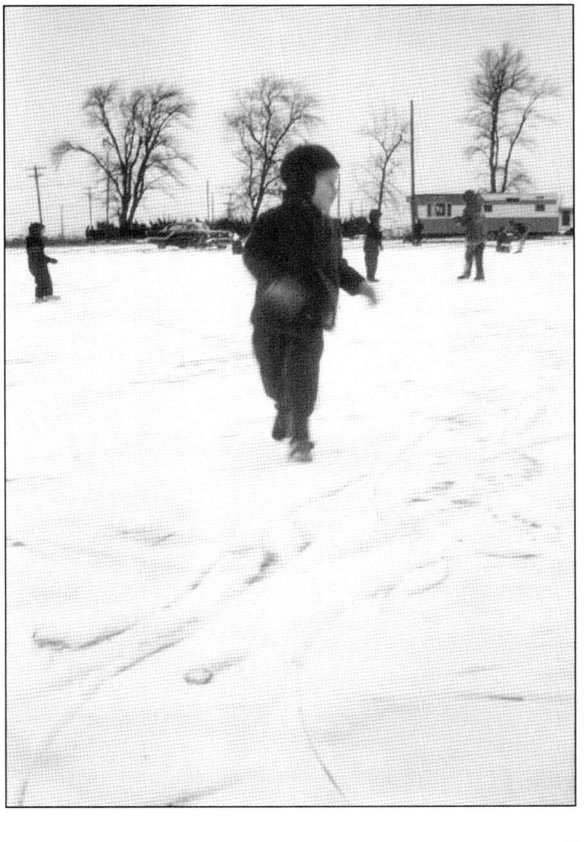

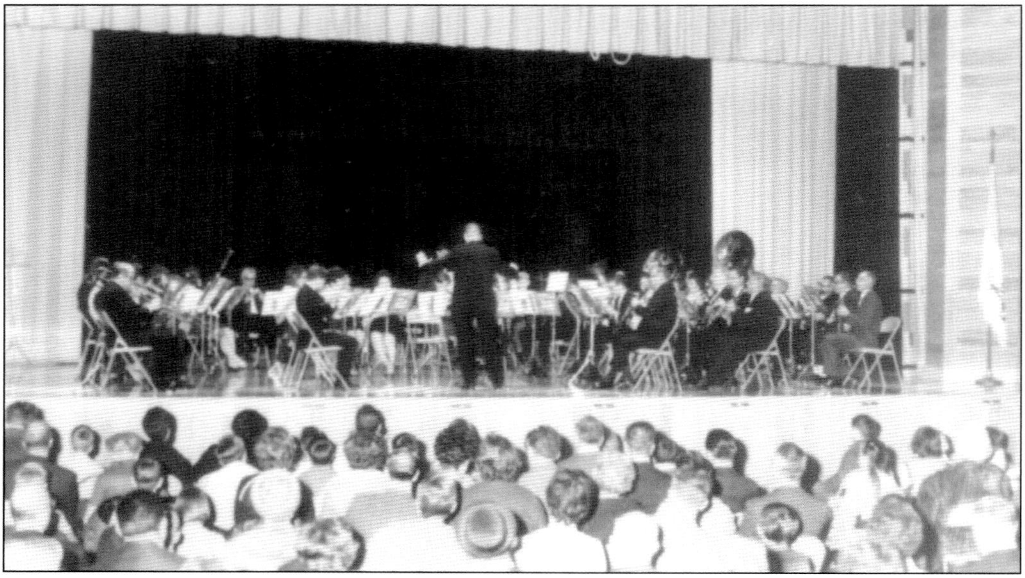

Bert and Eleanor Splichal had an idea to start a local band. They started hosting the Chicago Boys Club Band for local concerts on their front lawn. After three free concerts, they had attracted the attention of a good deal of the residents, as well as city officials. A band of 41 musicians was formed with George Yingst, the band director at Carl Sandburg School, as director. (By Bert Splichal; courtesy of RML.)

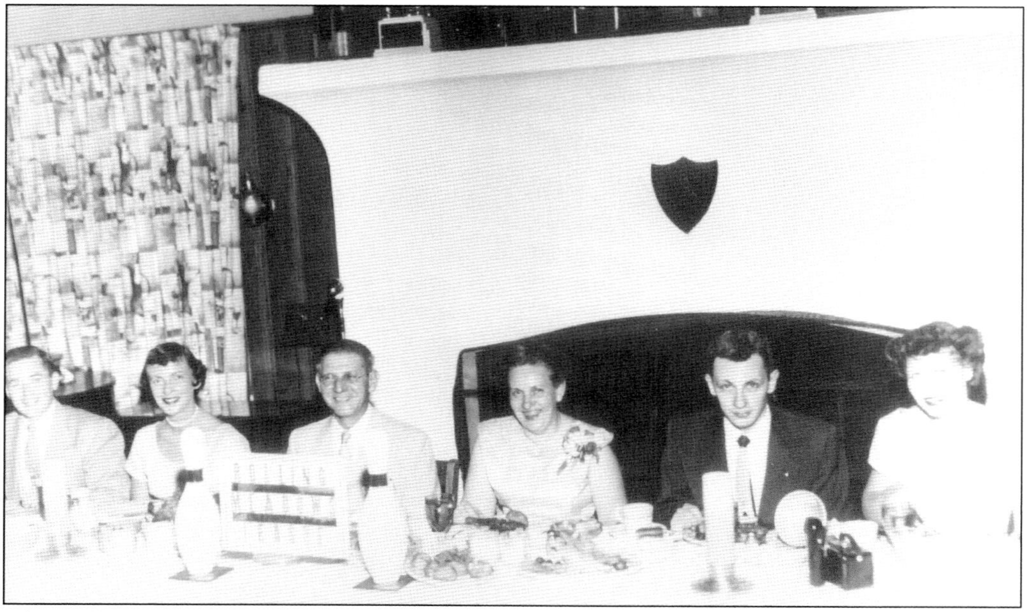

The Rolling Meadows Bowling League first started with weekly meets at the nearby Mount Prospect Bowling Lanes. During the league's second year, the team consisted of half of the Rolling Meadows Police Department and half of the fire department. This photograph was taken at one of the league's banquets. From left to right are Bob Zimmanck (secretary), Mae Zimmanck, Bert Splichal (president), Eleanor Splichal, Henry Leal (treasurer), and Leal's wife. (By Bert Splichal; courtesy of RML.)

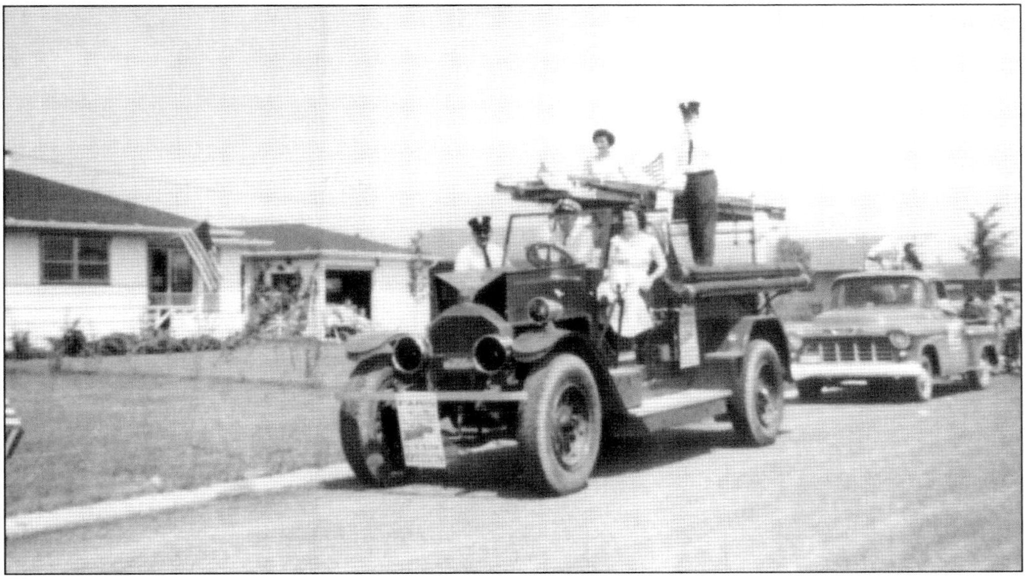

Every year, the Rolling Meadows fire district (for it was not yet a "department") offered a fundraising carnival. The carnivals were organized by Bert Traeger, pictured here behind the wheel. The community's support was felt by all the firefighters, who provided amusement park rides, carnival games, merchandise booths, and concessions for both children and adults alike. The district hosted a Fire Equipment Drive Publicity Parade every year, which always meant that the carnival was just around the corner. Here some volunteer firefighters drive through a residential area to get the community excited for that year's fundraising carnival. (By Capt. Ralph Evans; courtesy of RML.)

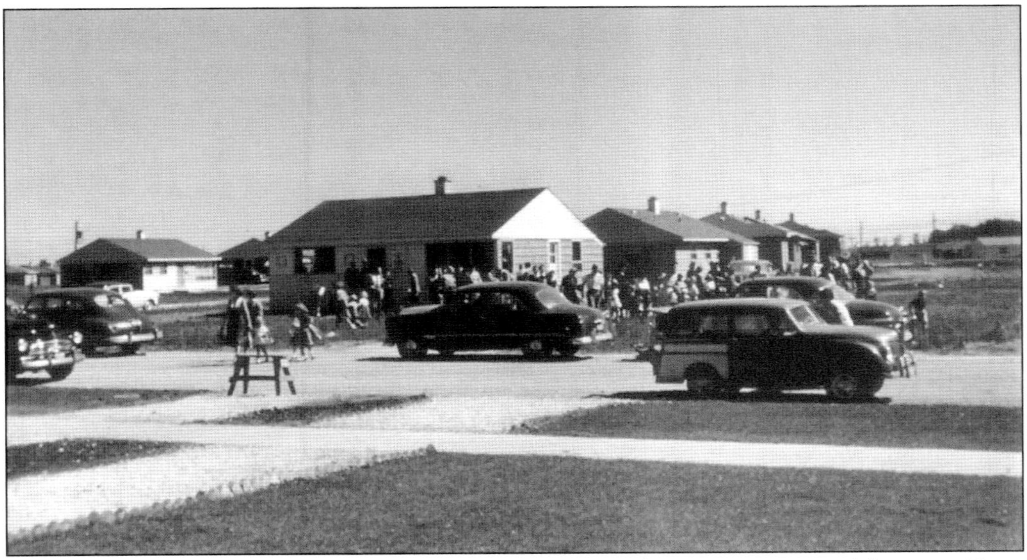

Parades have always been an important part of Rolling Meadows' community celebrations. From Fourth of July and Memorial Day Parades to Rolling Meadows High School's annual Homecoming Parade, the residents of the city make a point of attending and supporting local parades. Here, a parade sponsored by the Community Church of Rolling Meadows is underway. (By Emily Berglund; courtesy of RML.)

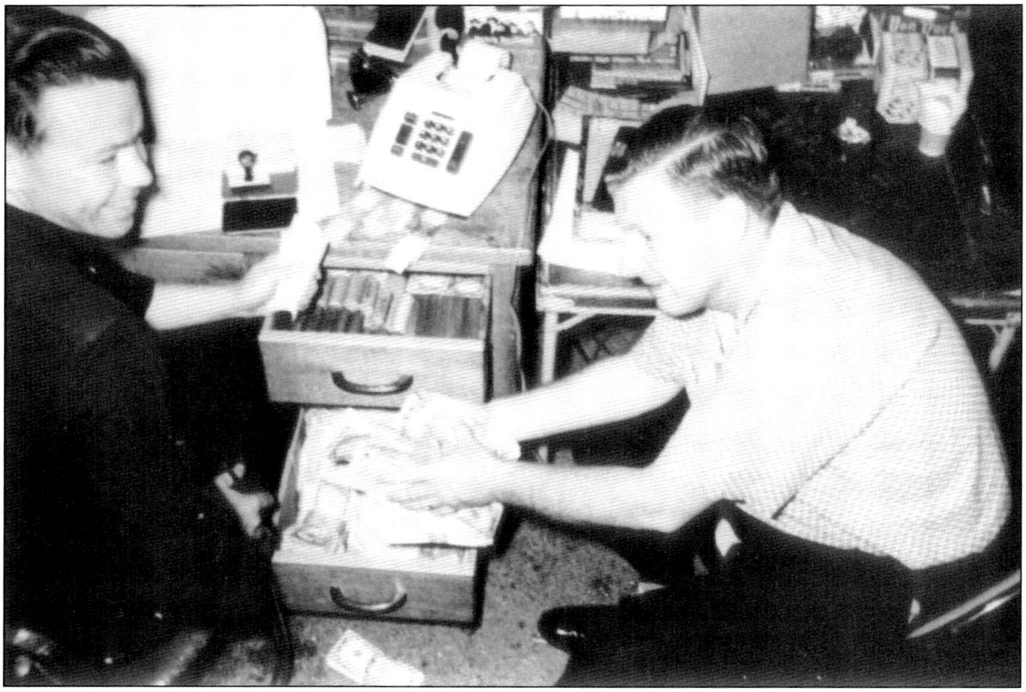

The fire district's fundraising carnival was one of the community's favorite activities. Children, especially, enjoyed the games and attractions. The volunteer firefighters pulled out all the stops to ensure that the community enjoyed itself at the carnival. At one of the early fundraisers, volunteer firefighter Ernie Pieron (below) really got into the carnival spirit, posing as the strong man. Above, in the city's first firehouse, John Delana and Ed Martin count the funds collected over several days of the carnival. The raised money allowed the fire district to purchase much-needed firefighting equipment. (Both by Thomas Fogarty; courtesy of RML.)

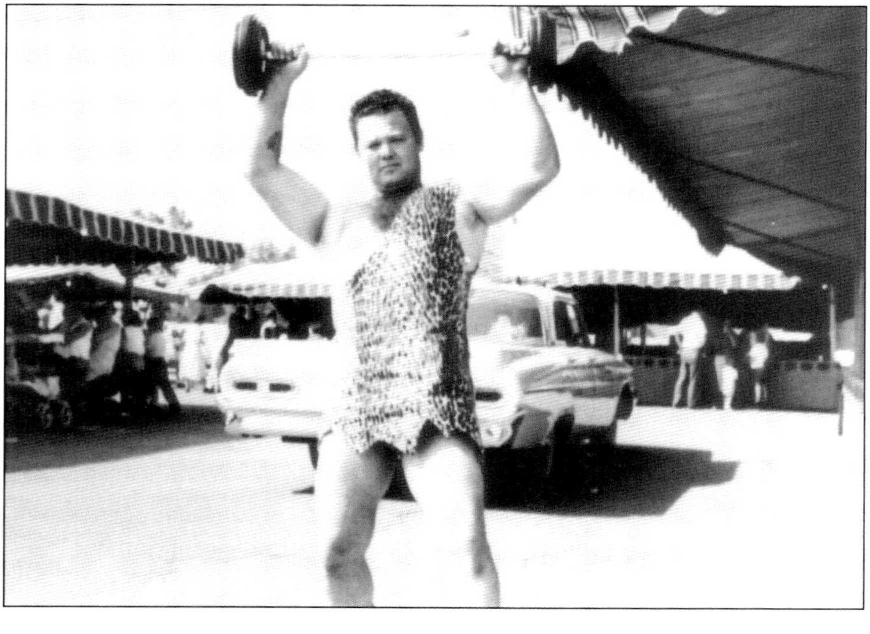

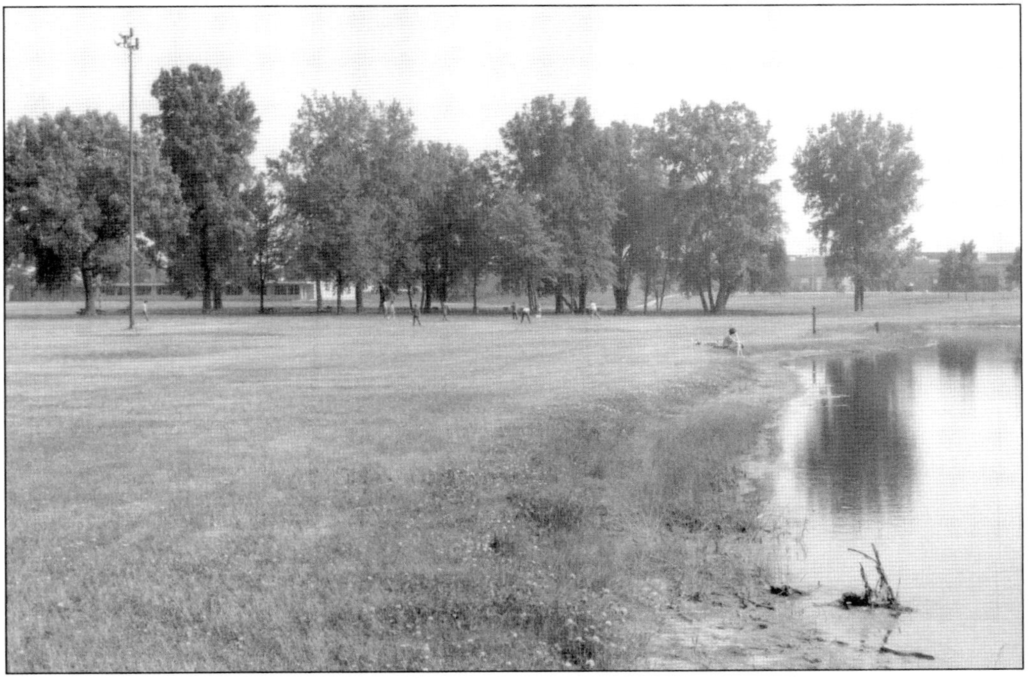

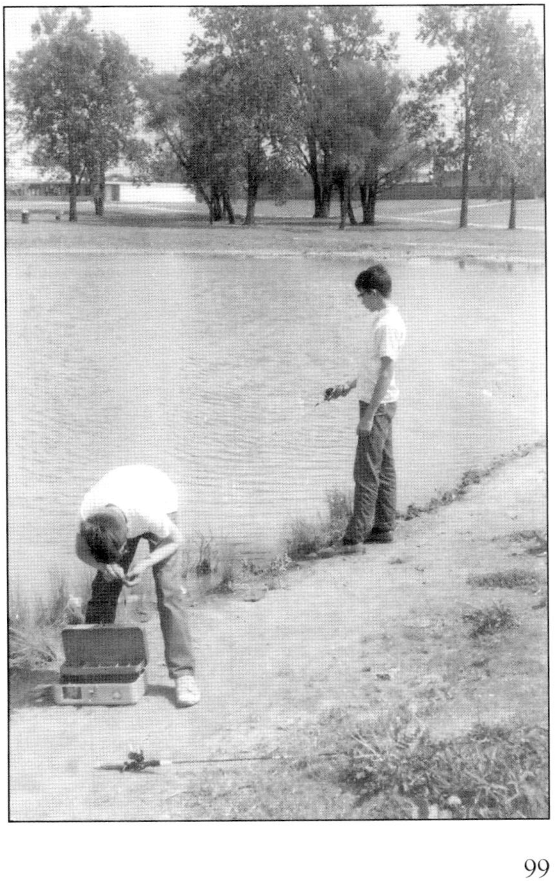

Kimball Hill designated land along Salt Creek for parks and recreational areas. Before plans for a pool or recreational facilities were funded, the new Rolling Meadows Park District committed to creating a park and playground area on the east side of the creek (above), south of Campbell Street and north of Kirchoff Road. The park district entered into negotiations with Kimball Hill and Cardinal Drive Schools to use this land as a public recreational area. The park district agreed to cut grass and plow snow, and the school facilities would be available after school hours to host community programs. This park area was named Kimball Hill Park, and the small flooded basin was named Kimball Hill Pond. This pond was used for ice skating in the winter and fishing in the summer (right). (Above by Rick Sutton, right by Emily Berglund; both courtesy of RML.)

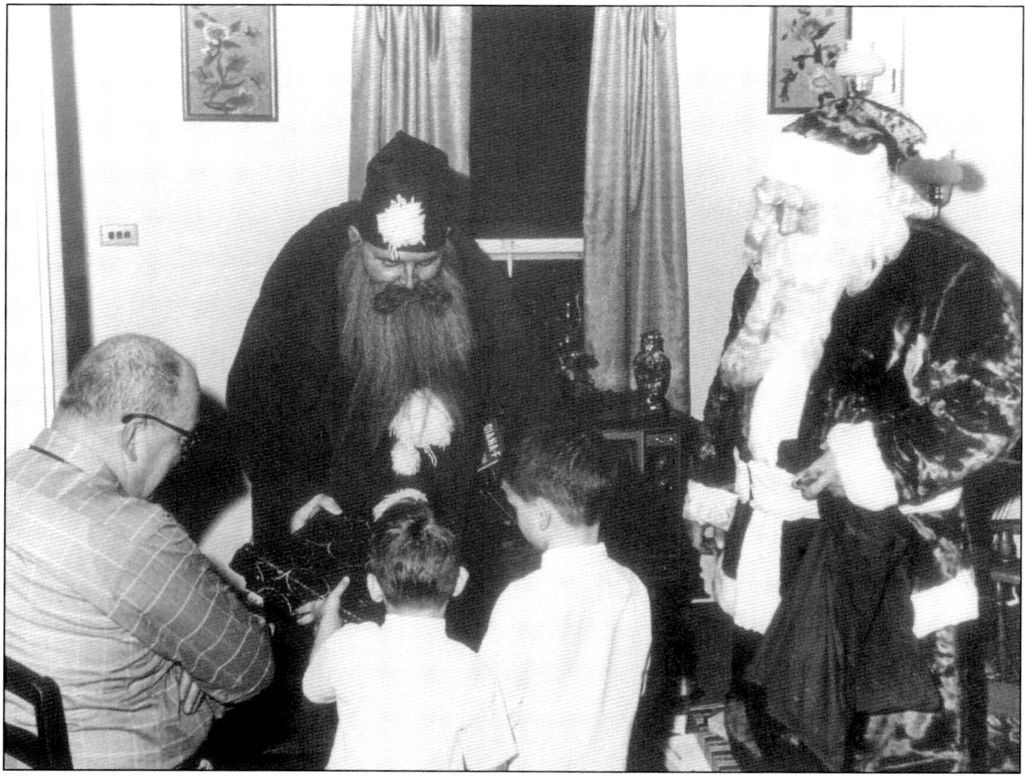

The Rolling Meadows Homeowners' Association scheduled community meet and greets with Santa Claus. In 1954, Kimball Hill appeared as the jolly man himself, but then Frank Knudsen (above right) took over the role. The Rolling Meadows Jaycees, a local volunteer group, sponsored a "Santa Visits Shut-Ins" program. Santa and his elf, portrayed by Anton Stieb (above left), visited children who were not able to attend the public meet and greet. On these visits, Santa and his elf would bring a gift to each child, provided by the Jaycees and residents of the city. Below, Santa pays a visit to a surprised young child. (Both by Frank Knudsen; courtesy of RML.)

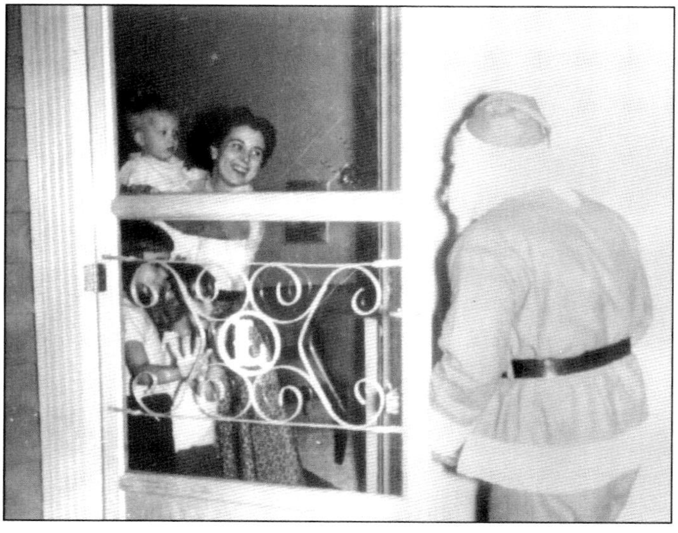

The City of Rolling Meadows' first true historian was Esther Perica. Here she sits with Kimball Hill, the "father" of Rolling Meadows, during a July 1977 interview. Perica spent several years interviewing Rolling Meadows' first residents and city officials to compile information about the first 25 years of the city's existence. Hill remained closely tied to the community that sprang forth from his housing development. He consistently donated land for civic buildings and community spaces, continually helping the new and maturing city to thrive. Hill passed away in 1993, but his legacy lives on in Rolling Meadows. (Courtesy of Esther Perica.)

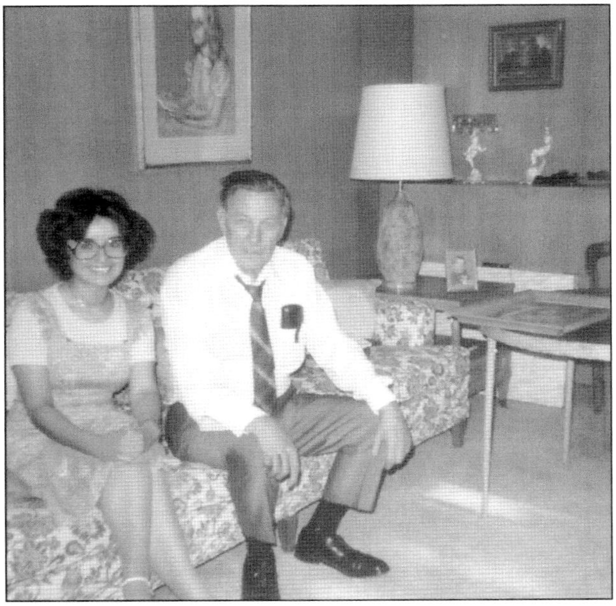

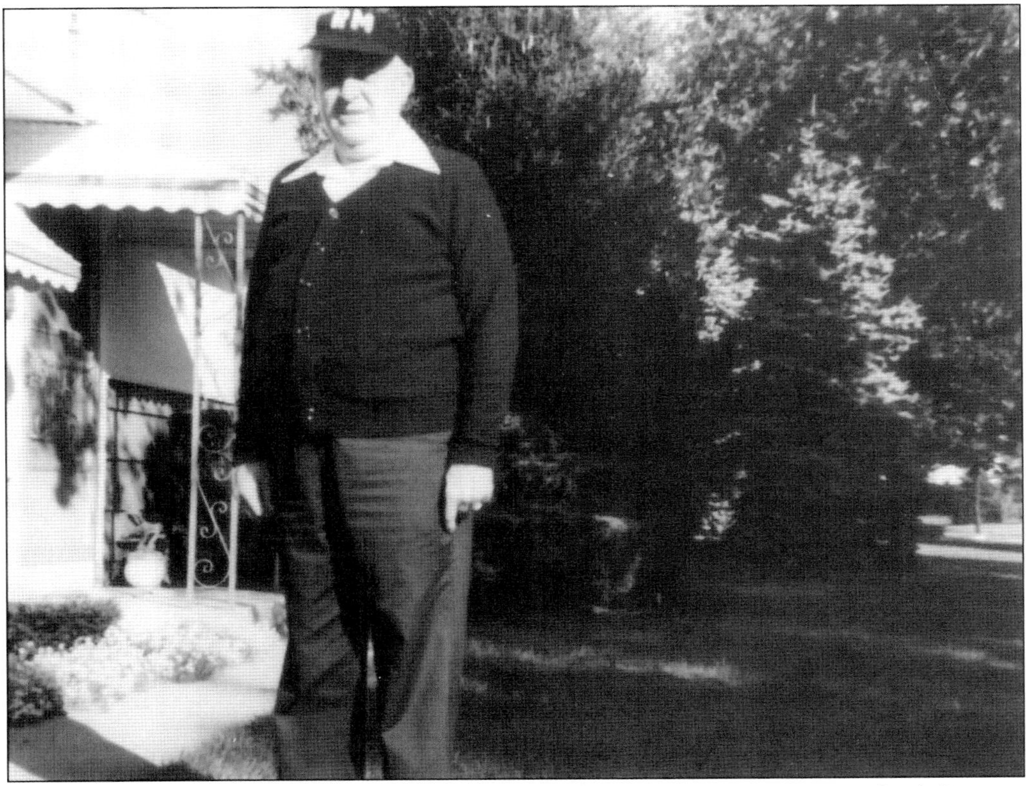

Before Rolling Meadows was even an official city, residents were anxious to start a Little League. As was the custom in Rolling Meadows, adults and children alike responded with such enthusiasm that the new Little League grew very large quite quickly. Here, coach Art Nyblin poses in 1978 with his Little League hat, reliving the glory days. (By Art Nyblin; courtesy of RML.)

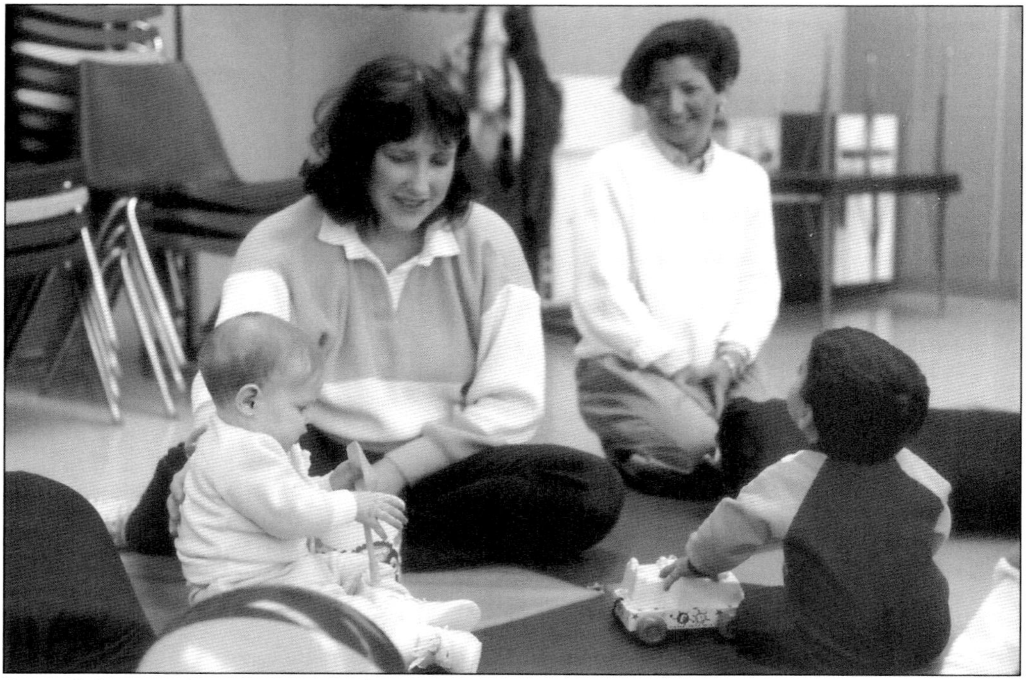

One of the popular programs at the Rolling Meadows Park District on weekday mornings was Baby Motions led by Jan Nowotarski, whom everyone lovingly called "Miss Jan." Young Rolling Meadows residents under the age of one and their mothers came to the Community Center building one morning a week to play and socialize with other babies. (Courtesy of Robin Schroeder.)

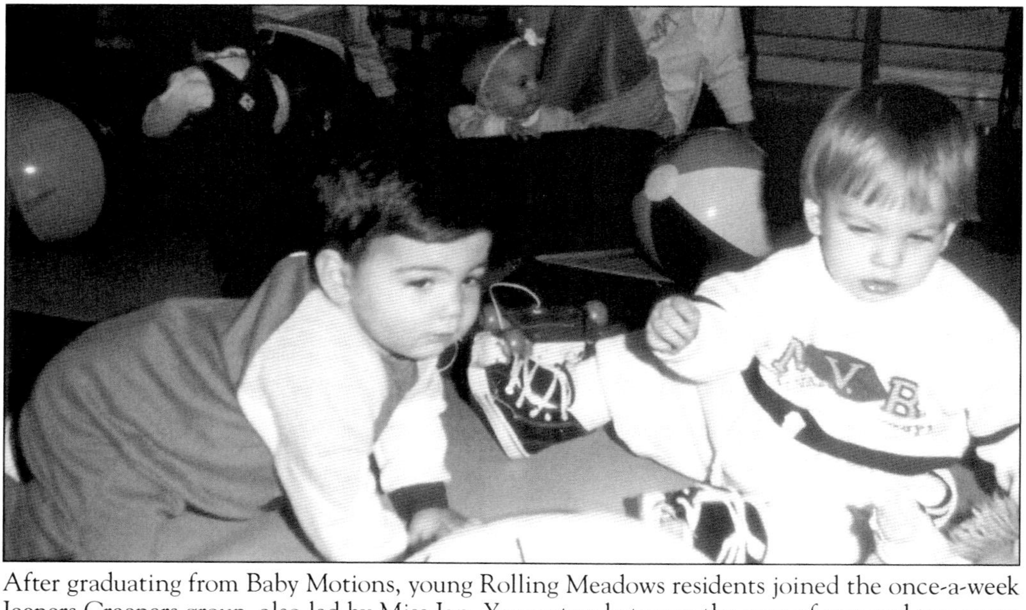

After graduating from Baby Motions, young Rolling Meadows residents joined the once-a-week Jeepers Creepers group, also led by Miss Jan. Youngsters between the ages of one and two came to play and explore, and their mothers came to mingle with other young mothers. Miss Jan would take play mats and build tunnels for the babies to crawl through, their favorite program activity. (Courtesy of Robin Schroeder.)

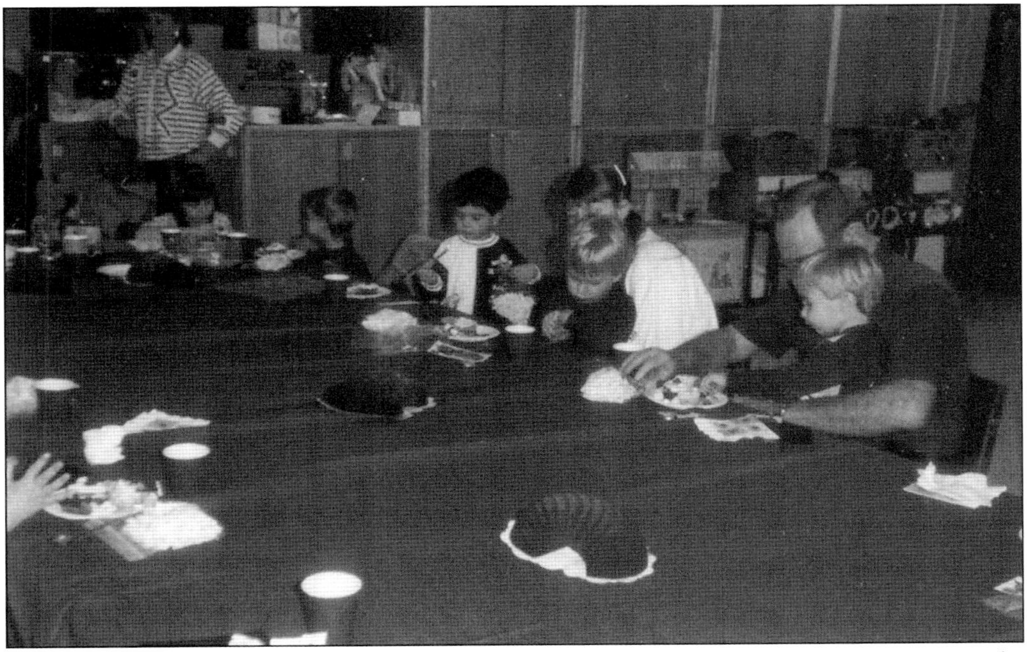

Every holiday, Dorie Schroeder from the Rolling Meadows Park District would host a party for children between the ages of two and three. The parties began with open play time to make sure that all the little boys and girls had arrived. Then "Miss Dorie" would gather everyone on a bright blue play mat for a holiday-themed story. Afterwards, children engaged in a simple craft and enjoyed snacks together, continuing the holiday theme. Above, toddlers celebrate Valentine's Day with red and white cupcakes. Below, children share the Thanksgiving table with some cheerful turkey decorations. (Both courtesy of Robin Schroeder.)

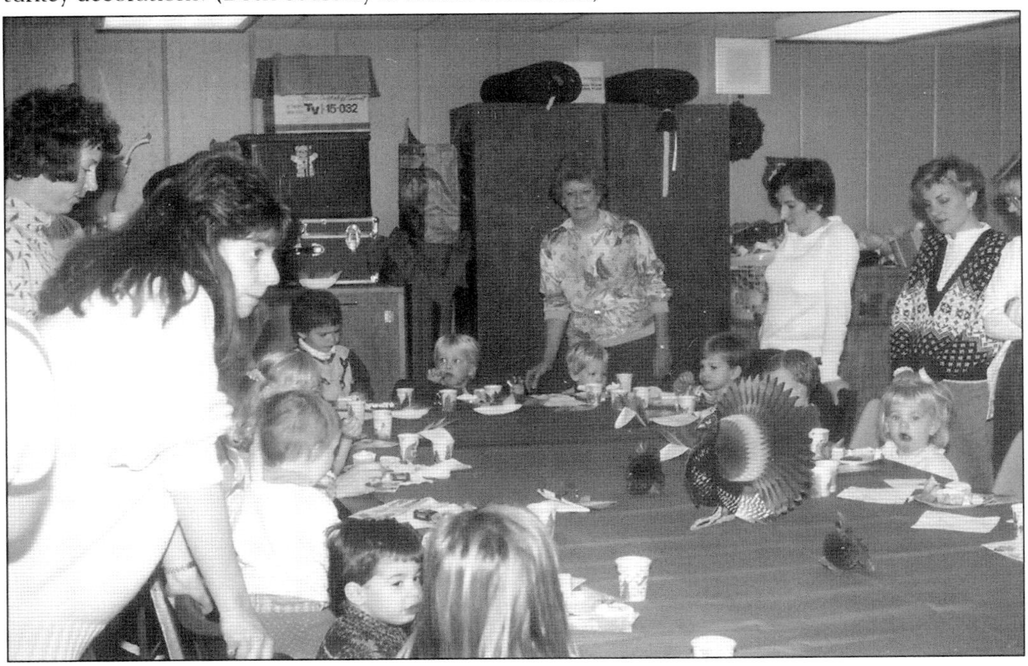

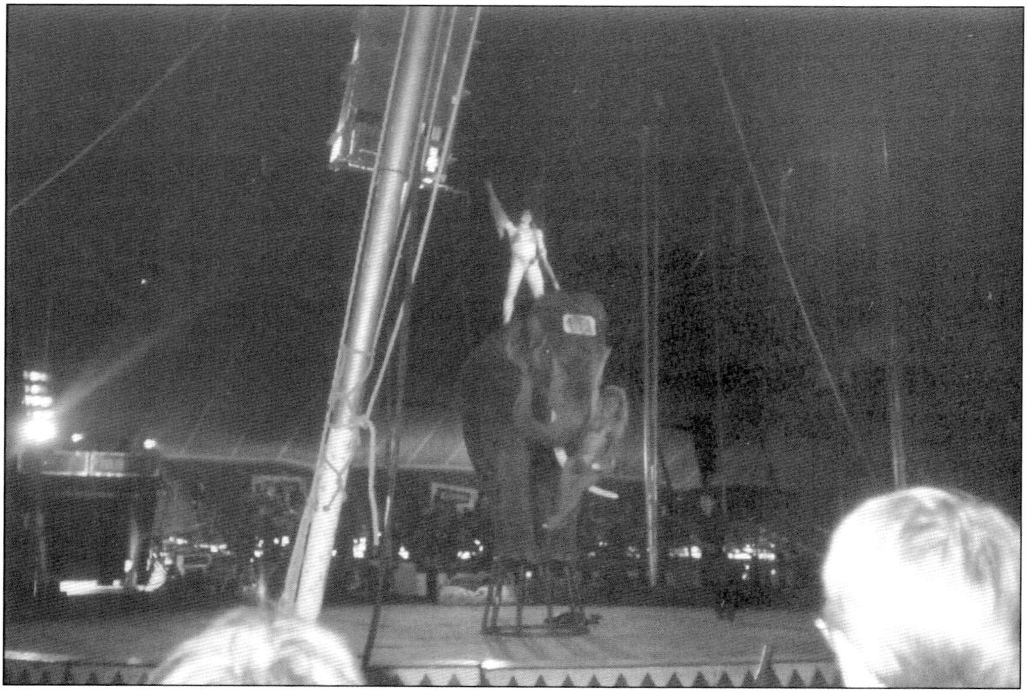

A summer staple in Rolling Meadows was the annual circus in the Waccamaw Pottery Mall's parking lot near the south end of the city, on the corner of Algonquin and Golf Roads. Children and parents of all ages came to enjoy a couple hours of awe and amusement with clowns, elephants, trapeze artists, and, most importantly, each other. (Courtesy of Robin Schroeder.)

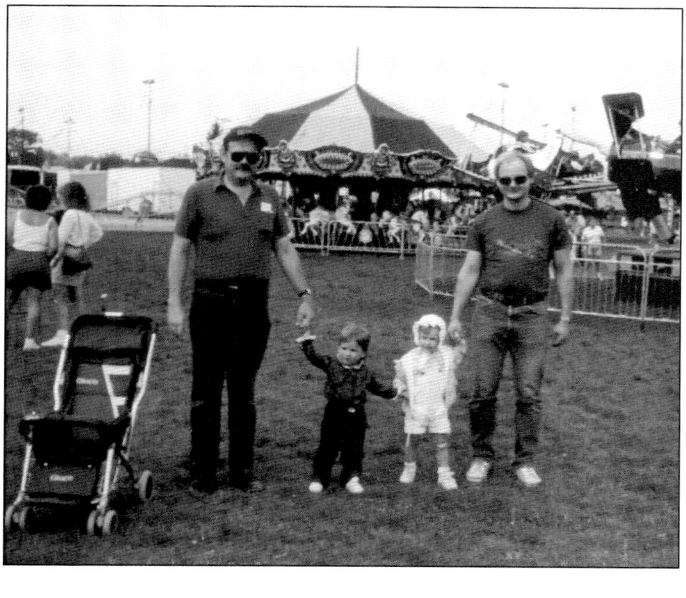

Most northwest suburban towns hosted a local carnival for the Fourth of July, but Rolling Meadows would instead celebrate Labor Day Weekend with its Diamondfest festival. Every night of the weekend, the city hosted a different musical group. The carnival attracted children and adults alike, and the city made sure to have rides to accommodate children of all ages. Here two fathers pose with their daughters in the center of all the amusement rides. (Courtesy of Robin Schroeder.)

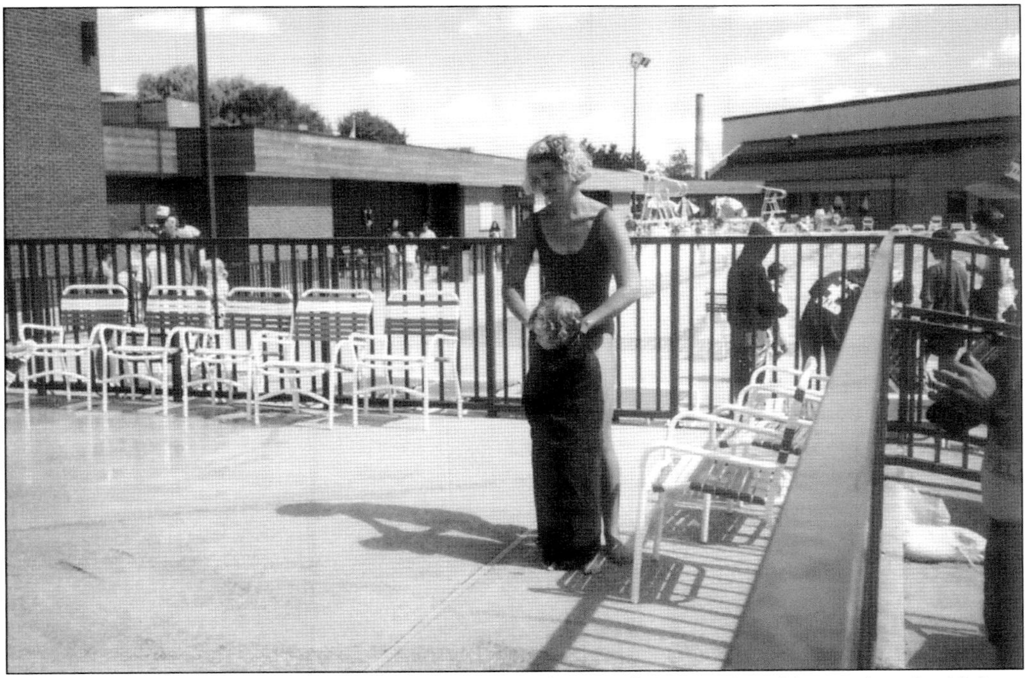

On evenings during the summer, the Rolling Meadows Park District's public pool at the Nelson Sports Complex is open to the public to enjoy the pool, waterslides, diving boards, kiddie pool, and hot tub. During the morning hours, the pool is only available for group swimming lessons. Children of all ages can sign up for lessons based on their skill level. To give smaller children an early advantage with swimming skills, the pool would offer lessons in the kiddie pool and work with children to get them comfortable using the "big" pool. Above, a swimming instructor helps dry off a young waterlogged swimmer. Below, a group of young children play around "the mushroom," which trickled water about every 10 minutes. (Both courtesy of Robin Schroeder.)

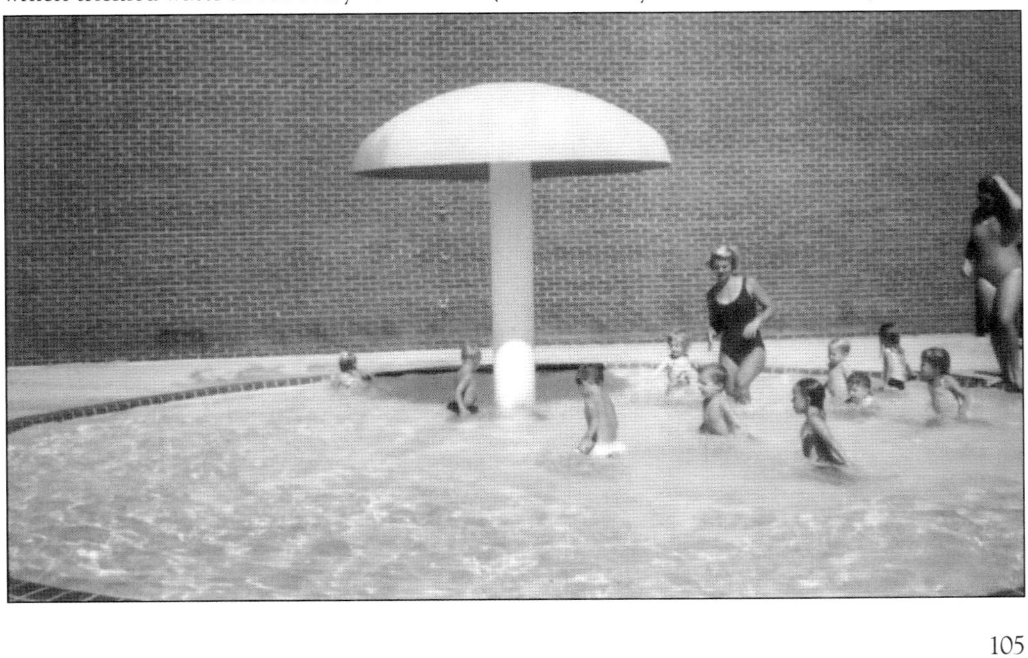

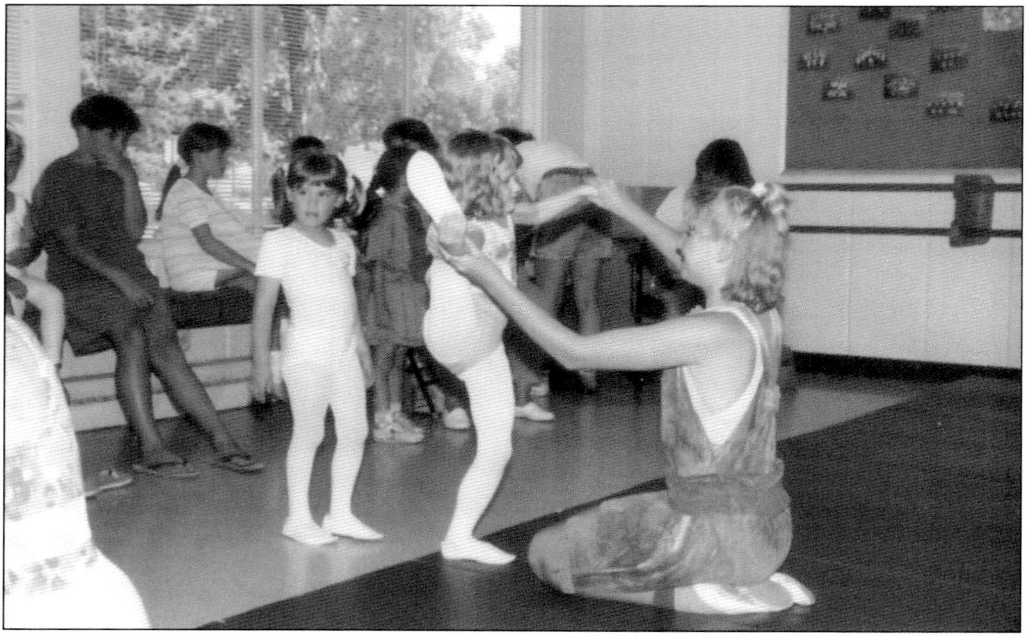

The park district offered many dance and gymnastics classes for the city's youth based on children's dance skills. Classes included acrobatics, ballet, country line dancing, gymnastics, jazz, modern, and tap. In this acrobatics class photograph, taught by Karen Halsne, students work on their flexibility and technique with the teacher's assistant, Gretchen. (Courtesy of Robin Schroeder.)

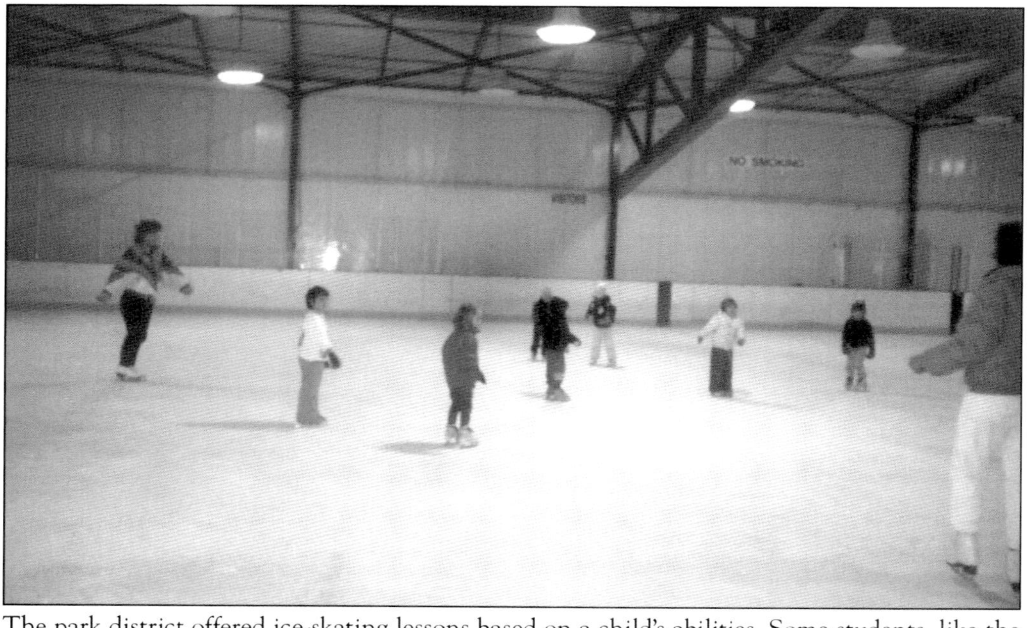

The park district offered ice-skating lessons based on a child's abilities. Some students, like the ones pictured here, simply learned how to balance on ice skates and move comfortably across the ice. On most nights, the ice arena hosted open skates. However, on special nights, people would pack the bleachers for local hockey games. One of the favorite field trips for students enrolled at schools in Rolling Meadows was an afternoon at the ice rink. (Courtesy of Robin Schroeder.)

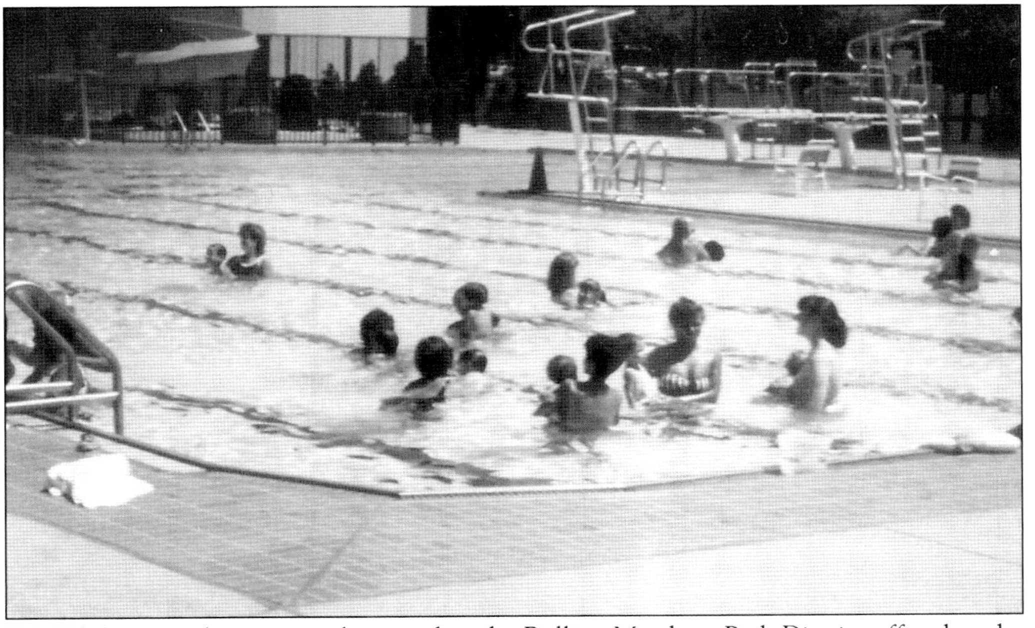

One of the special swimming lessons that the Rolling Meadows Park District offered at the Sports Complex was just for babies and their mothers. Moms would hold their children while encouraging them to kick, blow bubbles, and put their faces in the water. The class was designed to help children become less afraid of the water so that they could someday learn how to swim and have safe fun in the water. Lessons were held at special times, when older children were not at the pool. This helped to prevent the babies from accidentally getting splashed and becoming afraid of the water. (Courtesy of Robin Schroeder.)

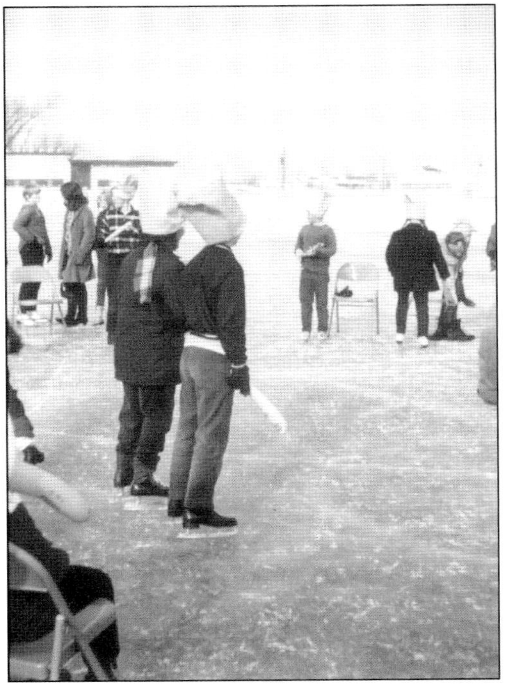

The Rolling Meadows Park District has always had a special interest in promoting activities and programs for the city's youth. Throughout the calendar year, the park district offers activities that reflect the season. Here, Rolling Meadows children skate around on Kimball Hill Pond for the park district's first ice carnival in 1961. (By Ronald Brightwell; courtesy of RML.)

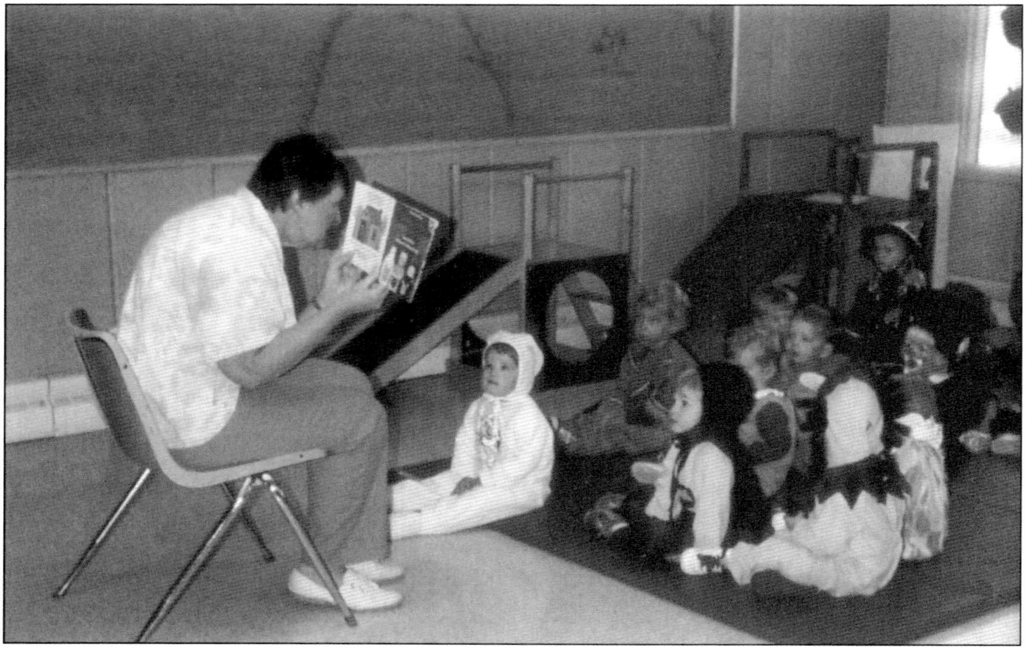

Every year around Halloween, the youth of Rolling Meadows would gather with their parents at the park district to show off their costumes and listen to spooky stories. Above, younger children would meet in one of the Community Center's small, intimate classrooms. Below, older children would crowd around the stage in the Community Center's multipurpose room and listen to Miss Dorie recount chilling tales. Afterwards, children would form a circle and parade around the room, allowing everyone to get a good look at their costumes. (Both courtesy of Robin Schroeder.)

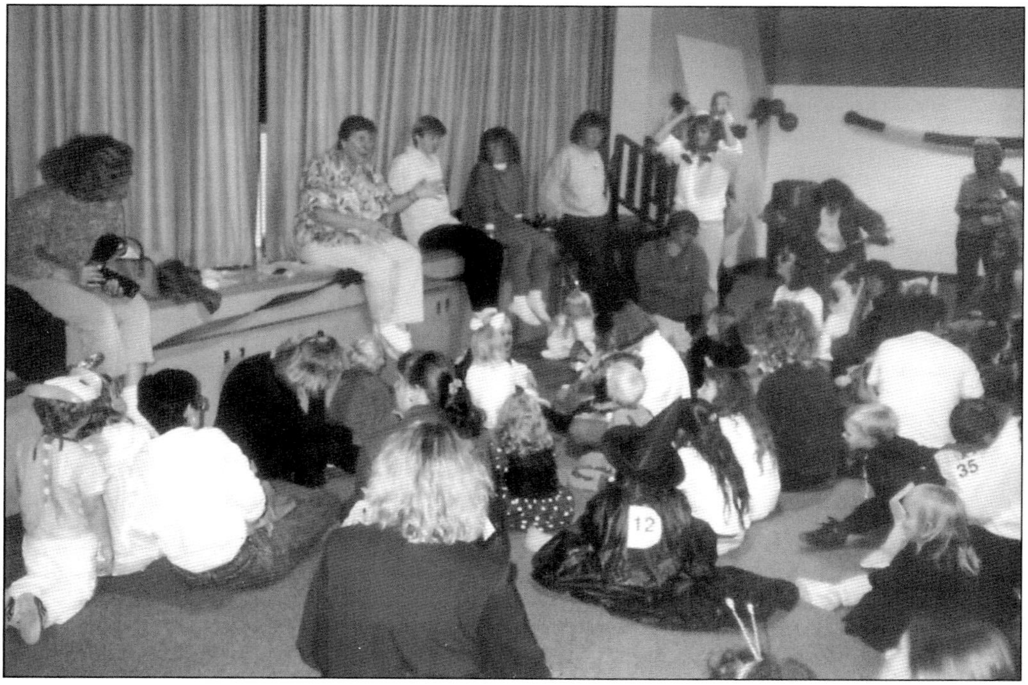

The residents of Rolling Meadows take great pride in their city and make a point of supporting it and celebrating its successes and achievements. May 1960 brought with it the fifth anniversary of Rolling Meadows as an incorporated city, and city officials worked to create a weekend full of entertainment for the entire community to enjoy. At right is a letter sent by Mayor John J. Woods cordially inviting each and every resident to join in the festivities. Five years later, for the city's 10th anniversary, Rolling Meadows threw a grand parade highlighting the various civic and cultural organizations of the city. Below, a group of teenagers from a local youth committee cruises in the 10th anniversary parade. (Below by Pat Hester; both courtesy of RML.)

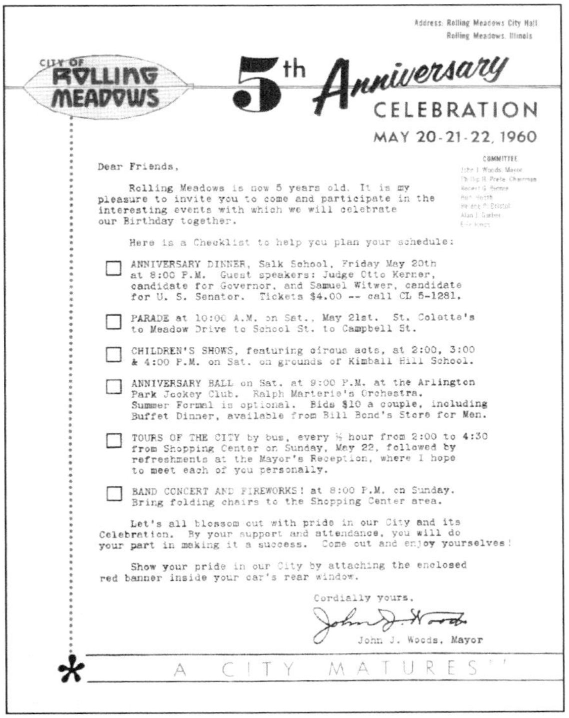

Address: Rolling Meadows City Hall
Rolling Meadows, Illinois

CITY OF ROLLING MEADOWS

5th Anniversary CELEBRATION
MAY 20-21-22, 1960

COMMITTEE
John J. Woods, Mayor

Dear Friends,

Rolling Meadows is now 5 years old. It is my pleasure to invite you to come and participate in the interesting events with which we will celebrate our Birthday together.

Here is a Checklist to help you plan your schedule:

- ☐ ANNIVERSARY DINNER, Salk School, Friday May 20th at 8:00 P.M. Guest speakers: Judge Otto Kerner, candidate for Governor, and Samuel Witwer, candidate for U. S. Senator. Tickets $4.00 -- call CL 5-1281.
- ☐ PARADE at 10:00 A.M. on Sat., May 21st. St. Colette's to Meadow Drive to School St. to Campbell St.
- ☐ CHILDREN'S SHOWS, featuring circus acts, at 2:00, 3:00 & 4:00 P.M. on Sat. on grounds of Kimball Hill School.
- ☐ ANNIVERSARY BALL on Sat. at 9:00 P.M. at the Arlington Park Jockey Club. Ralph Marterie's Orchestra. Summer Formal is optional. Bids $10 a couple, including Buffet Dinner, available from Bill Bond's Store for Men.
- ☐ TOURS OF THE CITY by bus, every ½ hour from 2:00 to 4:30 from Shopping Center on Sunday, May 22, followed by refreshments at the Mayor's Reception, where I hope to meet each of you personally.
- ☐ BAND CONCERT AND FIREWORKS! at 8:00 P.M. on Sunday. Bring folding chairs to the Shopping Center area.

Let's all blossom out with pride in our City and its Celebration. By your support and attendance, you will do your part in making it a success. Come out and enjoy yourselves!

Show your pride in our City by attaching the enclosed red banner inside your car's rear window.

Cordially yours,

John J. Woods

John J. Woods, Mayor

* A CITY MATURES''

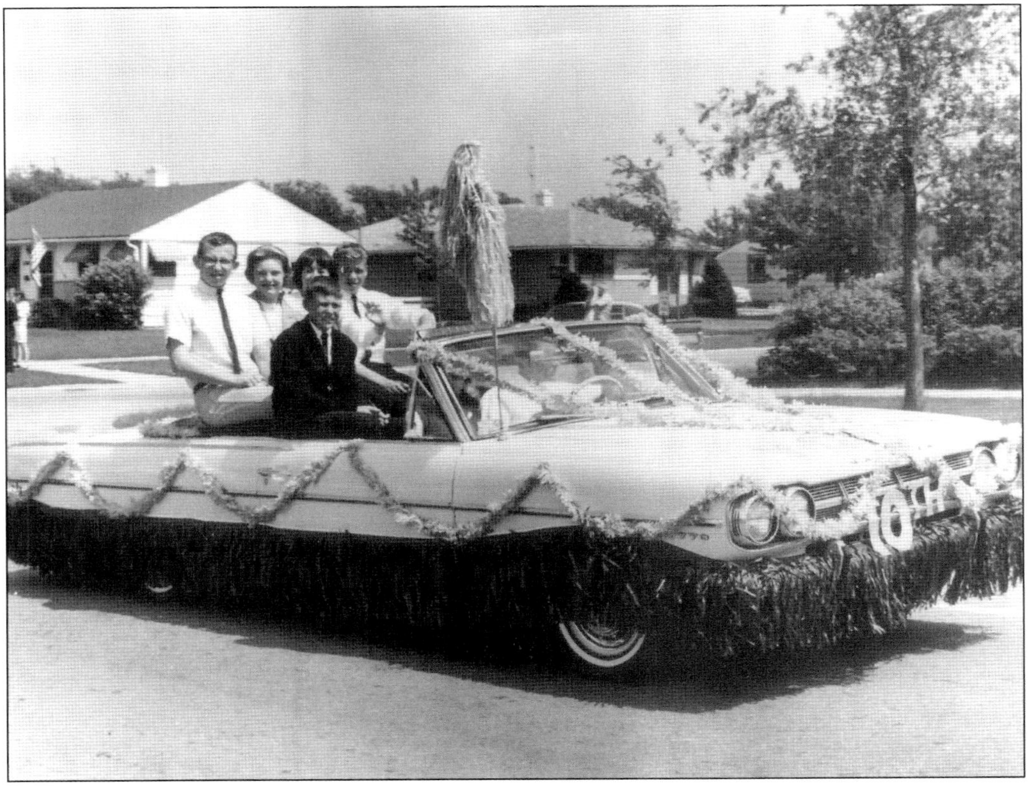

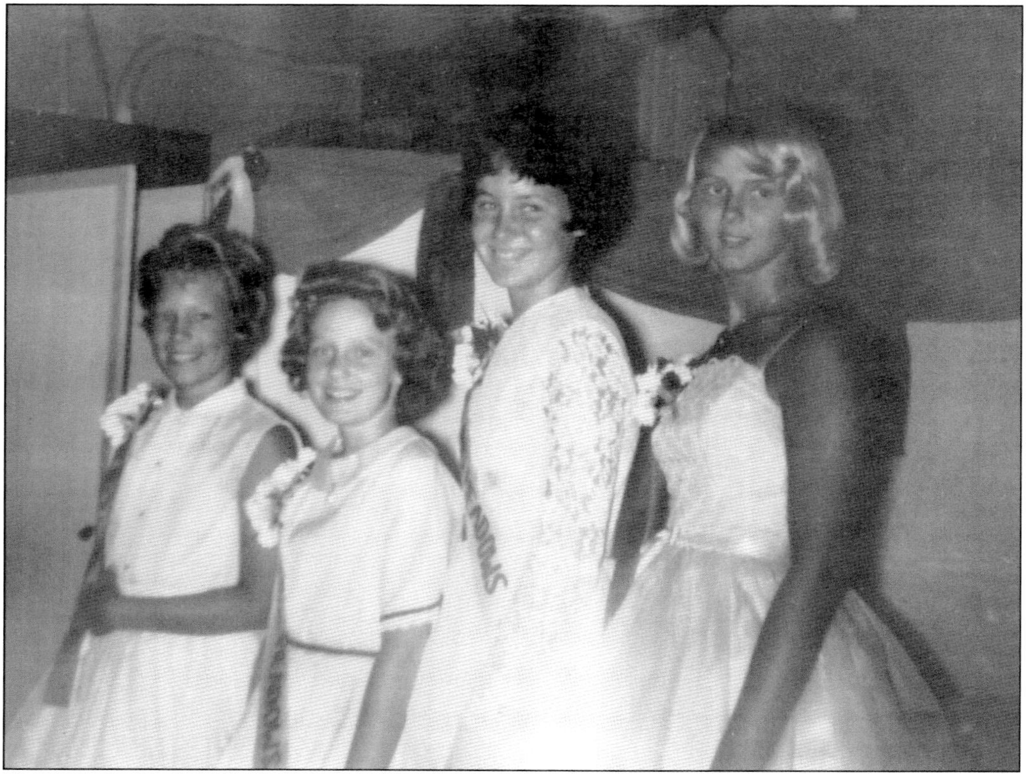

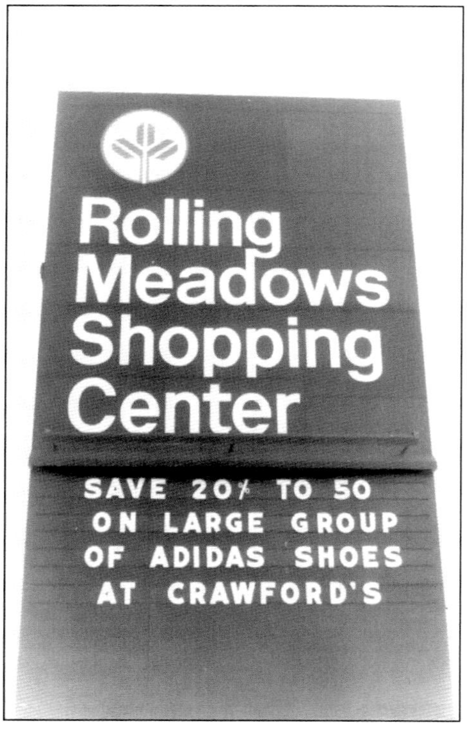

For some time, the city had its own beauty contest with both junior high school and senior high school divisions. Pictured here are four contestants from the 1963 pageant. From left to right are Leslie Traub, Noreen O'Donnel (junior high school division winner), Kay Hester (senior high school division winner), and Pat Steir. (By Margaret Hester; courtesy of RML.)

Until the Rolling Meadows Shopping Center was built, Rolling Meadows residents had to travel to neighboring cities like Arlington Heights or Palatine to purchase goods. In April 1955, Kimball Hill had announced plans for a large shopping center on the corner of Kirchoff Road and Meadow Drive, and on May 2, 1957, the city celebrated the grand opening with a three-day event. Shoppers were greeted by ushers and clowns and enjoyed free live music and prize giveaways. Each store offered its own sales and giveaways. The crowning jewel of the complex was Crawford's Department Store; then, Rolling Meadows boasted the largest department store in the northwest suburbs of Chicago. (Courtesy of Esther Perica.)

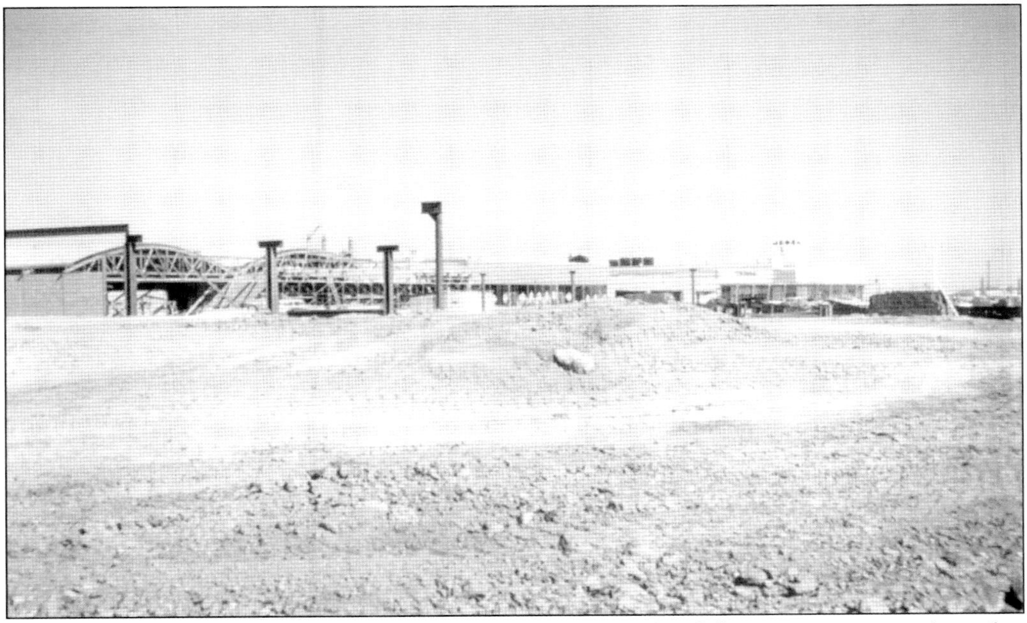

Construction on the Rolling Meadows Shopping Center took a full two years to complete after Kimball Hill had first announced plans. The 1950s ushered in a trend of suburban shopping centers. After Crawford's Department Store decided to place its third store in Rolling Meadows, it was only a matter of time before more stores would follow suit. Rounding out the largest one-stop shopping center in the northwest suburbs of Chicago at the time were A&W Foods, Ace Hardware, Flite Cleaners, Jewel Foods, Mellicks' Children's Shop, R&S Shoes, Rolling Meadows Currency Exchange, Suburban Casuals, Suburban Drugs, Suburban Snack Shop, Walter's Pastry Shop, and, later, the Bank of Rolling Meadows. (Above by Ronald Brightwell, courtesy of RML; below courtesy of Dom Najolia.)

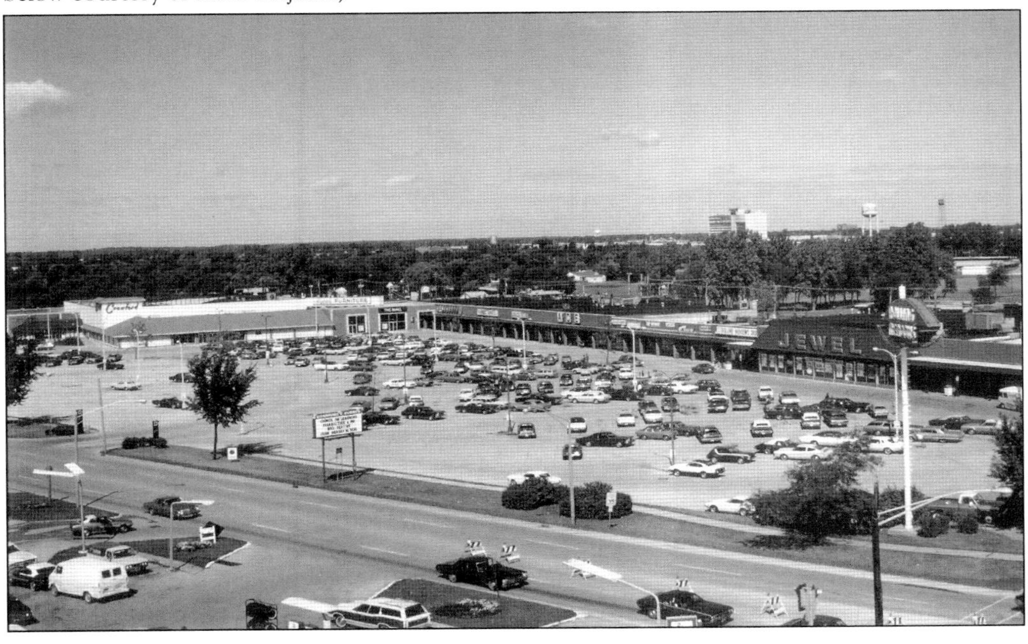

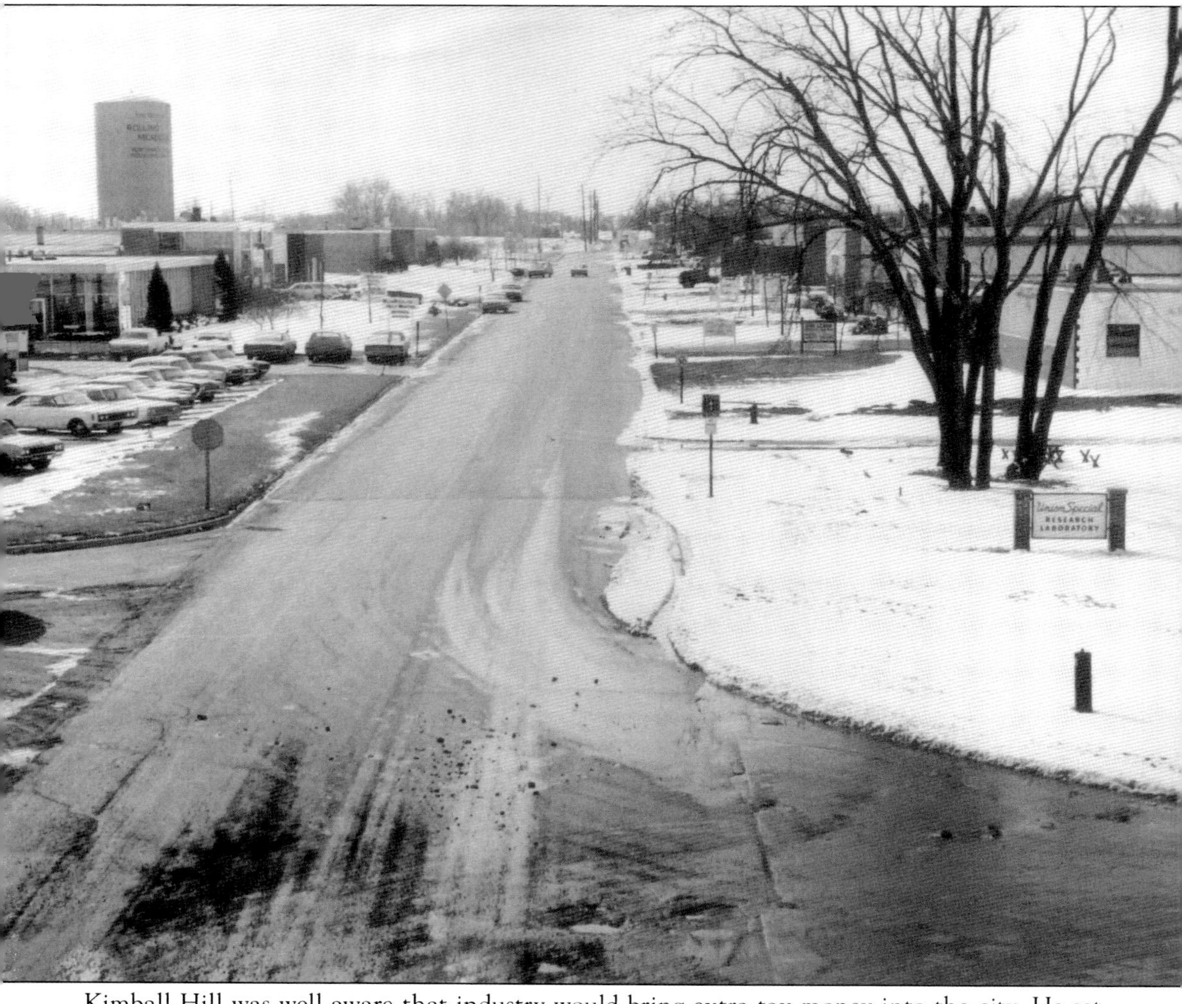

Kimball Hill was well aware that industry would bring extra tax money into the city. He set aside land along the northern boundary of Rolling Meadows for an industrial park. Here is the intersection of Rohlwing Road and Industrial Avenue. This area continues to be the industrial heart of the city. Just south of Northwest Highway and west of Illinois Route 53, this industrial park is connected to both local neighborhoods and more distant ones thanks to its proximity to the highway, allowing this industrial area to thrive for decades. (By Charles Poellien; courtesy of RML.)

Five

Welcome to Rolling Meadows

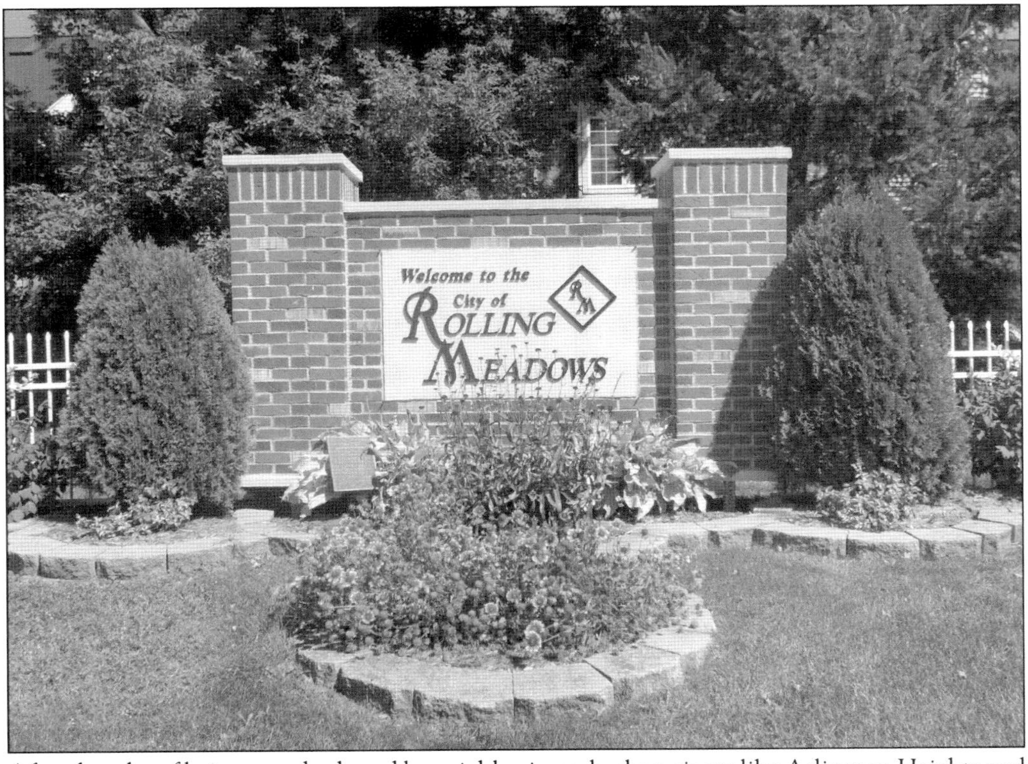

After decades of being overshadowed by neighboring suburban giants like Arlington Heights and Schaumburg, Rolling Meadows decided to update and promote its image. In 1997, city officials commissioned half a dozen brick and cement welcome signs to greet visitors as they travel down any of the main roads that run through town. This particular sign welcomes motorists as they exit Illinois Route 53 via the Kirchoff Road exit ramp. (Courtesy of the author.)

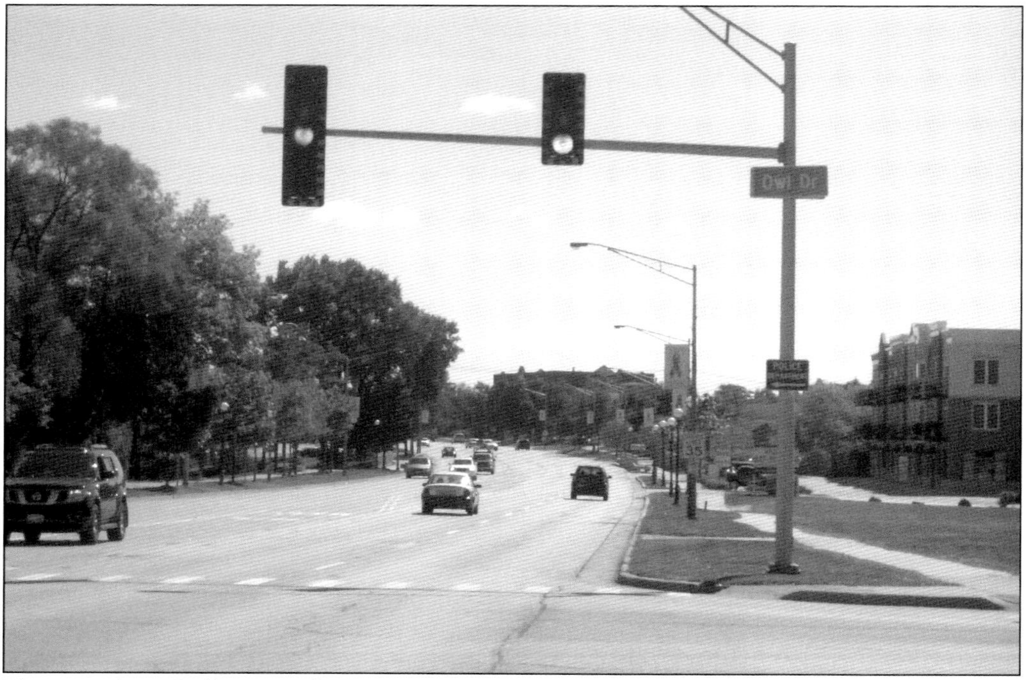

The view down Rolling Meadows' main street, Kirchoff Road, is drastically different than it was 50 years ago. Now with bricked-in sidewalks, bicycle paths, a carillon tower, new light posts, and new park benches lining Kirchoff Road's parkway, Rolling Meadows' main thoroughfare looks modern and stylish. The city now looks like an experienced, thriving, and breathing community. (Courtesy of the author.)

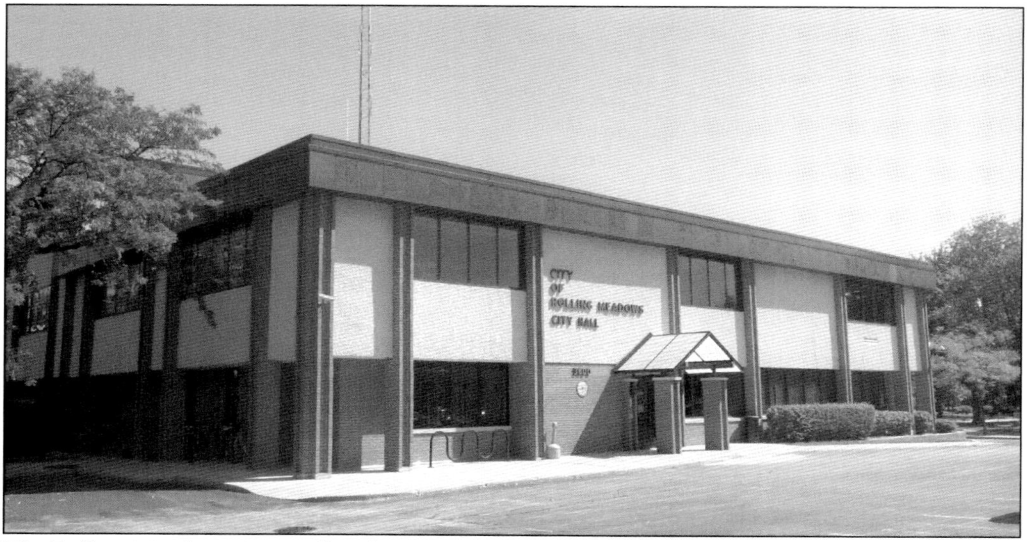

The Rolling Meadows City Hall and Police Department remain an important part of residents' daily lives. A new electronic marquee on the corner of Kirchoff Road and Owl Drive alerts passersby to civic and community events, including information about garbage collection, city parades, and the high school's craft show. Recent work to the front facade of the building now allows residents to enter the building through a covered, vaulted portico. (Courtesy of the author.)

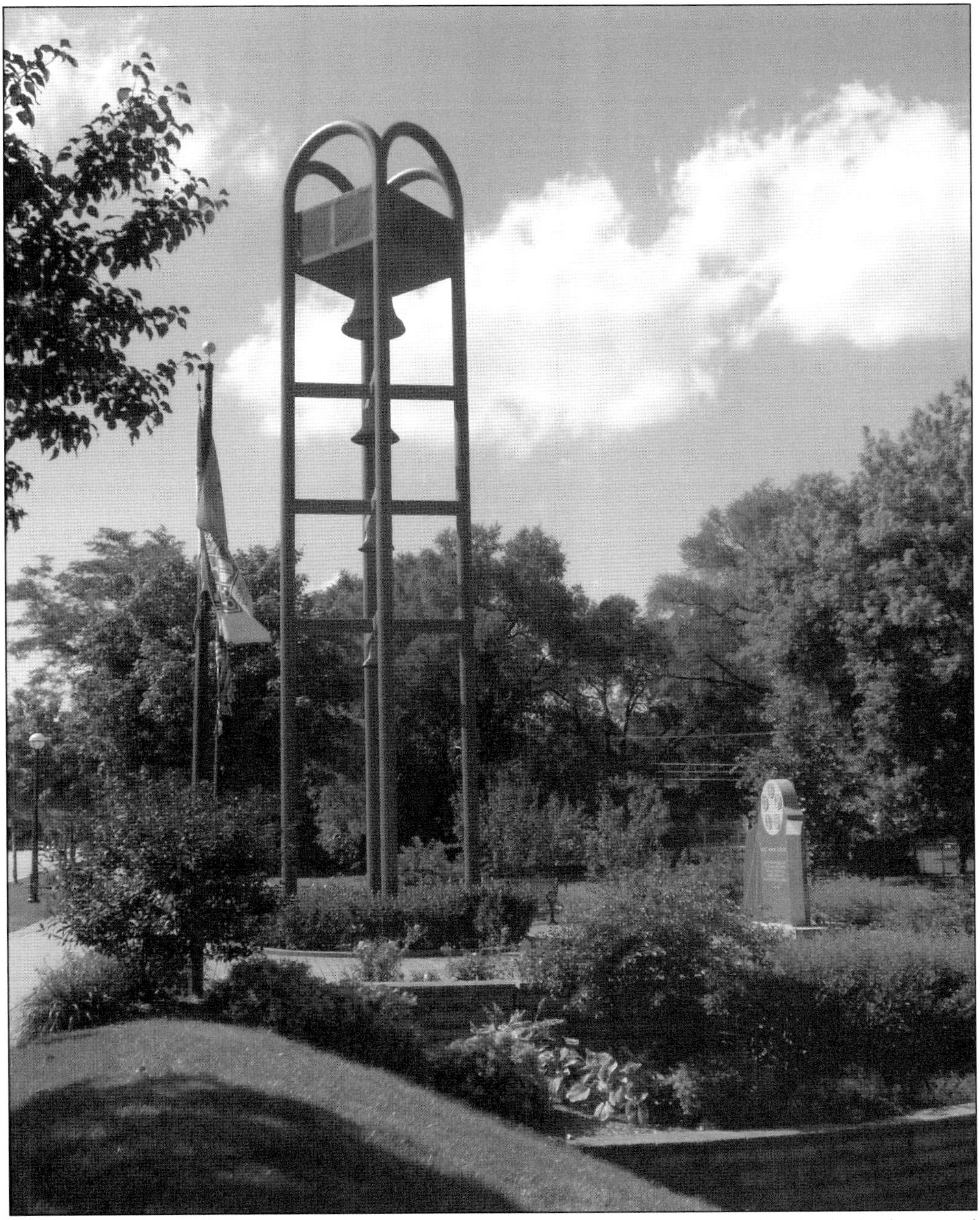

Rolling Meadows officials realized that, other than the city's water towers, the city lacked any real landmark. Plans were soon underway to construct a carillon tower on park district land close to both Kirchoff Road and Salt Creek so that residents and city visitors could enjoy its architecture and music daily. Originally painted a bright dandelion-yellow color, the Rolling Meadows Carillon was dedicated on October 10, 1998. It was later painted a deep bronze and has remained that color ever since. Throughout much of Rolling Meadows, the carillon's sweet music can be heard. Every 15 minutes, the carillon tower rings briefly, and on the hour, it plays a short melody and chimes the hour. (Courtesy of the author.)

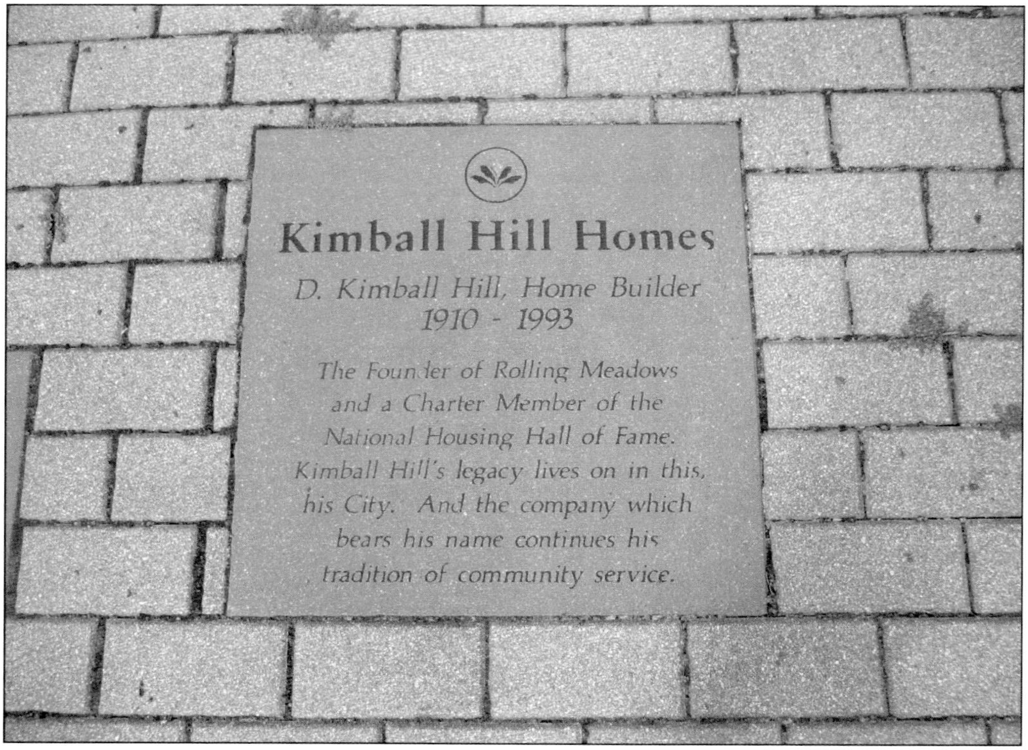

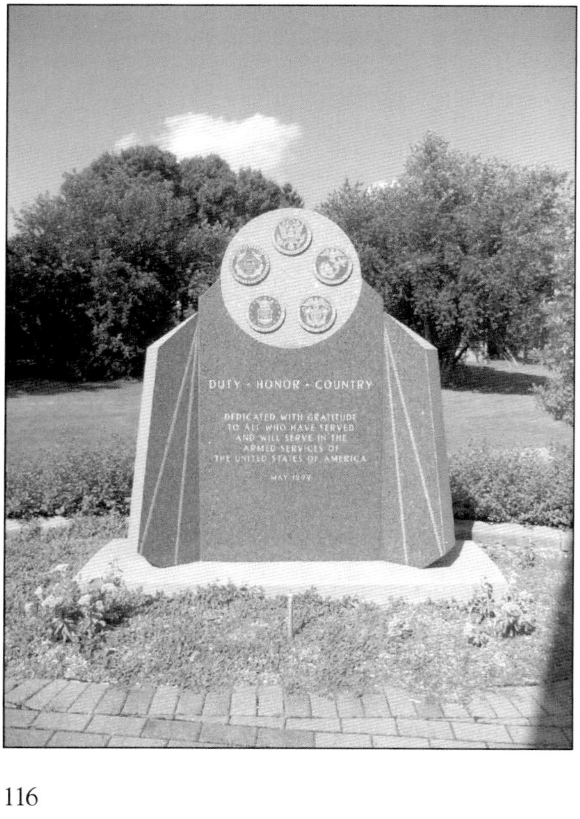

To help finance the carillon tower, Rolling Meadows sold bricks of varying sizes to be placed in the ground circling the bell tower. Many individuals and families, some who have been long-time residents of the city, purchased bricks, and their names have been immortalized at the city's new landmark. Several local businesses also purchased bricks, including Kimball Hill Homes, above. The company dedicated its brick to its namesake, the man who founded the housing development that later became the city of Rolling Meadows. In May 1999, the city erected a marble monument (left) honoring past, present, and future members of the US Air Force, Army, Coast Guard, Marine Corps, and Navy. The monument is positioned just behind the carillon. (Both courtesy of the author.)

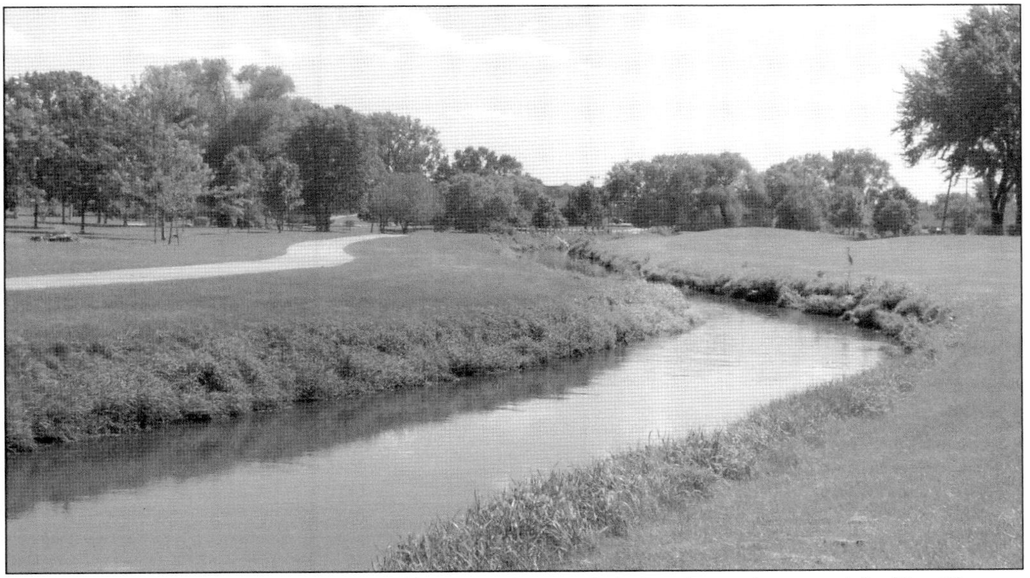

One of only two bodies of water in Rolling Meadows is Salt Creek, a tributary of the Des Plaines, Illinois, and Mississippi Rivers. It is known for the way it arcs and curves through the northwest suburbs. Salt Creek's shallow grassy shores are prone to flooding and, after a heavy rain, floodwaters will cover the nearby bicycle path for several days. (Courtesy of the author.)

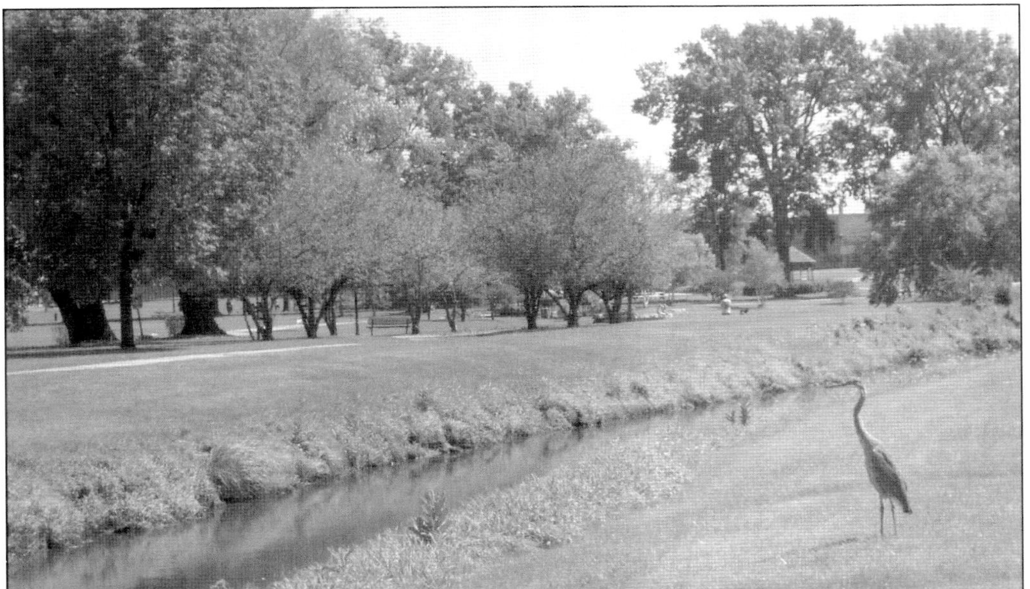

Kimball Hill had always intended that his housing development have parks and recreational areas, and he had set aside land along Salt Creek for that very purpose. North of Kirchoff Road, where this photograph was taken, playgrounds and public parks line the grassy hills along the creek. Here a great blue heron waits and watches for fish along the western bank, with Kimball Hill Park in the background. Birds of all sizes are often found near the creek, waiting for fish to swim past. (Courtesy of the author.)

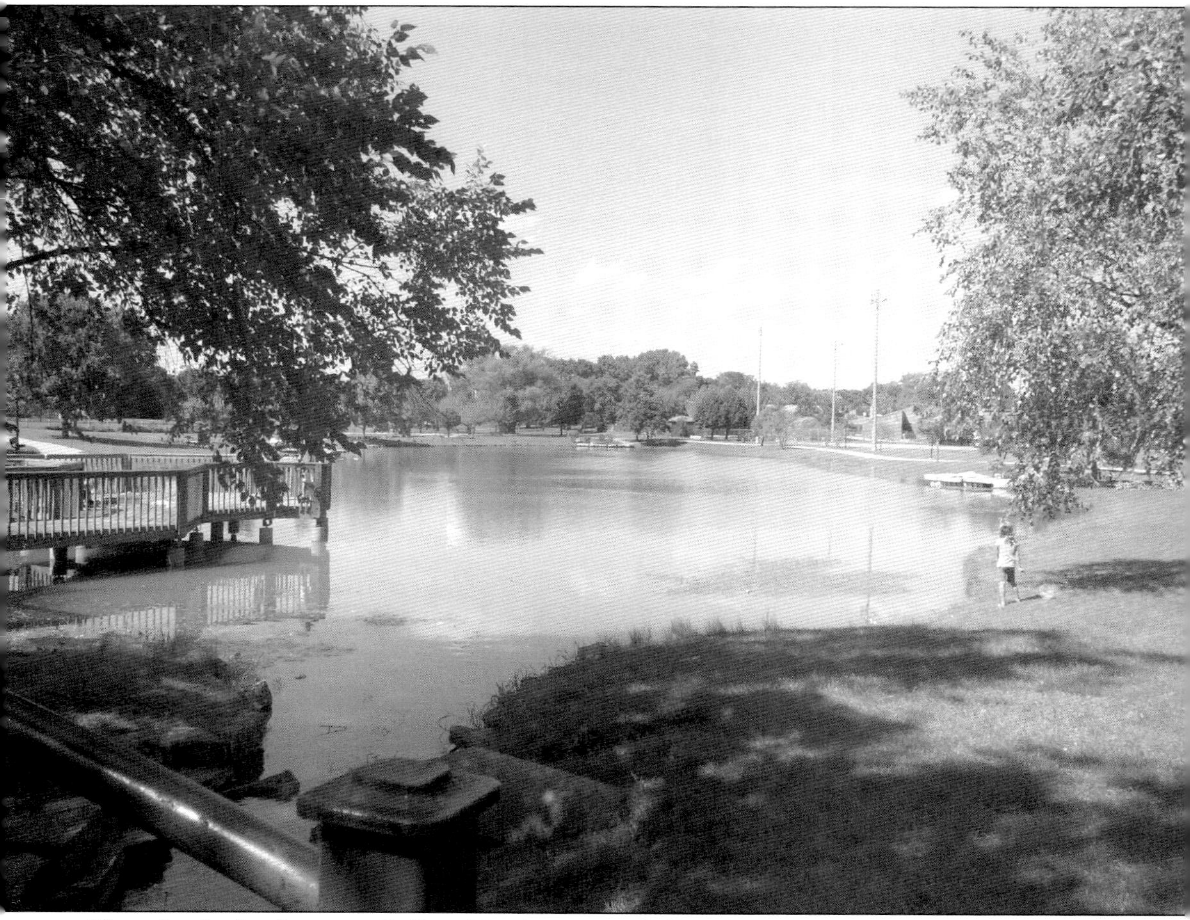

The other body of water in Rolling Meadows is Kimball Hill Pond, located in Kimball Hill Park behind the Rolling Meadows Shopping Center. The pond is home to many fish, namely bluegills and sunfish. Every year, the park district hosts a fishing derby for people of all ages, giving awards for largest and smallest fish caught as well as most and least amount of fish caught. Kimball Hill Park also consists of baseball fields and volleyball courts, a small waterfall, a gazebo, a covered pavilion with picnic tables, a playground (shared with Kimball Hill School), and park benches. The park is especially popular with residents in the summer. Here a family fishes off the large dock while a young girl chases butterflies with a small net. (Courtesy of the author.)

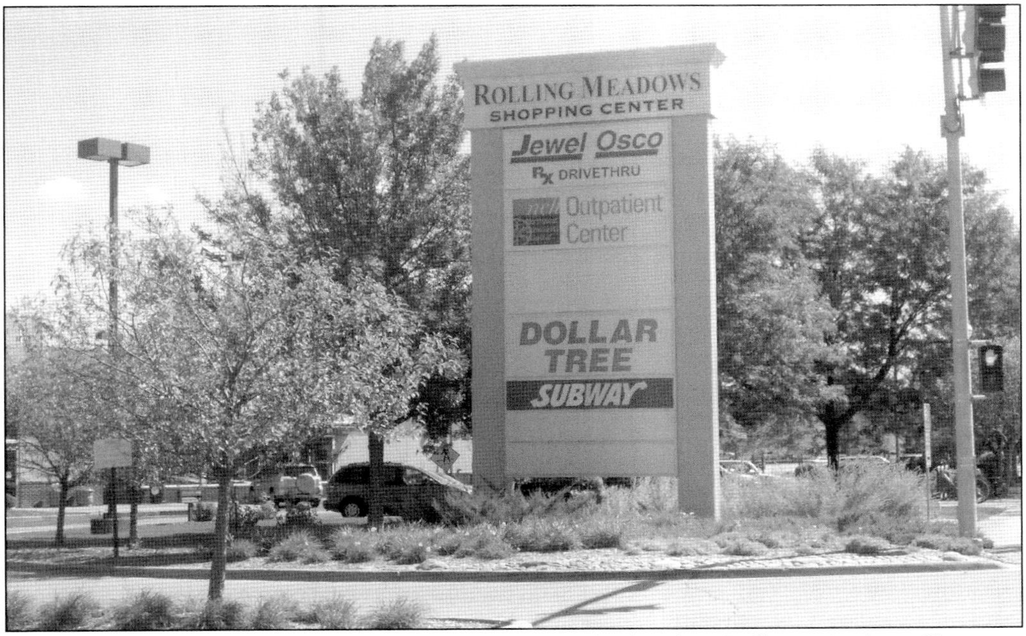

Right in the heart of downtown Rolling Meadows is the bustling Rolling Meadows Shopping Center, which has arguably seen the most obvious changes over the years. The large department store Crawford's (which would have been in the center background below) has since left, all of the stores in the adjoining indoor mall have moved, and the building was demolished. But the bare bones of the strip mall remain, with Jewel-Osco still as the strip's anchor store. Time has seen a McDonald's (far left background) and large warehouse (center background) built, the latter turned into a rehabilitation facility for the nearby Northwest Community Hospital. Today, Rolling Meadows residents continue to fulfill most of their shopping needs in this updated shopping center, as well as in additional strip malls on Central, Algonquin, and Golf Roads. (Both courtesy of the author.)

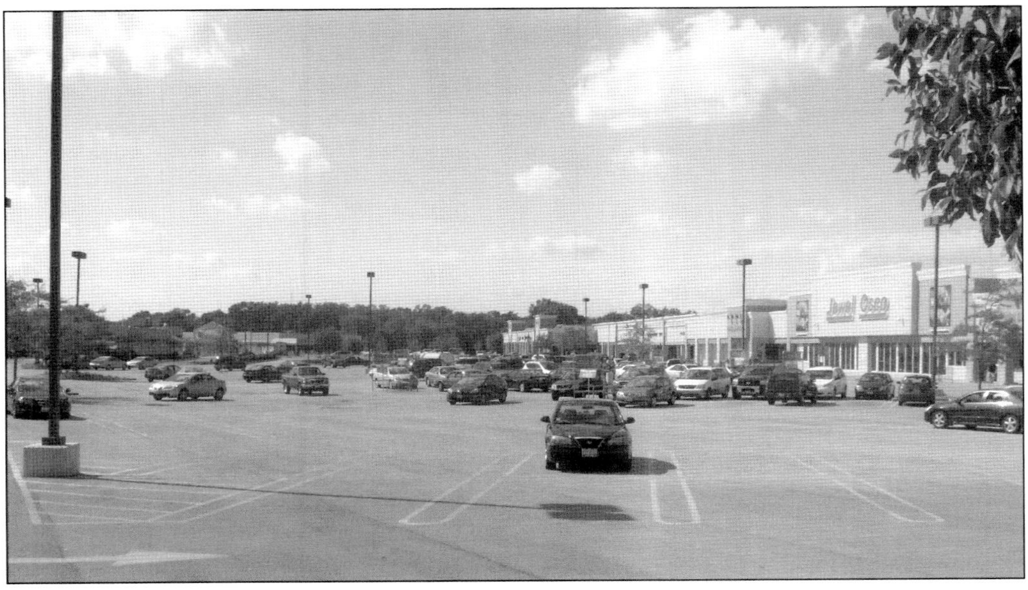

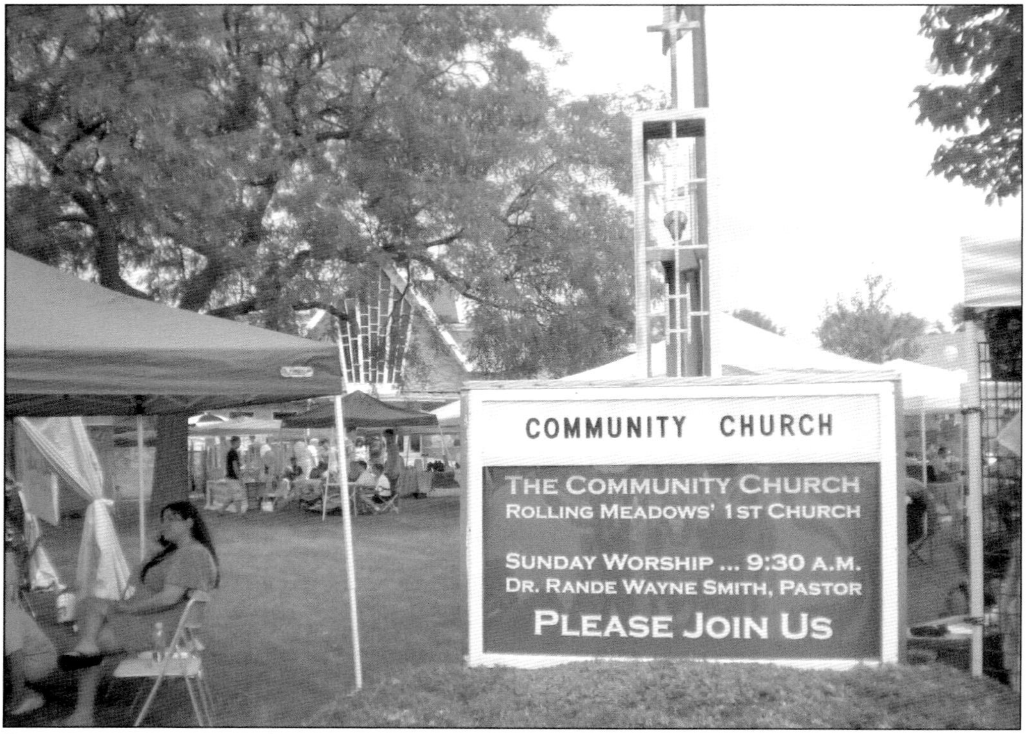

Every year since 1957 on the first Saturday in August, the Community Church of Rolling Meadows reaches out to the community by hosting Corn Fest. The church invites a favorite local singer or musical group to entertain residents while they enjoy hamburgers, hot dogs, fresh watermelon, and all-you-can-eat corn. Local crafters, artists, and business owners set up booths along Kirchoff Road and Meadow Drive on the church's front lawn, a tradition since the 1990s. This cookout and craft fair continues to be a community favorite and a summer must. (Both courtesy of the author.)

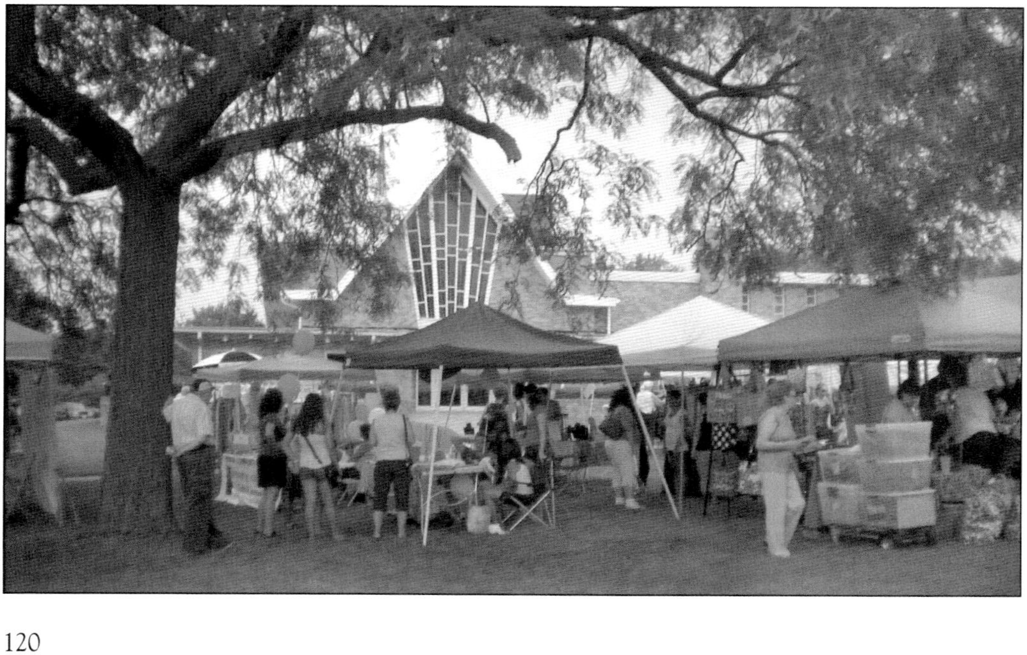

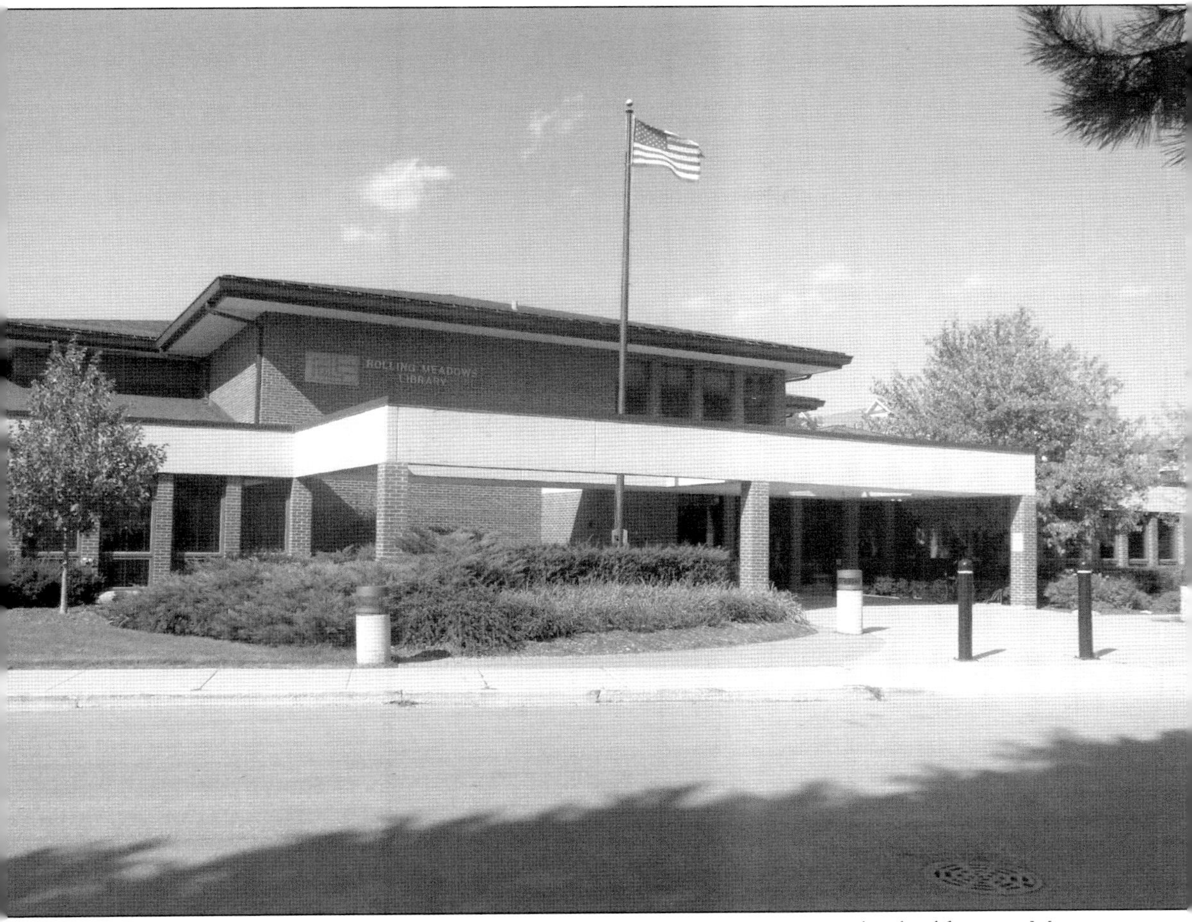

The Rolling Meadows Library has undergone several renovations since this building on Martin Lane opened its doors on October 31, 1967, including the addition of the west wing Reference Services area. As technology and media have evolved, so have the services and collection that the library offers its patrons. Equipped with multiple computer labs and an extensive audio and visual collection, the Rolling Meadows Library continues to meet the changing needs of the community and at the same time emphasizes the importance of books and reading in technology-driven times. After 50 years, the library remains one of the most important cultural centers of the city. (Courtesy of the author.)

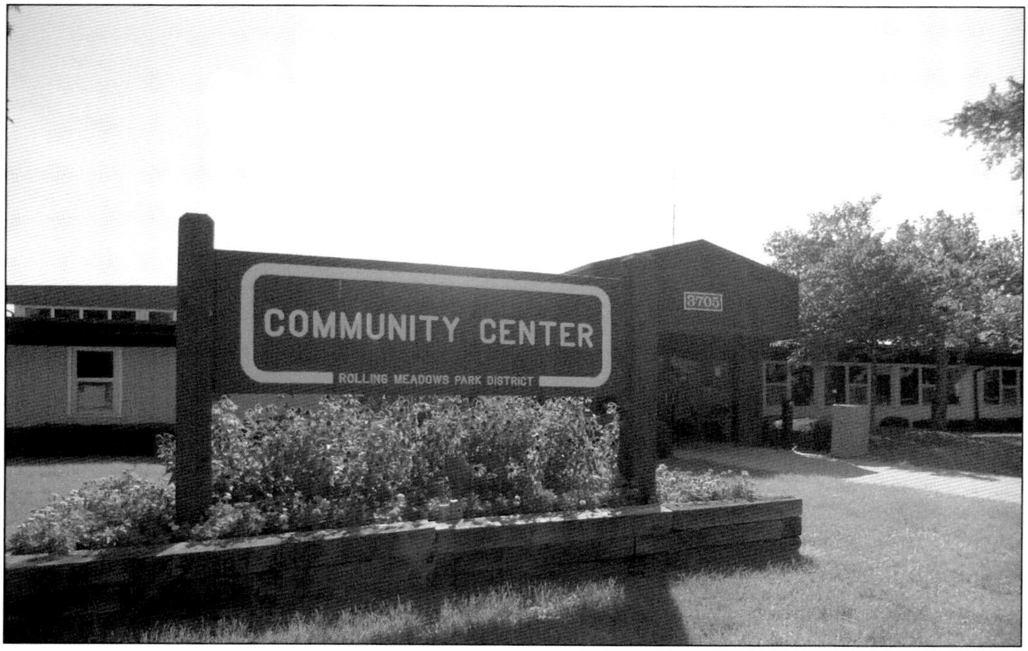

The Rolling Meadows Park District's community center (above) and senior center (below) continue to serve the youth, adults, and seniors of the city by offering new and interesting programs in fitness, crafting, and personal enrichment. The youth dance classes have developed into a reputable dance studio, allowing students to participate in area dance competitions. Seniors have their own wing of the community center where they can display and sell their handmade crafts as well as socialize with other community residents over games of bridge, Ping-Pong, and bingo. (Both courtesy of the author.)

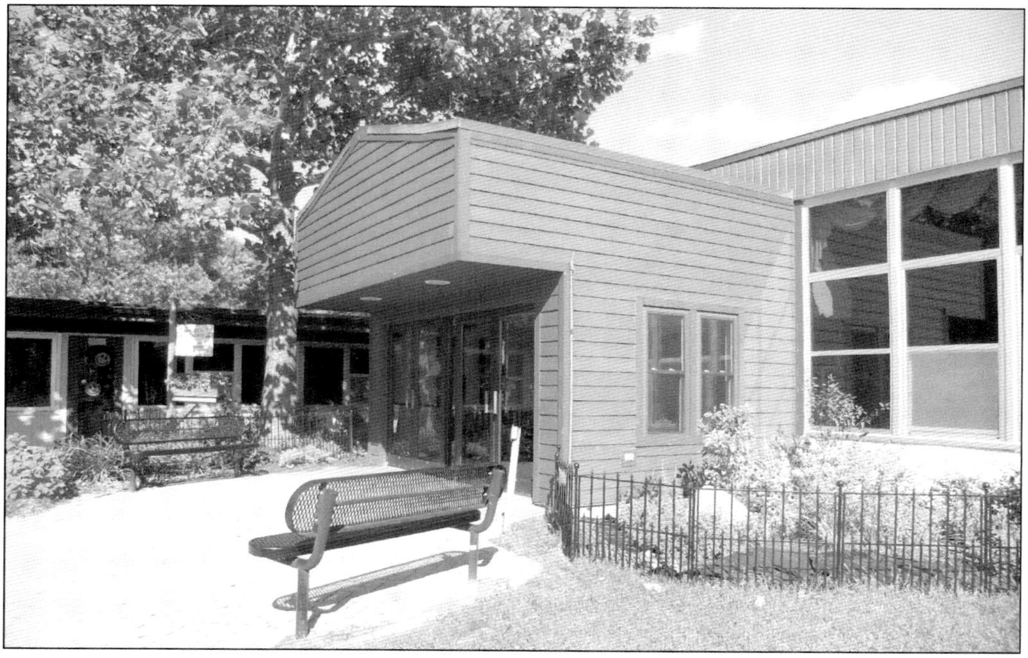

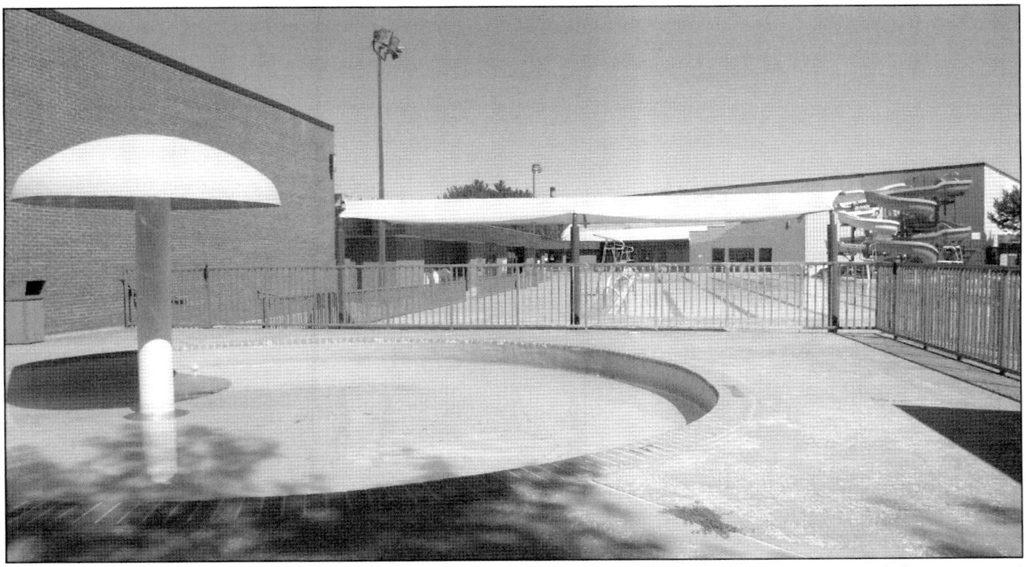

The Nelson Sports Complex has undergone many changes since the Olympic Pool first opened in 1962. Since then, the park district has added a wading pool, an adults-only hot tub, 2 two-story waterslides, and two diving boards. The park district also added an official-sized ice arena (far white building), a large gymnastics room, and a fitness center (left brick building). With all these additions, the Nelson Sports Complex has become a one-stop facility for fun and fitness in Rolling Meadows. (Courtesy of the author.)

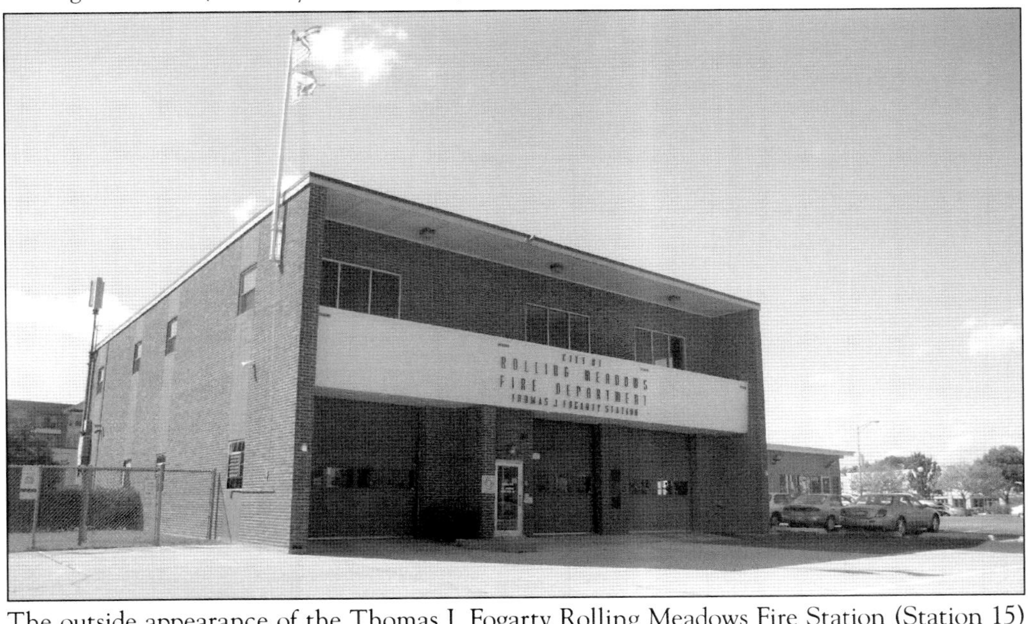

The outside appearance of the Thomas J. Fogarty Rolling Meadows Fire Station (Station 15) has not seen many changes over the years, but the fire department as a whole has. Starting with only part-time volunteers, the department has grown to see 43 full-time employees. A second fire station (Station 16) was built years ago on Plum Grove Road in order to better protect the entire city of Rolling Meadows. The department headquarters has since shifted from Station 15 to Station 16. (Courtesy of the author.)

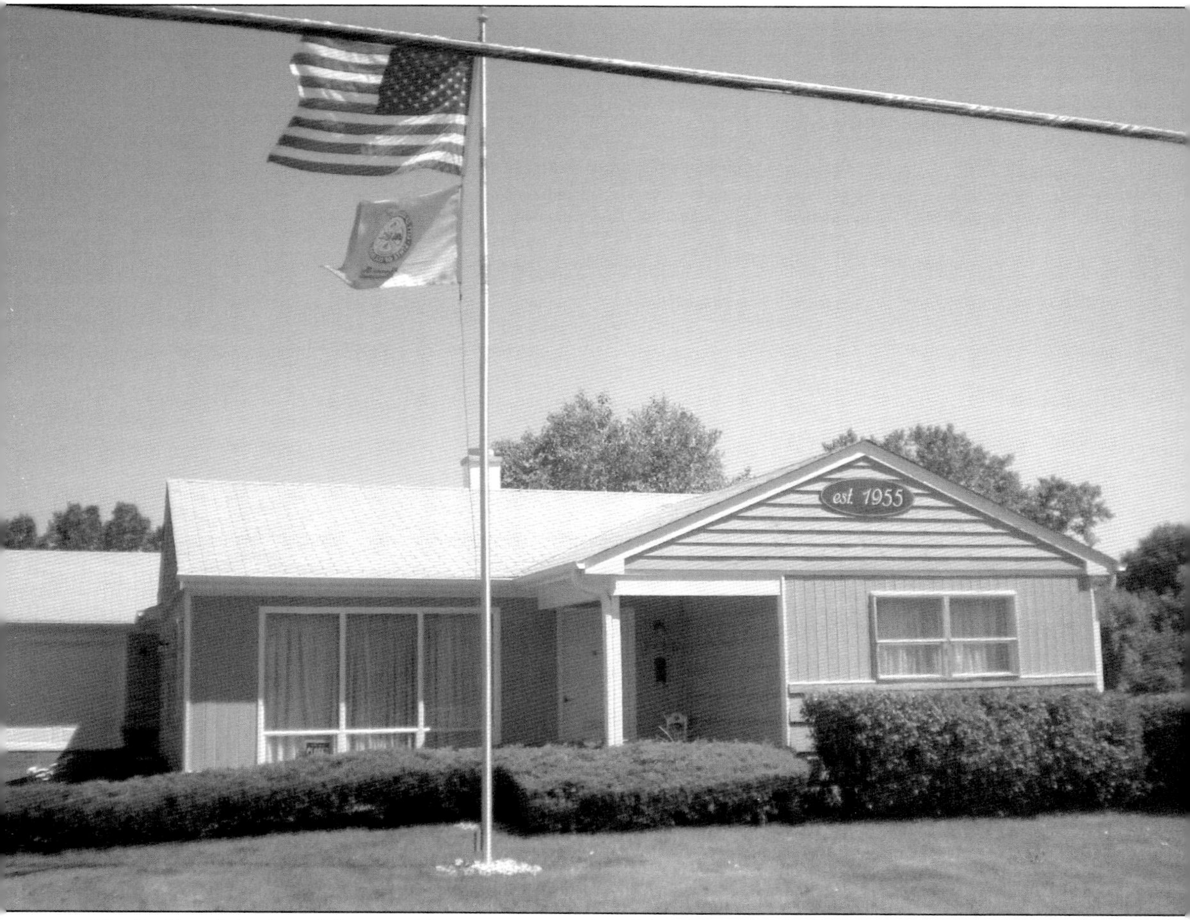

The Rolling Meadows Historical Museum opened in July 2002. The building design is modeled after the original Kimball Hill homes built in Rolling Meadows back in 1953. In the garage (left) is the Kimball Hill Family Educational Center, which displays information about Kimball Hill and early Rolling Meadows. The house was designed and furnished like a real Rolling Meadows house from the 1950s, complete with period furniture, children's toys, a black and white television set, and a silver aluminum tree that is displayed during the holiday season. The Rolling Meadows Historical Society continues to host its monthly meetings in the museum. (Courtesy of the author.)

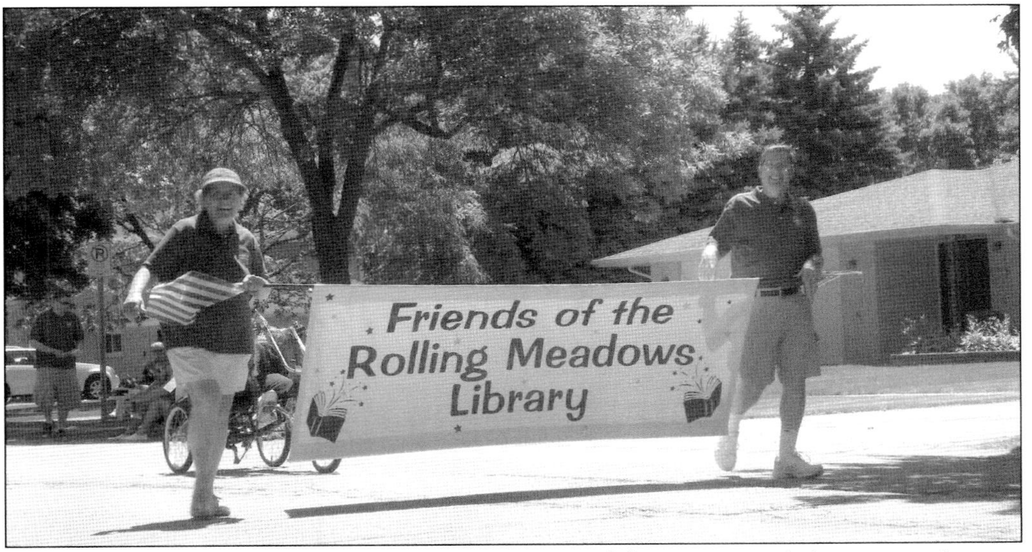

Rolling Meadows' Fourth of July Parade remains one of the most attended events in the city. Longtime residents continue to dress up as clowns, their identities "hidden" behind pancake circus makeup, and walk down the street to rouse the crowd before the parade kicks off. Every civic organization is represented, from the police and fire departments to public works and the Friends of the Rolling Meadows Library. Above, library director David Ruff and Friends of the Library treasurer Elizabeth "Liz" Vargas announce the eagerly anticipated summer book sale, hosted by the Friends of the Library. Below, Mayor Tom Rooney shows off his playful side as he pedals himself through his first parade as mayor. (Above courtesy of the author; below courtesy of Fred Schroeder.)

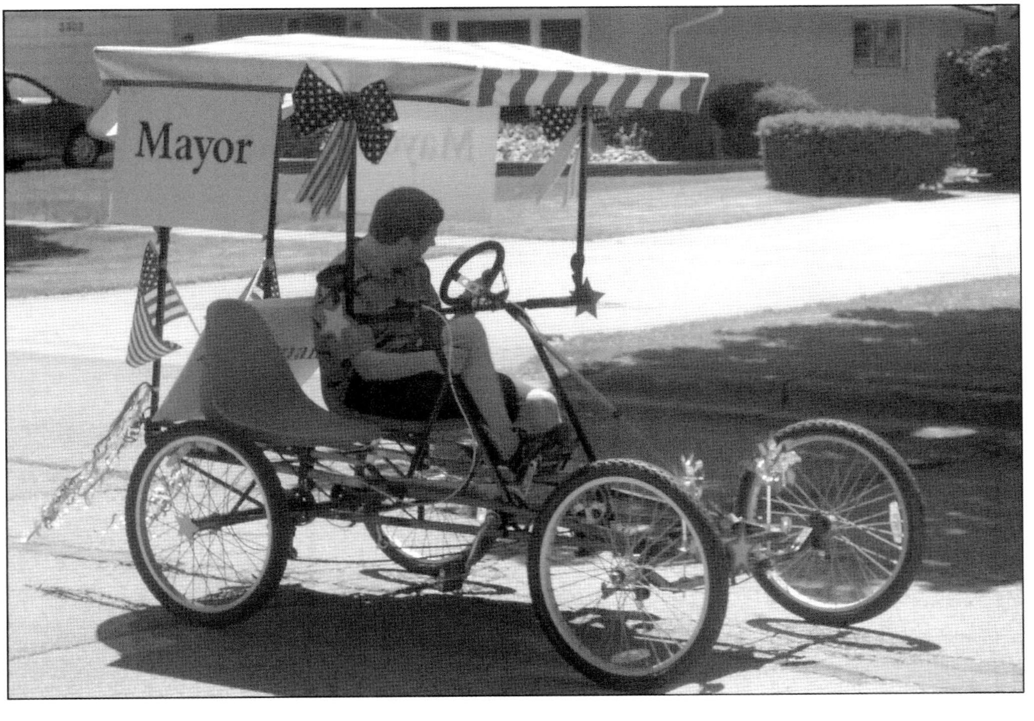

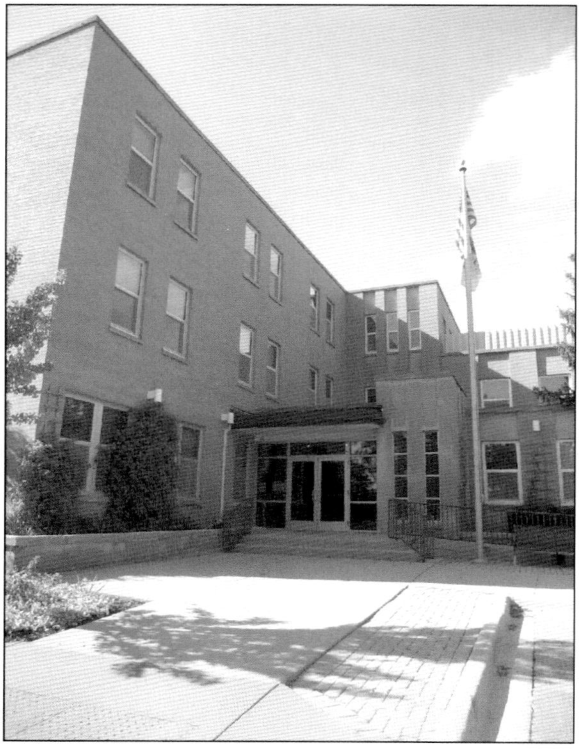

Park Central is home to the Rolling Meadows Park District's main offices. It is also one of the meeting places for the Northwest Special Recreation Association (NWSRA), an organization that provides people with disabilities opportunities to socialize, develop skills, and increase emotional and physical well being. Park Central is home to Opera in Focus, which presents scenes from famous operas, all performed by intricately expressive puppets. This building now boasts one of the most elegant banquet halls and courtyards in all of Rolling Meadows. (Courtesy of the author.)

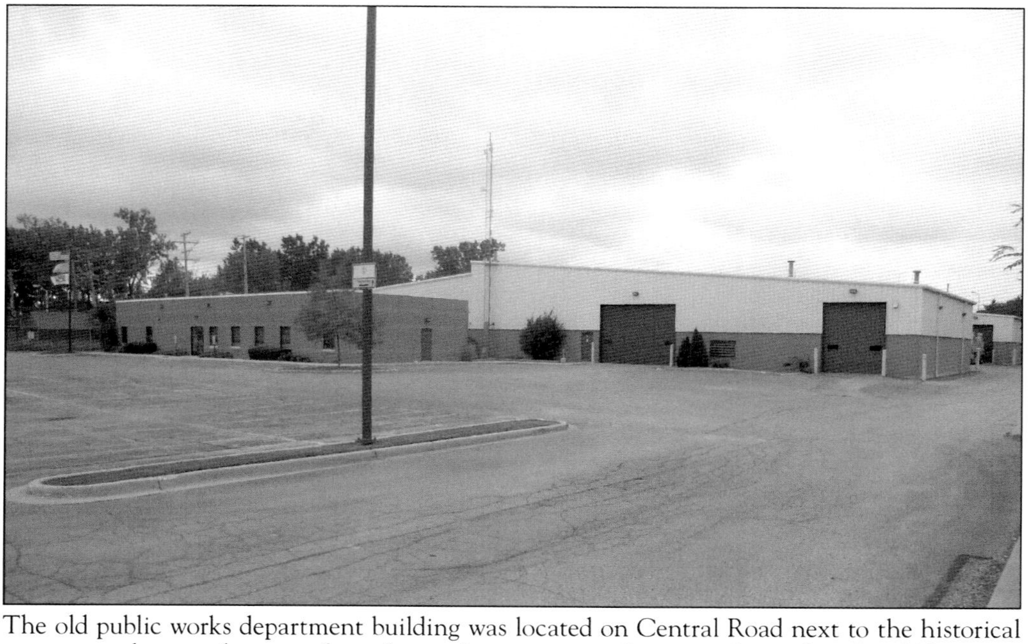

The old public works department building was located on Central Road next to the historical museum and across the street from the south water tower. Space was limited in the old location, so the department moved to the far north end of Rolling Meadows. The public works department remains one of the most active departments in the city, and its dedicated service to keeping the city clean, safe, and running efficiently is noted by residents. (Courtesy of Fred Schroeder.)

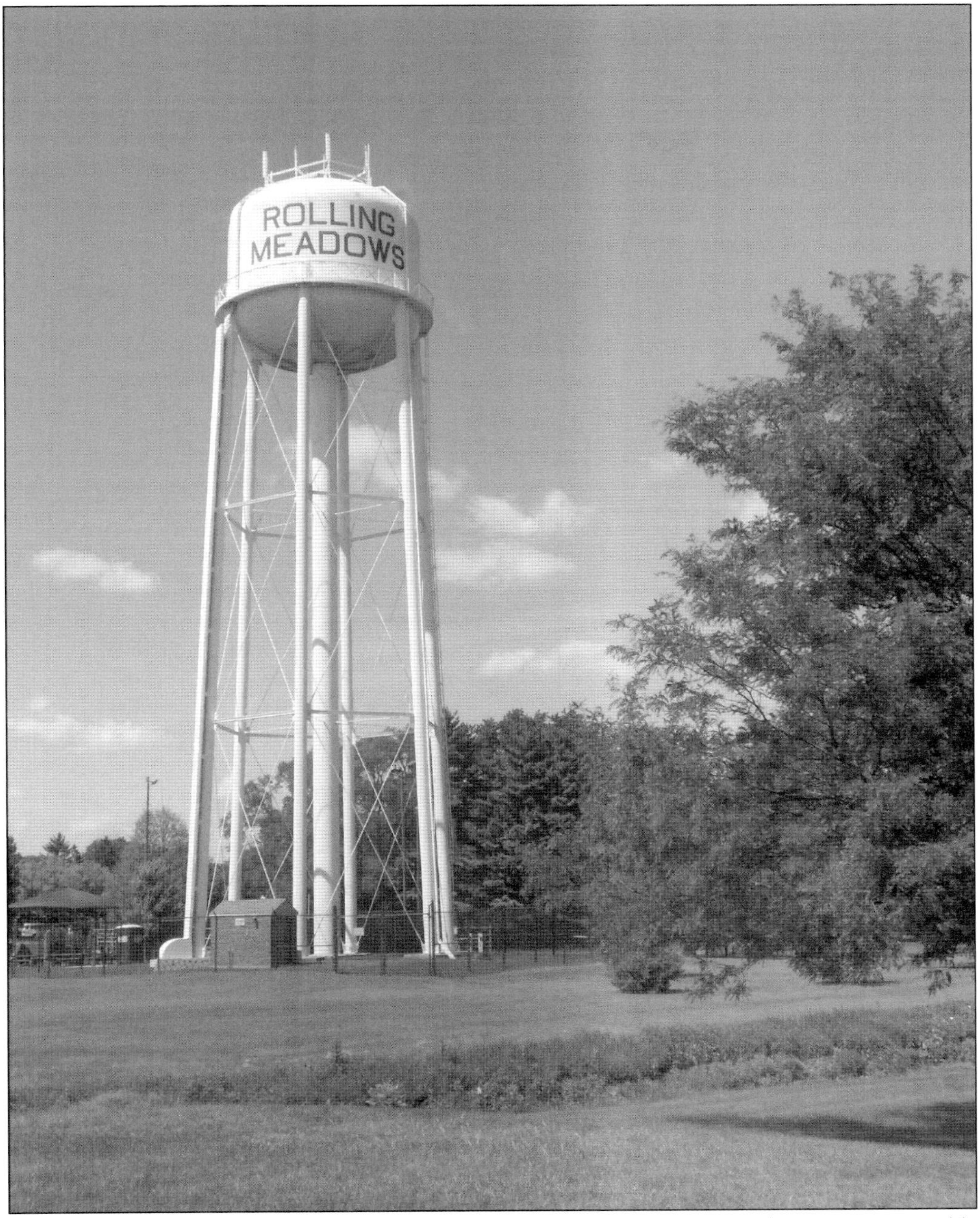

Other than the carillon tower, the two Rolling Meadows water towers are the most recognizable landmarks of the city. Pictured here is the north tower, positioned between Cardinal Drive Church and Salt Creek. Its sister tower is by a hill south of Central Road, across the street from the old public works building. Every year on the Fourth of July, residents swarm that hill to get one of the best views of the city's fireworks display. But the north water tower is the one that residents identify as a city landmark, the one that reflects in the gentle waters of Salt Creek. This water tower is one of the first things that visitors to the city notice, but residents and city officials are confident that it will not be the only thing worth noting in Rolling Meadows. (Courtesy of the author.)